U0611393

二语写作

Chinese Journal of Second Language Writing

主编 王俊菊

第三辑

外语教学与研究出版社
FOREIGN LANGUAGE TEACHING AND RESEARCH PRESS
北京 BEIJING

2021

图书在版编目（CIP）数据

二语写作. 第三辑. 2021 / 王俊菊主编. —— 北京：外语教学与研究出版社，
2021.12（2022.11 重印）
ISBN 978-7-5213-3040-3

I. ①二… II. ①王… III. ①第二语言－写作－文集 IV. ①H05-53

中国版本图书馆 CIP 数据核字 (2021) 第 280806 号

出 版 人　王　芳
责任编辑　解碧琰
责任校对　毕　争
助理编辑　周　娜
封面设计　李　高
出版发行　外语教学与研究出版社
社　　址　北京市西三环北路 19 号（100089）
网　　址　http://www.fltrp.com
印　　刷　北京天泽润科贸有限公司
开　　本　787×1092　1/16
印　　张　10
版　　次　2022 年 1 月第 1 版　2022 年 11 月第 2 次印刷
书　　号　ISBN 978-7-5213-3040-3
定　　价　40.00 元

购书咨询：（010）88819926　电子邮箱：club@fltrp.com
外研书店：https://waiyants.tmall.com
凡印刷、装订质量问题，请联系我社印制部
联系电话：（010）61207896　电子邮箱：zhijian@fltrp.com
凡侵权、盗版书籍线索，请联系我社法律事务部
举报电话：（010）88817519　电子邮箱：banquan@fltrp.com
物料号：330400001

《二语写作》第三辑
（2021 年 12 月）

目　录

Contents

卷首语

新时代、新文科背景下的中国二语写作研究面临新的历史机遇与发展契机。二语写作理论如何取得突破？二语写作与其他学科如何进一步交融？二语写作的优秀成果在国际学术话语体系中如何融入？这些问题的解决，需要广大二语写作学者与教师在不断提升教学、科研能力的同时，保持开阔的学术视野，加强国际交流与对话，充分把握全球化、多语言、跨学科、后疫情背景下二语写作教学与研究中的新问题、新特征和新趋势，共同探索二语写作教学与研究的创新发展之路。

《二语写作》第三辑的突出特点是兼具国际视野与本土特色。本辑汇集了13位国内外二语写作领域的知名专家学者、青年新秀和一线教师。研究成果充分体现了开阔的国际视野和各自话题的研究前沿；综述文章也具有"立足本土、放眼世界"的鲜明特色。

"特别约稿"栏目中，Icy Lee探讨了使用第二语言进行博客写作对新手外语教师合作学习和职业发展的促进作用。Neomy Storch借助活动理论分析了二语写作者在参与教师反馈和同伴反馈等活动中的能动性，剖析了反馈中影响二语作者能动性的主要因素，并为师生提供了教学与学习建议。

"写作研究"栏目中，Hani Albelihi和Ge Lan通过语料库手段对比分析了阿拉伯语母语作者与英语母语作者在英语学术写作中名词短语复杂性的异同。刘烨、董记华以自建工学和语言学学术语篇语料库为基础，从三个维度对两个语料库中的立场构建特征进行了对比分析。刘应亮、魏依基于中国学生英语硕士论文语料，参照期刊论文中转述词的使用特点，研究了中国学生在学术语篇中转述动词的使用情况。于万锁、郝媛通过自建英语专业高年级在校学生人物记叙语篇语料库，考察了英语专业高年级学生在人物记叙语篇中话语转述词词块运用的复杂性特征。

"研究述评"栏目中，牛瑞英界定了论证和论证能力等概念，阐释了议论文论证发展研究的理论视角，综述了国外目前关于英语议论文论证发展的实证研究。Yue Chen检索搜集了1949年至2019年间发表在国内核心期刊上的两千余篇论文，从发展趋势、研究主题、研究方法等层面进行了分析探讨。"新秀论坛"栏目中，周杰对2006年至2021年间国家社会科学基金和教育部人文社会科学研究项目立项的二语写作相关项目进行了多元分析，探讨了国内二语写作科研立项的现状和发展趋势。

作为本刊特色，本辑在附录中列出了2021年以来国内出版和发表的与二语写作相关的书籍与期刊文章，便于读者尽快了解相关领域的研究热点和发展动态。

以上栏目各具特色，既有理论角度的新尝试，也有方法层面的新应用。文章中的研究发现和学术思考对新时代背景下的二语写作教学与研究有较大的启示意义和借鉴价值，值得品鉴。

目前，《二语写作》已经成功出版两辑。《二语写作》的创刊得到了来自全国甚至全球二语写作研究者的关注。本刊不仅收到了来自国内学者的踊跃投稿，还收到了来自美国、比利时、澳大利亚、新西兰、泰国、沙特阿拉伯等国家的作者投稿。本刊自收录于中国知网以来，其论文也收获了不俗的阅读量、下载量和引用量。今后，《二语写作》还将继续为广大教师和研究人员搭建学术交流的渠道和平台，巩固已有的学术影响力，延续并加强在国内写作教学与研究中的引领作用。

Blogging as a Multi-purpose Tool for EFL Teacher Development

Icy LEE

The Chinese University of Hong Kong, China

Abstract: Recent years have witnessed the emergence of blogs as a tool for promoting second language (L2) teachers' development. However, the majority of studies have addressed the pre-service rather than in-service context. The study reported in this paper aims to examine the use of blogging in an in-service teacher education program in Hong Kong, China. Drawing upon data gathered from blog entries and comments as well as written self-reflections by 20 novice EFL teachers, this study investigates the extent of the teachers' participation in the class blog, the focuses of their blog entries and comments, as well as their perspectives on the benefits and problems of blogging. The paper concludes that blogging can enhance collaborative learning, promote professional exchange and serve as a multi-purpose tool that facilitates novice EFL teachers' professional development.

Keywords: blogging; in-service teacher; teacher education

1. Introduction

With technology advancement in society, social networking has figured prominently on the Internet and its place in second language (L2) teacher education is receiving more and more attention. Blogs based on the Web 2.0 technology allow computer users to express their ideas on the same platform (Soares 2008) and have the potential to serve as a powerful tool for teaching and learning, specifically to cultivate a learning community among the users. To date, research on blogging has focused on how blogs can be utilized as an instructional tool in K-12 or higher education classrooms (Dalgarno et al. 2015; Hall 2018; Justice et al. 2013), with less attention paid to L2 teacher education contexts. In L2 teacher education, while the majority of research studies on blogging are conducted with pre-service teachers, insufficient attention has been given to the use of blogs for fostering teacher learning and cultivating a learning community among practicing teachers attending in-service teacher education programs, particularly in EFL contexts. In Hong Kong of China, in-service English teachers are known to work under enormous pressure, having to cope with heavy workloads from teaching and non-teaching responsibilities that include pastoral care and extra-curricular activities. Asking novice teachers enrolled on an in-service teacher education program to participate in blog discussion, in addition to day-time teaching, evening class attendance, and coursework assignments, is a challenging task. The present study was designed to explore the extent to which novice English teachers engage in blogging in a part-time teacher education course, the focus of their blogging activities, as well as their perspectives regarding blogging in language teacher education.

1

2. Literature Review

Blogs, formerly called weblogs, are websites that can easily be created and updated without any knowledge of HTML programming. A blog is typically topic-oriented and consists of entries which are presented in reverse chronological order on a single page (Blood 2000). Broadly speaking, there are three types of blogs (Campbell 2003): the tutor blog, the learner blog and the class blog. The tutor blog is run by the class teacher, serving as a teacher's personal library for students and for parents to understand the school curriculum. It can also be used for disseminating information about extra-curricular activities and homework. The learner blog is operated individually by each student in the classroom and is regarded as an "online journal that an individual can continuously update with his or her own words, ideas, and thoughts" (Campbell 2003, para. 1). It can also help foster students' fluency in writing and develop their creative voice (Murray & Hourigan 2008). The class blog is run by both the teacher and students collaboratively and can be used as a platform to promote a feeling of community among the members of the class, as well as a collaborative space for discussion, exchange of ideas and self-reflection (Campbell 2003), promoting problem-solving and higher-order thinking skills at the same time (Murray & Hourigan 2008). In the study, the class blog was used.

In language education, blogs can be used as a useful tool for promoting language learning. Not only do they allow teachers and students to post language-related content instantly on the web and interact with each other with just one touch of the comment function button, but they also afford students the opportunities to use the target language for authentic communication (Arena 2008; Godwin-Jones 2003; Richardson 2006; Ward 2004). From a pedagogical perspective, blogs can enhance knowledge conceptualization, promote knowledge generation and develop a reflective learning culture through meaning making and social interaction (Oravec 2002, 2003). They can allow learners to connect to contexts beyond the classroom and foster social knowledge construction (Du & Wagner 2007). When blogging is integrated into the course content and assignment requirements, students can actively engage in conversations with their classmates on an ongoing basis, thereby promoting exchange of ideas and learning (Laurillard 2002), enhancing learner interaction, and building a sense of community (Miceli et al. 2010). Additionally, blogging can enhance learners' writing performance and promote learner autonomy (Bhattacharya & Chauhan 2010).

A growing body of literature has evinced the positive role of blogs in pre-service language teacher education. For example, Tang (2009) and Tang and Lam (2014) introduced an online blog-based teaching portfolio in the pre-service language teacher education program in Hong Kong, China, showing that the online portfolio could attract instant and interactive feedback from peers, encourage the pre-service teachers to actively participate in the blog-based discussion, foster a reflective culture within the learning community, and create opportunities for pre-service teachers to get emotional support and advice from their peers. In a similar vein, Bener and Yildiz (2019) demonstrated that blogs can promote pre-service teachers' reflection during ELT practicum. While the above studies have addressed blogging in the pre-service context, blogging among in-service teachers of English has received much less attention, except recent research that investigates teacher reflection through blogging (e.g., Hall 2018; Tajeddin & Aghababazadeh 2018). By focusing blogging in the in-service EFL teacher education context, the present study aims to contribute new knowledge to the current research base about blogging and L2 teacher education and address the following research questions:

(1) To what extent did the EFL teachers participate in blogging, and what did they focus on in their blog discussions?

(2) What were the perceived benefits and problems regarding blogging among the in-service EFL teachers?

3. The Study

3.1 Context and participants

In Hong Kong, China, in-service teachers of English without a professional teaching qualification are required to attain the Postgraduate Diploma in Education (PGDE) with a major in English soon after their entry into the teaching profession. These teachers are mostly novice teachers with no or little teaching experience. The part-time PGDE for teachers of English in Hong Kong is a two-year program that equips teachers with knowledge and skills in English language teaching as well as education in general. The 20 novice teachers of English who participated in the study were in their first or second year of teaching, all serving in secondary schools in Hong Kong. All of them are Cantonese-speaking, with half of them holding a Bachelor's degree in English and the other half with a non-English major.

The PGDE program in which the study was conducted has a 17-week English language teaching (ELT) methodology course in the first year of the part-time program, which is a compulsory course for participants who major in English. The ELT methodology course includes topics like teaching approaches and methodologies, the teaching of grammar, vocabulary, speaking, listening, reading and writing, classroom communication, lesson planning and evaluation, etc. Participants of the part-time PGDE program have to attend evening classes two to three times a week for two semesters each year (four semesters in total for the two-year program), including three hours of ELT methodology course per week over a total of 17 weeks in their first year of study.

As the instructor/teacher educator of the ELT methodology course, I designed a class blog with a view to fostering learning and promoting professional development among my novice English teachers. To improve the participation rate, the class blog was introduced as part of the coursework assessment, taking up 10% of the total score (the other assignments included an essay study assignment, a mini-project and a post-course written reflection on the class blog). Scoring was based on the teachers' level of participation in the class blog, as well as the depth of analysis and reflection as manifested in the blogposts and comments. I created and co-ran the class blog with the novice teachers. A login name and password were created for the class blog and shared among the novice teachers.

At the beginning of the ELT methodology course, the novice teachers were introduced to the class blog and encouraged to actively participate in the online discussion by adding entries on the blogs and/or posting comments on their peers' blogposts. At the end of each ELT methodology class, a few questions were posed in the course handouts to stimulate blog discussion, but the novice teachers were reminded that they were free to write on topics not raised in the questions. They were encouraged to visit the class blog each week after class and discuss with their peers any issues relating to English language teaching through posting entries and/or comments on their peers' posts. At the end of the course, also as part of coursework assessment, they were required to submit a post-course written reflection on their blogging experience, taking up 10% of the total score. Assessment was primarily based on their critical ability to reflect on their blogging experience.

3.2 Data collection and analysis

The study relied on three main data sources: the blog entries (i.e., blogposts), blog comments, and the novice teachers' post-course written reflections on the blogging experience. To answer the first research question (about the extent of participation and the focuses of blog discussion), the blog entries and comments posted by each novice teacher were counted. A content analysis approach was employed to ascertain the focuses of the blog discussion. The data analysis was conducted without preconceived categories but instead I let the codes emerge from the data, yielding a total of 12 themes that illuminate the blog focuses. The percentages of the blogposts and comments that are related to each of the 12 themes were calculated. Examples that are relevant to the themes were extracted from the blogposts and the comments to further support the themes. The second research question is examined by means of content analysis of the post-course written reflections triangulated with blogposts and comments, the benefits and problems of the class blog as perceived by the novice teachers.

4. Findings

4.1 Novice teachers' participation in blog discussion

In terms of the novice teachers' participation in the class blog, the findings show that the class blog was generally well-received, especially given the heavy workload of the participants, some of whom having to cope with a new teaching job and a part-time course. There were in total 20 blogposts, 90% (18) of which were written by the novice teachers (two by me as the teacher educator), and 80% (16) of the novice teachers had their individual blogposts (with two teachers having two blogposts each). Among the 90 comments on the blog, 85.5% (77) were posted by the novice teachers (the rest by me as the teacher educator). All of the 20 teachers had given comments on the blog and the average number of comments made by each teacher was 3.9. The maximum number of people involved in a blogpost discussion was 11, whereas the minimum number was two. The details of the teachers' participation on the blog are shown in Table 1.

In light of the fact that the participants were busy teachers undertaking a part-time teacher education program during the study, their participation in the class blog was considered satisfactory. Although two teachers did not post any individual entries and 16 teachers posted only one blogpost each, there were a great many comments (totaling 77), averaging 3.9 each participant.

Table 1. Novice teachers' participation in the blog

Details	Number
Total number of novice teachers in the course	20
Total number of blogposts	20
Total number of comments	90
Number of blogposts written by teachers	18 (90%)
Number of comments written by teachers	77 (85.5%)
Number of teachers who had their individual blogposts	16 (80%)
Number of teachers who had their individual comments	20 (100%)
Average number of blogposts that each teacher wrote	1
Average number of comments that each teacher wrote	3.9
Maximum number of people (including the teacher educator) involved in a blogpost discussion	11
Minimum number of people (including the teacher educator) involved in a blogpost discussion	2

4.2 Foci of novice teachers' blog discussion

The findings show that the novice teachers covered a wide range of issues in their blog discussion. All together 12 themes were identified from the blog entries and comments. Table 2 shows a breakdown of the 12 themes, as well as the percentages of the blogposts and comments that fell within each of the themes.

A number of entries and comments were about self-introduction and greeting (posted early in the course) — 33.3% of the blogposts and 3.9% of the comments, which was the third most popular theme in the blogposts. Most teachers started introducing themselves by commenting on the first blogpost written by the teacher educator. For example, Teacher C wrote:

> *Hello everyone! Thanks T (the teacher educator) so much for the blog. It is a wonderful platform for us to sharing (share) and exchanging (exchange ideas), isn't it?*

It is noteworthy that Teacher A, who missed the first session of the course, made use of the class blog to introduce herself to the rest of the class:

> *Hi there! I'm A — the late comer ... I feel terribly sorry that I missed the first lecture since I had to bring my students to the mainland at (in) that weekend. Anyways, I joined all of you on last Friday finally.*

Table 2. Themes of blogposts and comments by novice teachers

Themes of the Posts	Percentage (Number) of Blogposts	Percentage (Number) of Comments (%)
1. Socializing/relationship-building	33.3% (6)*	3.9% (3)
2. General views on students' learning of English	5.6% (1)	6.5% (5)
3. Background and prior education experience	33.3% (6)*	2.6% (2)
4. Personal teaching beliefs	22.2% (4)	22.1% (17)**
5. Growth in teachers' expertise	27.8% (5)	2.6% (2)
6. School culture	11.1% (2)	2.6% (2)
7. Sharing of teaching methods and teaching materials	44.4% (8)**	19.5% (15)
8. Posing problems and seeking help	16.7% (3)	3.9% (3)
9. Giving solutions and advice	0	20.8% (16)*
10. Emotional support and empathy	0	72.7% (56)***
11. Learning from others	0	13.0% (10)
12. Self-reflection	55.6% (10)***	16.9% (13)

*** The most popular; ** The second most popular; * The third most popular

The novice teachers also made use of the class blog to share their views on students' learning of English. 5.6% of the blogposts and 6.5% of the comments were about the participants' views on their own students' problems in learning English, what makes effective student learning and what teachers should do to help students learn better. For example, Teacher B expressed her view on what Hong Kong students think about English learning by responding to Teacher A's comments on students' problems in learning English. She commented as follows:

I agree with Teacher A that being unable to speak the language in their daily lives is one of the reasons why some students cannot speak English well ... I noticed that most of the students who do not do well in English found learning English boring as they usually learn English only from the textbooks. They thought there was no other way to learn English, but the fact is they rejected finding some other ways in learning the language.

Such a comment was taken up by Teacher C, who commented as follows:

I do agree that the reason why students cannot express themselves well in English is they do not use the language once they are out of class ... We need to sort of brainwash our students that using English in and out of class is something natural ... and if we English teachers do not stress on grammatical accuracy and interrupt students' speech too much, students will hopefully be more and more confident in speaking in English.

While Teacher B agreed with Teacher A's comments about the students' lack of exposure to the English language outside class and also offered the reasons behind the students' inability to speak English well, Teacher C proposed solutions to get around the problem.

Apart from talking about their students, the novice teachers shared with others their own background and prior education experience — comprising 33.3% of the blogposts and 2.6% of the comments, which was the third most popular theme in the blogposts. Within this theme, the in-service teachers blogged about the schools they were teaching, the reasons why they became teachers and their previous education experiences. For instance, Teacher C explained why he wanted to become a teacher even though his first degree is not related to education. He reflected as follows:

> *My major is hotel and tourism management in University A (sounds nothing to do with language). But as I worked in a hotel before, I couldn't help wondering why our local students, who studied English for some 10 years, can't express well when it comes to something very simple, or hardly show a sense of hospitality by using the language in a too formal way? I knew I needed to do something instead of just serving my guests, by making a little more difference.*

It was found that blogposts and comments related to this theme tended to find a great deal of support from their peers. For example, Teacher B expressed in a blogpost that she was thinking to quit her teaching job because she failed to get support from her students, and she got 12 comments from 10 peers giving her emotional support and encouragement, including one from Teacher H, who wrote:

> *I'm very sorry to hear that. But I feel one thing should cheer you up for sure, that is, your students really love you, or else, they wouldn't have written you the thank you card. That must be a sweet memory of yours which would never been taken away by anyone.*

Added to their background and prior education experience was a focus on their personal teaching beliefs, which accounted for 22.2% of the blogposts and 22.1% of the comments. Novice teachers shared how they perceived education and teaching and the beliefs underlying their choice of certain pedagogy. This was the second most popular theme in the comments. Teacher D shared her teaching belief in the blogpost as follows:

> *No matter it's a 'tough' school or 'non-tough' school, we are teachers. We are here to teach, to inspire and to enlighten students. We can choose to teach for money and status or we can choose to teach for love and hope.*

Mid-way into the ELT methodology course, a theme that emerged was the growth in teachers' expertise, which took up 27.8% of the blogposts and 2.6% of the comments. This theme documents how the participants' teaching effectiveness/practice was enhanced as a result of the ELT course. Teacher H shared her experience of how she became a better teacher after taking the course. She explained in this way:

> *In the past, when it comes to speaking lessons, I will let students do the speaking, but having little idea on how I can help them improve. Now, I come to understand that there are different aspects of speaking which can be taught, and I try to work on one area each time.*

As the novice teachers established a better relationship with as well as trust for their peers, they also began to talk about their school culture. This theme accounted for 11.1% of the blogposts and 2.6% of the comments. Specifically, the novice teachers discussed how school policies as well as teachers, students and parents' attitudes towards education shaped the school culture. Teacher D shared in a blogpost about the culture in her former school:

> *The culture of this school is interesting. The principal is an authoritarian. Students are like teachers, working all day long to finish their homework and revisions. It is common for students to stay at school until seven and work on their homework until one at night.*

Through taking the ELT methodology course, the novice teachers acquired new ideas about language teaching. They made use of the class blog to share different teaching methods and material — 44.4% of the blogposts (the second most popular theme) and 19.5% of the comments. The participants shared about their current practice, their attempts at implementing new pedagogies learnt from the course and the teaching materials that they found useful. Teacher G shared her vocabulary teaching method in her blogpost as follows:

> *To let them learn more vocabulary, I have tried out the following methods to encourage them to widen their vocabulary bank...teaching them prefixes and suffixes...providing examples of synonyms and antonyms...making them use the words...keeping on recalling their memories.*

The establishment of trust in the learning community also saw the teachers opening up by posing problems and seeking help (16.7% of the blogposts and 3.9% of the comments). A few novice teachers shared about the problems they encountered in teaching and how they sought help from the others. An example to illustrate this theme is a question posed by Teacher I in a blogpost about how to teach the senior secondary English Language curriculum:

How do you teach senior secondary English? I am currently teaching two F.4 classes English and I really do not have much idea of what to teach in class.

Related to the theme about posing problems and seeking help is giving solutions and advice, which accounted for 20.8% of the comments. Aside from attempting to suggest solutions to the problems posed by their peers, the teachers gave advice to those who shared their teaching stories, beliefs and pedagogy. Teacher J, in response to Teacher I's question about how to teach senior secondary English, offered her advice:

Sometimes I try to find a connection between things they learn and their interested topics (i.e., how to use wh-questions to catch a girl's attention); or to show them how they can use or find a particular Grammar item in real life situation (i.e., use a recipe/mobile phone manual to teach Imperatives). In other words, to make them think that 'this could be useful in the future' so that they would do everything to memorize it!

In addition to giving concrete suggestions and advice to help their peers address their problems, the participants showed emotional support and empathy on the class blog. This theme had the highest percentage in the comments — 72.7%. For instance, the blogpost about a novice teacher thinking of quitting her job attracted a number of comments from the teachers, including one of the most inactive bloggers in the class, Teacher K:

Keep your chin up! I think you're a bright teacher with a loving heart! It's good to share any thoughts here — be it good or bad!

A number of the themes in the above (e.g., sharing teaching methods and materials, posing problems and seeking help, giving solutions and advice) resulted in the novice teachers' learning from others, which comprised 13% of the comments. This theme refers to the teachers' newly learnt teaching ideas from their peers on the blog. For instance, Teacher H replied to Teacher G's blogpost by talking about useful teaching ideas learnt from the peers on the blog:

Thanks for G's sharing. These are all good strategies to help students learn vocabulary. M's suggestion also sounds very interesting, and I'll try out with my students later.

Another teacher (Teacher J) appreciated Teacher H's idea of using digital storytelling in class and also sought advice from him.

I think that is a great idea. Definitely very well thought out. I like your scaffolding technique of introducing new concepts to improve on their writing skills. Like you, I was inspired to have my students complete something similar in Photo Story as well. I think that S.4 students would benefit greatly from this activity ... I am still debating on whether I should go with a fictional story or have them tell a real story of their childhood, or something non-fiction. Also, I am still debating on whether to have it as a class activity or something voluntary, like part of the school's writing club.

Finally, self-reflection, the highest percentage in the blogposts (55.6%) was evident in the blog discussion. The novice teachers blogged about their reflection on personal growth, teaching beliefs as well as pedagogy. Teacher H wrote:

I would like to take this opportunity to reflect on my personal development after I entered the teaching profession ... Teaching has gradually transformed my personality, adding positive elements to my being and my life ... Suggestions from colleagues and the PGDE courses have helped me to make improvements on my teaching. Now, I come to understand that there are different aspects of speaking which can be taught, and I try to work on one area each time ... Self-reflection has been quite useful in helping me to improve. I used to have a journal called "My teaching career 123".

Sometimes peers' blogposts triggered the teachers' self-reflection, as shown in 16.9% of the comments. For example, Teacher K responded to Teacher H's comments about the idea of keeping a self-reflection journal:

Thanks very much for your sharing, which makes me think that it's time for me to keep a journal as well. As teachers, we always give students' feedback about how they have been doing but ironically, sometimes, we tend to forget the need of self-reflection. Thanks for your message which highlights a key point that we should also keep growing up together with the kids instead of simply watching them grow ... self-reflection is particularly important for new teachers like us. When we reflect upon our teaching effectiveness, we can realize our strengths and weaknesses in teaching which allows us to improve our teaching effectiveness. Unfortunately, with the amount of work we have, we seldom have time to do so. Thanks for reminding me that self-reflection is crucial for teacher's development.

4.3 Novice teachers' perspectives on blogging

An analysis of the teachers' written reflections revealed the novice teachers' favorable attitude towards blogging. Specifically, the data demonstrated four main benefits as perceived by the teachers, as well as a small number of problems associated with blogging.

First, all the teachers found that blogging provided opportunities for them to exchange ideas about English language education and to seek advice from the teacher educator and their peers without the restriction of time and space. Some teachers regarded the blog as "a treasure full of ideas" and "a resource bank". The following extracts from the teachers' written reflections illustrate the value of blogging:

> *I posted my predicament on the class blog. Soon I got some constructive suggestions which I had never thought of.* (Teacher B)
> *The class blog gives me inspiration in teaching.* (Teacher F)
> *All their ideas shed light on me when I have come to a bottle-neck of my teaching.* (Teacher T)

Second, the class blog was considered a useful platform for the expression of personal thoughts and a source of emotional support, as shown by the majority of the teachers' reflections. The novice teachers believed that the class blog is a "strong learning community" because "everyone can participate and pitch in to help solve each other's difficulties in the teaching of English". It can serve as a network for teachers of different backgrounds to express their views and get resonance and encouragement from the peers:

> *What we need is a genuine support network like this, with people who are able to identify with our difficulties and challenges, and who are able to offer encouragement, and even more, possible solutions to our problems.* (Teacher R)
> *The class blog is a place where I can find people who would understand my feelings and give me some support ... reading others' successful stories of personal development or students' improvement is a way to motivate me to move on. Also, others' words of encouragement make me feel that my heart and effort are appreciated.* (Teacher E)
> *The class blog serves the purpose of relieving us from the great pressure.* (Teacher O)

The third benefit, according to the teachers (half of them), is that blogging provided a useful impetus for self-reflection and helped develop their critical reflection through asking questions about theory and practice and examining issues raised by their peers, and hence helping them develop insights into teaching:

> *Sharing on the blog helped me to reflect on my role as a teacher.* (Teacher M)
> *Frequent self-reflection can guide us to concentrate on the real value of education and help our students learn and grow.* (Teacher P)

Lastly, all teachers, in one way or another, expressed the view that blogging enhanced their professional learning and development, as they could learn new ideas and teaching methods through reading the entries of their peers. For example, Teacher H shared a self-made digital storytelling (DST) video on the blog and one of their peers (Teacher J) learned to use DST to teach her students. He wrote:

> *Seeing someone successfully carrying out greatly encourages me to try it with my students.* (Teacher J)

Another teacher referred explicitly her own professional development as the main benefit of the blog:

> *(It is) a place to enhance my professional development as a teacher.* (Teacher B)

Despite the above benefits, two novice teachers, Teachers L and N, had negative feelings about the use of blogging as an assessment task when they first learnt about it at the beginning of the course. The class blog was perceived as a source of pressure for the busy in-service teachers. Teacher N wrote:

> *I was not used to share my personal feelings to others through posting online blogs ... It was weird and strange for me to write something, which is usually emotional and sentimental ... I was shocked to see the sentence 'if you do not participate at all, you will not get any mark'. I felt the pressure and lots of workload was coming towards me ... At first, I did not like the idea at all thinking how I am supposed to find time to write blog ...*

In his post-course written reflection, however, Teacher N acknowledged the value of blogging:

> *Despite the lack of posts, I did read the blog from time to time ... I was once inspired by M's work and I tried making a similar one but of a different topic ... To my surprise, my kids were attracted to this sort of activity.*

Teacher L, another passive blogger, had the following to say:

> *I seldom blog and I never leave comments to any posts ... It's like a difficult task for me.*

Nevertheless, Teacher L showed her understanding of the potential benefits of blogging:

> *We can all share our views and opinions about teaching and learning*

through the class blog ... Once I tried out something, thinking that it was the most suitable method to the learning for my students but it turned out that I was wrong ... I was told by our classmates that my concept needed to be changed ... I am also amused by the new ideas by our classmates.

Even though Teacher L was not an active blogger, she benefited from sharing one teaching episode and from reading the comments.

5. Discussion

This study examined the application of a class blog as part of coursework assessment for in-service teachers in a teacher education course in Hong Kong, China. All the novice teachers showed positive attitude towards blogging at the end of the course. The findings of the study demonstrate that blogging provides a platform for the novice teachers to share their beliefs, exchange ideas, pose questions and get advice and support from their peers, which in turn facilitates their social interactions and professional learning (Hodgson & Wong 2011). Blogging could also promote a sense of community and provide a place for discussion, reflection, and problem-solving (Campbell 2003). In the physical classroom, it is not easy for the teacher educator to involve all teacher learners in asking questions, exchanging ideas, sharing experience etc., especially in the Asian context where students are used to the passive way of learning, and to working in isolation without much cooperative group work (Mok & Ko 2003). However, blogging can provide a virtual platform that fosters active participation of all members in the class. In the study, for instance, every novice teacher had either written a blogpost (or more) and/or given comments to their peers, which was regarded by one of the novice teachers as "a closely-knitted learning community which would otherwise not exist in the real world".

Although increased workload was raised as a potential problem of blogging, arguably it is the time constraint that renders blogging a valuable tool for novice teachers' professional development. This is because through blogging the busy novice teachers could get support from peers regardless of time and place — as long as they have access to the Internet. In Hong Kong, China, teaching is a busy and stressful job. Many in-service teachers do not have time to share their problems with others in their workplace, not to mention the fact that they may feel uneasy to do so lest they will be looked upon as incompetent and incapable. Interacting with peers who are not their colleagues on the class blog can take some of the pressure off novice teachers as the platform offers a virtual space for them to share their concerns freely and conveniently as long as they are hooked up to the Internet. In the words of one teacher:

In today's generation of smartphones, tablet computers and wireless internet, blogging allows for virtual interaction which is not restricted by time and place where we can choose to participate at our convenience, which is perfect for the situation of student teachers who already have a heavy workload and may not have the time to sit down and converse professionally. (Teacher D)

Above all, reflection is a cornerstone of teachers' professional development (Baird 1993). The study has demonstrated that blogging can facilitate the development of a reflective culture among teachers. Very often, teachers spend most of their time teaching in the classroom without taking time to reflect on their work. Blogging allows teachers to reflect on their own beliefs, practices and experiences, which can enhance their reflective abilities and facilitate their professional development.

6. Implications and Conclusion

Despite the small sample size, the relatively short duration of the study, and the limited number of blogposts and comments collected, this study has shed light on the potential value of blogs in EFL teacher education. The findings suggest that the incorporation of blogging into teacher education programs can enhance the learning experience of teachers and bring a number of benefits. Not only does the class blog serve as a communication platform and a support tool for the teachers, but it can also provide teachers with advice and guidance on how to address the conflicts and problems they face in their workplace, serving as a great inspirational source of encouragement, insights and teaching pedagogy. Moreover, it is a useful resource for the teachers to share their knowledge and experience in the teaching of English as well as to reflect upon and improve their practices.

Although the participants in the study were novice teachers of English, a number of implications can be drawn from the study which may be applicable to more experienced teachers or those working in similar contexts. First, in-service teacher education programs can capitalize on social networking sites such as blogs to foster critical reflection, build a professional learning community, and enhance teachers' professional development. To encourage participation, in the study the class blog was linked to coursework assessment. Although a small number of teachers resisted the idea initially, as they discovered the benefits of blogging they gradually began to buy into the idea and participated in the class blog more actively than before. Teacher educators in similar contexts can continue to explore ways to maximize participation in blog discussion, particularly among in-service teachers who have multiple tasks to juggle with. Second, blogging can overcome material challenges in teacher education contexts constrained by the lack of teaching time and large class sizes, since participants, as many as 30 to 40, can take part in blog discussion not restricted by time and place. Third, blogging demonstrates that teaching and learning need not be confined by the classroom but it can take place outside and beyond class time. Online discussion can even be sustained after the completion of a teacher education course (though this is not the focus of the study). Future research can explore the value of blogging among more experienced in-service teachers — e.g., how blogging can help foster school-based professional learning communities.

References

Arena, C. 2008. Blogging in the language classroom: It doesn't "simply happen" [J]. *TESL-EJ* 11(44): 1-7.

Baird, J. R. 1993. Collaborative reflection, systematic inquiry, better learning [A]. In T. Russell & H. Munby (eds.). *Teachers and Teaching: From Classroom to Reflection* [C]. New York: Falmer Press, Taylor & Francis Incorp. 33-48.

Bener, E. & S. Yildiz. 2019. The use of blog activities to promote reflection in an ELT practicum [J]. *Australian Journal of Teacher Education* 44(8): 38-56.

Bhattacharya, A. & K. Chauhan. 2010. Augmenting learner autonomy through blogging [J]. *ELT Journal* 64(4): 376-384.

Blood, R. 2000. Weblogs: A history and perspective [OL]. http://www.rebeccablood.net/essays/weblog_history.html (accessed 15/09/2021)

Campbell, A. P. 2003. Weblogs for use with ESL classes [J]. *The Internet TESL Journal* 9(2): http://iteslj.org/Techniques/Campbell-Weblogs.html

Dalgarno, B., A. Reupert & A. Bishop. 2015. Blogging while on professional placement: Explaining the diversity in student attitudes and engagement [J]. *Technology, Pedagogy, & Education* 24: 189-209.

Du, H. S. & C. Wagner. 2007. Learning with weblogs: Enhancing cognitive and social knowledge construction [J]. *Professional Communication, IEEE Transactions on Professional Communication* 50(1): 1-16.

Godwin-Jones, R. 2003. Blogs and wikis: Environments for on-line collaboration [J]. *Language, Learning and Technology* 7(2): 12-16.

Hall, L. A. 2018. Using blogs to support reflection in teacher education [J]. *Literacy Research and Instruction* 57(1): 26-43.

Hodgson, P. & D. Wong. 2011. Developing professional skills in journalism through blogs [J]. *Assessment & Evaluation in Higher Education* 36(2): 197-211.

Justice, J. E., J. Anderson & K. Nichols. 2013. The affordance of blogging on establishing communities of practice in a pre-service elementary teacher education program [J]. *Journal of Technology and Teacher Education* 21: 49-88.

Laurillard, D. 2002. *Rethinking University Teaching: A Conversational Framework for the Effective Use of Learning Technologies* [M]. Routledge: Psychology Press.

Miceli, T., S. V. Murray & C. Kennedy. 2010. Using an L2 blog to enhance learners' participation and sense of community [J]. *Computer Assisted Language Learning* 23(4): 321-341.

Mok, I. A. C. & P. Y. Ko. 2003. Beyond labels- teacher-centered and pupil-centered activities [A]. In P. Stimpson, P. Morris, Y. Fung & R. Carr (eds.). *Curriculum, Learning and Assessment: The Hong Kong Experience* [C]. Hong Kong: Open University of Hong Kong Press. 307-328.

Murray, L. & T. Hourigan. 2008. Blogs for specific purposes: Expressivist or socio-cognitivist approach? [J]. *ReCALL* 20(1): 82-97.

Oravec, J. A. 2002. Bookmarking the world: Weblog applications in education [J]. *Journal of Adolescent and Adult Literacy* 45(7): 616-621.

Oravec, J. A. 2003. Blending by blogging: Weblogs in blended learning initiatives [J]. *Journal of Educational Media* 28(2-3): 225-233.

Richardson, W. 2006. *Blogs, Wikis, Podcasts, and Other Powerful Web Tools for Classrooms* [M].

Thousand Oaks, California: Corwin Press.

Soares, D. 2008. Understanding class blogs as a tool for language development[J]. *Language Teaching Research* 12(4): 517-533.

Tajeddin, Z. & Y. Aghababazadeh. 2018. Blog-mediated reflection for professional development: Themes and criticality of L2 teachers' reflective practice [J]. *TESL Canada Journal* 35(2): 26-50.

Tang, E. 2009. Introduction and development of a blog-based teaching portfolio: A case study in a pre-service teacher education programme [J]. *International Journal of Learning* 16(8): 89-100.

Tang, E. & C. Lam. 2014. Building an effective online learning community (OLC) in blog-based teaching portfolios [J]. *The Internet and Higher Education* 20: 79-85.

Ward, J. M. 2004. Blog assisted language learning (BALL): Push button publishing for the pupils[J]. *TEFL Web Journal* 3(1): 1-16.

About the Author

Icy LEE is a professor at the Department of Curriculum and Instruction of the Faculty of Education, The Chinese University of Hong Kong, China. Her research areas include second language writing, error correction and feedback in writing, classroom writing assessment, and second language teacher education. Email: icylee@cuhk.edu.hk

Feedback on Writing: A Learner Agency Perspective[1]

Neomy STORCH

University of Melbourne, Australia

Abstract: In this paper, I focus on learner agency in two activities associated with feedback on L2 writing: learners' engagement with and response to teacher feedback and learners' stances as givers or receivers of feedback in peer response activities. This paper begins by discussing what agency means and its key attributes. Adopting an activity theory perspective, I show how these attributes can be mapped onto a model of activity. Then, drawing on a number of studies that I and my colleagues have conducted with English language learners, I interpret the salient learner behavior observed in these studies using the construct of learner agency. Using activity theory I highlight the individual and contextual factors that could explain these observed behaviors. I conclude by suggesting some strategies that could encourage learners to take a more active role in feedback activities and call on teachers to reflect on their practices in order to promote learner agency in L2 feedback activities.

Keywords: feedback; learner agency; L2 writing; enactment

1. Introduction

Feedback on second language (L2) writing, and particularly feedback on language errors, referred to as written corrective feedback (WCF), continues to receive much research attention in the field of L2 writing. Two distinct strands in this body of research can be identified. One large strand, consisting predominantly of experimental studies, has tried to identify the most effective type of WCF. For example, a number of studies compared the impact of direct (correct forms given) versus indirect corrective feedback (errors signalled) or targeted (feedback given on a selected number of errors) versus comprehensive feedback (see review in Bitchener & Storch 2016; Ferris & Kurzer 2019). This research has been largely informed by cognitive theoretical perspective, where learning begins with noticing of new linguistic information (input) and culminates in uptake (e.g., Gass 1997; Leow 2015). From this theoretical perspective, feedback is viewed as new input that the learner's brain needs to notice and then process (e.g., Bitchener 2019). Overall, the results of this body of research have been quite inconclusive, precluding researchers from determining which type of WCF is the most effective.

The second strand includes a relatively small number of more recent studies investigating learners' engagement with the feedback they receive. This research (e.g., Han & Xu 2019; Zhang & Hyland 2018; Zheng & Yu 2018), often consists of small-scale case studies, uses retrospective interviews to investigate how students process and react

---

1 This paper is based on a presentation delivered at the 12th Conference on Teaching and Researching EFL Writing, delivered in October 2020.

to the feedback received. These studies deploy an engagement framework first proposed by Ellis (2010) and since elaborated on by others (e.g., Zhang & Hyland 2018), which distinguishes between three dimensions of engagement with feedback: cognitive (depth of processing), behavioral (uptake or rejection of the feedback, strategies used) and affective (emotional reaction). What stands out in these studies is the individual variations in learners' engagement with feedback. It is these variations that may explain why research on which type of WCF is best has yielded mixed results. However, although the engagement framework is a useful heuristic, it is not theoretically driven. Furthermore, the engagement framework ignores the context in which the feedback is provided.

Thus, in this paper, I would like to propose that a more theoretically informed way of investigating and trying to understand learners' engagement with and response to feedback is to consider learner actions as an enactment of their agency. I begin by discussing the term agency, including why it has become an important focus of scholarship in the field of L2 writing and applied linguistics more broadly. I also suggest that activity theory can provide a useful heuristic to identify important individual and contextual factors to explain agentive learner behavior. Using excerpts from studies that I have conducted with colleagues, I illustrate how we can explain agentive learner behavior when responding to teacher feedback and when engaging in peer feedback activities using the model of activity provided by activity theory. I conclude by describing two activities that I have implemented in the English for Academic Purposes (EAP) classes that I teach, which, I believe, provide learners with greater opportunities to enact their agency in feedback activities.

2. What is Agency?

The term agency has only relatively recently gained attention in the field of applied linguistics and language learning (e.g., Deters et al. 2015; Douglas Fir Group 2016; Gao 2010, 2013). Yet agency is not a new term. Agency has been a topic of much discussion and debate in disciplines such as sociology, anthropology, and philosophy (see Ahearn 2001), disciplines that often inform research in applied linguistics.

This relatively new interest in agency in applied linguistics is linked to a number of major shifts. One such shift is in how we view the learner. There has been an observed move away from a view of the learner as a disembodied processor of language input, to a view of the learner as a complex individual (Pavlenko & Lantolf 2000) whose language learning success may be explained by reference to emotions, goals, and a sense of identity. Ahearn (2001) documents another shift — the move away from a view of language as merely a set of structures (e.g., Chomsky 1975) to a view of language as a form of social action, with meaning co-constructed by interlocutors in a particular social context. These shifts are also evident in research on L2 writing, with a move away from focusing only on the written product to investigations of increasingly more complex and less quantifiable issues such as authorial voice (e.g., Matsuda 2015; Morton & Storch 2019) and digital identity (e.g., Smith et al. 2017).

Yet, despite the greater research interest in learner agency, the definition of the term is quite elusive and a number of definitions have been offered by scholars, depending very much on the theoretical perspective guiding the scholar's work. Ahearn (2001), a linguistic anthropologist, offers the shortest definition "a socioculturally mediated capacity to act" (p. 112), a definition that attempts to acknowledge the social nature of agency and the impact of culture on human intentions. However, Ahearn admits that this definition needs further unpacking. Duff (2012), coming from a language socialization perspective, defines agency as "people's ability to make choices, take control, self-regulate, and thereby pursue their goals as individuals leading, potentially, to personal or social transformation" (p. 417). What this definition emphasizes is human intentionality; that is, the individual's ability to make deliberate choices in pursuit of their goals. It also suggests that when individuals are able to pursue their goals, their actions lead to positive outcomes. However, others, such as Lantolf and Pavlenko (2001) reject the idea that agency is linked only to an individual's volition because it seems to equate agency with free will. Informed by a sociocultural perspective, Lantolf and Pavlenko (2001, p. 148) argue that "agency is never a property of the individual but a relationship that is constantly constructed and renegotiated with those around the individual and with society at large." In other words, the key traits of agency are that it is relational (indicated by the term relationship); that it is dynamic and dialogic (constantly constructed and renegotiated); and that it is situated (renegotiated with others and society at large). In a subsequent publication, Lantolf and Thorne (2006) admit that agency has components of individual intentionality but continue to emphasize the social and dynamic nature of the construct.

If we synthesize these definitions, we gain, I believe, a better understanding of agency. Agency has both individual and situated dimensions. Agency can be viewed as an individual's capacity to act, to choose actions which are driven by individual goals and beliefs. However, this choice is context specific and occurs in interaction with others, and as such it is mitigated by relational and contextual factors (see also Larsen-Freeman 2019). In other words, how and whether an individual learner exercises their capacity to act is made possible, encouraged or stifled, depending on key people and factors in the specific context in which learning activities take place. We can observe instantiation of learners' enactment of their agency in a range of classroom activities. These include, for example, whether and how learners participate in small group activities, such as collaborative writing or peer feedback activities, whether they communicate to each other in the classroom in their shared first language (L1) or the L2, and whether they choose to take up or ignore peer or teacher feedback on their writing.

3. Activity Theory and the Model of Activity

The theoretical framework that can perhaps best captures this definition of agency is activity theory (AT). The theory has its roots in Vygotsky's (1978) sociocultural theory. Briefly, sociocultural theory views human cognitive development as occurring during social interaction between a novice and a more expert member of society who provides the novice with appropriate assistance. This assistance is enabled or mediated by a range of artefacts or tools. Activity theory extends Vygtosky's work by focusing on purposeful human activity (e.g., work, education), activities which provide conditions for further development, and attempting to understand the outcomes of an activity by considering the behavior of all those involved and the role of the meditational tools (for a more detailed discussion see Bitchener & Storch 2016). A model of activity, which is a graphical representation of activity theory, identifies the key elements in any activity. This model has undergone a number of iterations, but the one that is most often referred to in research on L2 writing is that developed by Engeström (2001) and reproduced below.

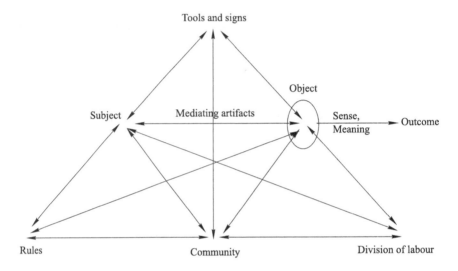

Figure 1. A model of activity (Engeström 2001, p. 135)

The underlying premise of this model is that humans who participate in a purposeful activity (*subjects*) are agentive in the sense that their actions are intentional. They come into an activity with their own social history, beliefs, and sense of identity which shape their goals. Subjects' actions are driven by their goals and ultimate *object* leading to a desired *outcome* but are mediated (enhanced or hindered) by various artefacts which can be physical or psychological. Physical artefacts (*tools*) include, for example, textbooks, handouts or computers; psychological tools include semiotic *signs* such as language. As these actions take place within a broader context, to fully understand human behavior we also need to consider other participants in the activity (*community*), the implicit or explicit conventions that regulate behavior in this particular community (*rules*), and the distribution of responsibilities and power within this community (*division of labor*).

The double headed arrows in the model denote that each of the key elements can influence and be influenced by the other elements in the activity. Thus the model highlights the situated, dynamic and goal directed nature of human activity. The advantage of using this model is that it enables researchers to simultaneously consider the multiple factors that can influence behavior and identify which factors best explain human behavior in a particular situation. In this paper, I identify elements in feedback activities that can help explain how and why agency is enacted.

The enactment of human agency is important, because as Pavlenko and Lantof (2000) argue "the ultimate attainment in second language learning relies on one's agency" (pp. 169-170). As I will illustrate in the excerpts that follow, it is learners' action in pursuit of their goals that can impact on language learning opportunities. It can also have another important outcome: it can affect learners' sense of achievement, of the ability to fulfil their own goals, as intimated by Duff's (2012) definition of agency.

In the next section, I draw on a small number of studies I have conducted with colleagues and graduate students which investigated feedback activities in different contexts. I reanalyze some of the findings from a learner agency perspective. I begin with discussing studies investigating learner response to feedback provided by an expert (e.g., native speaker researcher, teacher) and then discuss a study which analyzed learner behavior in a peer response activity.

4. Learner Response to Expert Feedback: A Learner Agency Perspective

In this section, I draw on the findings of two studies where feedback was provided by an expert member of the community. I begin by providing some details about the studies and their main findings. I then use excerpts from these studies to illustrate some salient learner behaviors which illustrate learners' agentive behavior. Using the model of activity, I identify the elements that seemed to play a key role in explaining the observed behaviors in a given context.

The first study was part of a large-scale research project which investigated the efficacy of direct versus indirect feedback (see Storch & Wigglesworth 2010a, b; Wigglesworth & Storch 2012). The participants (n=48), all volunteers who were paid for their participation in this research project, were international students in a large university in Australia who were undertaking degree courses in different disciplines. Their English proficiency was advanced (IELTS scores of 6.5 or above).

The design of our study was informed by a small case study conducted by Brooks and Swain (2009). Our study had three stages. In Stage 1 (Day 1), the participants were given a graphic prompt (similar to an IELTS task 1) and asked to compose a report in pairs. In the second stage (Day 5) the pairs processed the feedback they received and revised their original text. One group of participants received direct feedback (reformulated texts); the other group received indirect feedback (errors underlined with a code denoting the kind of error made). The pairs were given 15 minutes to discuss the feedback. The text with the feedback was then removed and the pairs were given 30 minutes to rewrite their original (unmarked) version. All rewritten texts were collected. The third stage (Day 28) required the students to compose a report on the same prompt as in Day 1, but this time individually. All pair talk (Day 1 and 5) was audio recorded. All feedback was provided by a research assistant, a native speaker of English who was a trained and experienced

ESL teacher.

Our study found that indirect feedback elicited greater engagement with the feedback received than direct feedback. This was evident in the number and length of language related episodes generated when learners processed the feedback received (Stage 2 of the study). However, the learners who received direct feedback produced more accurate texts on Day 28, when they wrote new texts individually. These results led us to look more closely at the participants' behavior in Stage 2 of the study.

The pair talk data showed two interesting phenomena. One was that several learners, particularly those who received direct feedback (reformulations) tried to memorize the reformulated texts and then reproduced it in Stage 2, when rewriting their original text in pairs. Many seemed to retain these memorized chunks and used them in Stage 3, when writing a text in response to the same prompt individually. Excerpt 1 illustrates the memorization strategy adopted by several pairs. Haan suggested to Chay that they divide the reformulated text between them (Turn 14, 18), with each memorizing one part of the text to make it easier, and Chay readily agreed.

Excerpt 1

14	Haan:	We try to remember the mistakes. I remember the first part, you remember the second part, OK? From this sentence
15	Chay:	Ah, which one? "The rainfall in autumn"
16	Haan:	Ah, yeah. You know
17	Chay:	"the rainfall in autumn"
18	Haan:	Yeah, you remember this. If we remember the separately, it will be much more easy

Gus and Jon were another pair who memorized the reformulated text. However, as the excerpt from their pair talk illustrates (Excerpt 2), Gus and Jon held negative attitudes to reformulations as a form of feedback (Turn 41, 64) because they felt that learners would memorize the feedback rather than work out how to correct their errors. Yet they then proceeded to do just that, dividing the four paragraph texts between them (Turn 65). The adoption of this strategy could be related to the fact that they held their own writing in such low esteem (Turn 44).

Excerpt 2

41	Gus	huh? I don't think this kind of feedback is good, because ...
42	Jon	Yeah
43	Gus:	people will tend to memorize this
44	Jon:	yeah this still crap
...		
64	Gus:	Yeah a feedback should not just give away the answer. Yeah that's ... that's my opinion. Ok, so, are we supposed to memorize this?
65	Jon:	Yea, you got paragraph 1 and 2, I got paragraph 3 and 4

Thus what seems to explain the better performance of the direct feedback group was the memorization strategy adopted by several pairs. The texts produced for this task were relatively short and by dividing the text between themselves the learners made the memorization of the reformulated text manageable. I should note here that this strategy of memorization was not unique to our study. Sachs and Polio (2007) reported similar observations in their study.

The other interesting observation was that the learners at times questioned the feedback and perhaps the expertise of the researcher and then rejected the feedback provided, whether direct or indirect. Excerpt 3 and 4 illustrate this behavior. For example, in Excerpt 3 Hong and Van recalled that the word "fluctuative" was underlined with a code indicating that this was an error in word form. The two students engaged in a lengthy discussion about the feedback on their error (Turns 10-15), digressed to discuss another feedback point before returning to this error (Turns 34-38) when they finally decided that the feedback they received was incorrect. They then decided to use a different adjective as a form of compromise.

Excerpt 3

10	Hong:	"fluctuate"? "fluctuative" wrong form
11	Van:	um ...
12	Hong:	"fluctuation ... had more fluctuative"
13	Van:	what's wrong with "fluctuative"?
14	Hong:	"fluctuate", I think. "fluctuate ... more fluctuate levels"
15	Van:	No
...		
34	Hong:	fluctuative
35	Van:	fluctuation ... Fluctuative
36	Hong:	It's right
37	Van:	Yeah, I think she wrong with that. I just change it into "unstable"
38	Hong:	OK, OK, OK

Excerpt 4 comes from a pair of students who received direct feedback. They evaluated the reformulated phrase but decided that it does not improve their text. They rejected the offered suggestion and use a different structure.

Excerpt 4

| 187 | Feng: | No I don't think that is an improvement. I think that make this sentence more complicated but provide nothing |
| 188 | Mai: | yeah yeah ... just you use different structure |

The behaviors we witness in the pair talk are manifestations of learners' agency when responding to feedback. This includes engaging with the feedback or just memorizing it, accepting or questioning and rejecting expert feedback. Activity theory enables us to identify the key elements that mediate this behavior (see Figure 2). Agency, as noted earlier, is an individual's socially mediated capacity to choose actions in order to pursue their ultimate goals (*object*). In retrospect, I assume that these participants agreed to participate in this study in order to improve their writing, however there is no interview data to ascertain that this was indeed their goals (hence the question mark). The pair talk data suggested that another goal may have been to simply complete the tasks promptly, and hence they chose to memorize the reformulated text. This pragmatic strategy was also adopted perhaps because the learners did not think highly of direct feedback (an artifact) or of the quality of the writing they produced. The task they produced was not one on which they were going to be graded on. Another key element in this activity is the researcher, the other important member in this context (*community*). The participants did not know her very well and because she was not their teacher, the relationship they had with her was inconsequential. There was no clear power hierarchy in this context. Similarly, learners were expected to complete the tasks (an implied expectation) but there were no expectations for the participants to necessarily accept the feedback. Hence the participants were at liberty to question and reject the feedback (and expertise). Thus the key elements in this activity system (in bold) are the learners' goals and beliefs and relationship with the feedback provider. The other elements, rules and division of labor, enhanced their ability to pursue actions that aligned with their goals and beliefs.

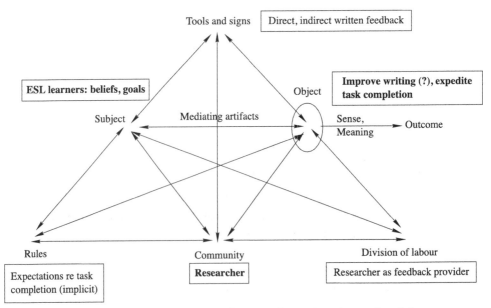

Figure 2. Learner enactment of agency in an experimental activity

Thus, what these observed behaviors suggest is that in experimental studies, learners may have a greater capacity to enact their agency, and this makes the response to feedback activity in an experimental study very different to the response to teacher feedback in a regular classroom, as is evident in the next study I discuss.

The second study I draw on is a more recent one (Liu & Storch, under review). It investigated learners' response to teacher feedback on the first drafts of their assignments.

The study was small scale (n=9) and conducted with intermediate students enrolled in a credit bearing EAP elective offered to graduate students across the university. The assessment tasks are based on topics related to students' fields of study. Students receive feedback on penultimate drafts of their assignments and are then given about a week to revise and submit the final version to be assessed. The study investigated students' response to feedback on their draft Assignment 2, a critical summary of two texts from their field of study, which contributed 20% to their overall grade for this subject. The data consisted of the students' first draft with teacher comments, revised drafts submitted for assessment, and recorded retrospective interviews conducted with each student about five days after they submitted their final draft of this assignment. In these text-based interviews, students were asked to comment on how and why they respond to feedback generally and to the specific feedback points on their drafts.

Our analysis of learners' first drafts with feedback showed that although the feedback was provided on all aspects of writing (content, structure, use of sources, language and mechanics), feedback on language and mechanics predominated (61% of all feedback points). WCF was approximately evenly split between direct and indirect feedback. Direct feedback was given as reformulations which at times were accompanied by explanations; indirect feedback was given as suggestions with symbols or abbreviations (familiar to the students) denoting the type of error made.

Analysis of the revised drafts showed that all nine learners took up the vast majority of all feedback (97%), particularly WCF. Retrospective interviews helped explain the high compliance rate. I report here on two cases whose interviews provide insights into the learners' behavior. The two case study participants were representative of the majority of the students in this subject. They were female, international students from China, with a high English proficiency (IELTS 6.5 average, writing 6) undertaking a Master of Applied Linguistics.

The first case study is Diane who received the most feedback on her draft (66 feedback points) and showed the highest uptake rate (97% of all comments). The second case study is Katherine who also received a large amount of feedback (53 feedback points). Her revised text also showed a high uptake rate, but it was slightly lower (91%) compared to her peers. Although we investigated learners' response to feedback on all aspects of writing, here I focus specifically on learners' response to WCF, the predominant focus of the feedback given.

Diane

Diane came across as a highly motivated student. Her ultimate goal was to improve her academic English writing, an aspiration that was closely linked to her idealized vision of herself, as she reported in the interview:

> *(I could imagine) myself could help other people, that's a very strong motivation in my academic writing, not only the exams that I need to pass ... but the ideal of myself encourage me to do more.*

She explained that she wanted to improve her accuracy in order to be able to communicate her ideas meaningfully. She was concerned that her grammatical errors distracted the teacher from looking "at my conclusion of my research, and what I think about this topic".

Diane explained that she engaged extensively with the feedback she received, considering carefully all the feedback comments, whether they were provided as indirect WCF or reformulations. Diane reported that she did not simply revise her expression based on what the teacher suggested. Instead, she thought deeply about the feedback, checked dictionaries, consulted the original articles she summarized, and asked the teacher for more explanations until she understood why revisions were needed.

Katherine

In contrast to Diane, Katherine did not enjoy writing and did not have a strong motivation to improve her writing. Her overall aim was "to get a high grade". She felt that she could achieve this by improving her critical thinking skills rather than accuracy, because she felt that as an adult L2 learner she could never achieve native speaker like accuracy. At the same time, she felt embarrassed by the amount of corrective feedback she received because she was a high school English teacher in China. The large volume of feedback she received seemed to threaten her identity as an English teacher:

> *Because I'm an English teacher in China, sometimes you find you have so many problems ... it's hard to admit that ...*

Katherine sometimes felt confused or disagreed with the direct WCF, yet she still accepted the suggestions noting the authority invested in the teacher and her desire to get a good grade. For example in response to the suggestions to delete the word 'completely' in one of her sentences she noted:

> *Why should I delete 'completely' ... I don't understand, because this is not a mistake ... (yet) because teacher marks your work ... I delete it ...*

Her lack of understanding became more acute with indirect WCF. She did not like indirect WCF because she did not know how to correct the identified error and sometimes the feedback contradicted her previously acquired knowledge of grammar rules. In such cases, she just made random choices or avoided the target error by rephrasing the whole sentence. For example, in response to a feedback comment that suggested that she should check her use of prepositions, Katherine admitted that:

> *I don't know how to correct it, I also ask my classmates, they don't know, because according to my own language system, I think it's correct ... and I can't find the example of the same structure ... I just randomly change ... try another (preposition) ...*

The retrospective interviews showed that the actions the learners took in response to the teacher feedback were goal driven and closely linked to their sense of identity, whether an existing professional identity (Katherine) or an idealized one (Diane). Diane's goal was to improve her accuracy and thus she engaged deeply with the feedback provided and sought assistance. Her ability to pursue her goals was also relational. She clearly considered the teacher as approachable and a source of expert advice. Her actions provided her with language learning opportunities as well as a sense of achievement. In contrast, Katherine's goal was to gain a better grade and thus she simply took up the feedback, even when she did not understand or agree with it. She was acutely aware of the perceived power hierarchy in the classroom and expected norms of behavior. Unlike the experimental studies discussed above, in this study the revised text was assessed by the teacher. This clearly constrained the learners' choice of actions, explaining the high take up rate for all nine participants. A number of classroom-based studies have indeed noted that students are likely to accept their teacher's feedback even if they do not fully understand it (e.g., Lee 2014; Zhao 2010). Katherine's interview also suggested that the compliance with the feedback led at times to a sense of frustration rather than achievement.

Using activity theory, we can again map the key elements that mediated these EAP learners' choice of actions in response to the teacher's feedback, highlighting (in bold) the key elements shaping learners' agency. This is illustrated in Figure 3.

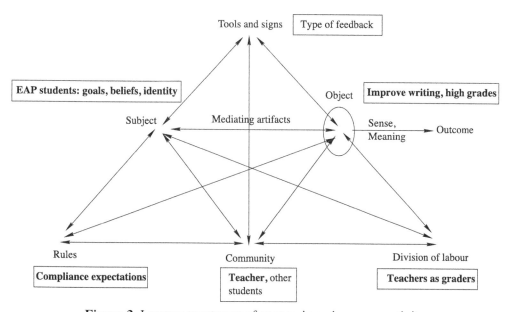

Figure 3. Learner enactment of agency in a classroom activity

In this feedback activity taking place in a regular classroom, subjects' actions in pursuit of attaining their ultimate goals (*object*), whether to improve their writing and/ or achieve high grades, were shaped by goals, beliefs, and their sense of identity. These actions were mediated by their relationship with other members of the community, other students (who can be consulted) and the teacher — the key member of this community. In the classroom, unlike the experimental context described earlier, the teacher marks the students' work and this power hierarchy (*division of labor*) and entrenched expectations concerning compliance with the feedback given (*rules*) mediated learners' choice of actions.

The findings in these studies show that learner response to teacher/expert feedback is agentive. It is driven by individual learner goals, goals that are perhaps shaped by prior learning experiences and beliefs. However, this ability to pursue one's goals is relational and situated, as implied by the definition of agency. In these studies, the relationship with the feedback provider, the importance of the task and whether it is high stakes (graded), and the expected norms of behavior in a particular setting all mediated learners' ability to enact their agency. The differences between the classroom and experimental contexts have implications not only for learners' ability to enact their agency, but also for language learning opportunities. When learners simply follow the feedback provided, without understanding the source of their errors or simply memorise it without engaging with it, they are unlikely to learn from the feedback nor derive a sense of satisfaction from the activity.

5. Peer Response Activities: A Learner Agency Perspective

Another source of feedback in L2 writing classes is peers. Peer response activities, also referred to as peer feedback or peer review activities, involve learners in providing feedback on each other's writing. Many scholars have identified the potential benefits of this activity, both for language learning and learning to write (see Yu & Lee 2016). However, a small number of studies have also shown that the benefits of peer response activities may depend on the group dynamics and the type of stances learners adopt in this activity (e.g., Lockhart & Ng 1995; Yu & Lee 2015). Drawing on a study conducted in Saudi Arabia (Aldossary 2017; Storch & Aldossary 2019), I suggest that the stances learners adopt as givers or receivers of peer feedback are instantiations of learner agency, and in turn have implications for language learning opportunities.

The study was conducted in two English as a Foreign Language (EFL) classes at a large male only university. It sought to investigate whether it is better for a language learner to be a giver or receiver of peer feedback. The students, all of intermediate EFL proficiency, were randomly assigned to be either givers (n=24) or receivers (n=23) of peer feedback and maintained that role over an entire semester. All participants were trained and given extensive practice in peer feedback before the study was implemented. The writing and the peer feedback activities formed part of the regular language class (150 minutes in duration) but were not assessed. The feedback givers read the assigned peer's written text and were given a checklist to guide their review. The checklist directed their attention to consider errors in language, logical flow of content, and development of ideas. Pairs composed of a feedback giver and receiver then met (for approx. 30 minutes) and their pair talk was audio recorded. Once the peer feedback session was completed, all participants (givers and receivers) were asked to re-write their own drafts. There were six such sessions throughout the semester, and in each session a feedback giver worked with a different receiver. All students were interviewed at the end of the study.

Pre and post test results revealed that all learners improved their accuracy, regardless of whether they were assigned to be feedback givers or receivers. However, what seemed to impact on post-test gains was the stances learners adopted in these peer review activities. Analysis of the pair talk during these activities revealed that the learners adopted distinct and stable stances. Feedback givers adopted one of three stances: authoritative, cautious or probing. Feedback receivers adopted one of four stances: responsive, defensive, probing and passive. These giver and receiver stances were distinguished in terms of the learners' moves (e.g., frequency and type of requests), language (e.g., use of modals, imperatives, pronouns) and the tone used (see Storch & Aldossary 2019 for a detailed description of these stances). The most common stances adopted were authoritative by the givers and responsive by the receivers. Thus authoritative/responsive was the most frequent pattern of interaction in the peer review activities. The following excerpt illustrates this pattern of interaction.

As Excerpt 5 illustrates, the giver (Omar) dominated the session providing fairly prescriptive advice, directing the receiver (Matrodi) on how to improve his text. Directives were issued (e.g., Turn 3: you must say...; Turn 7: you have to put ...) to improve the structure (need for a topic sentence), syntax (sentence length) and mechanics (use of capitals and punctuation). The receiver seemed to be engaged with the feedback, seeking assistance (Turn 2) and confirmation for changes needed (Turn 10).

Excerpt 5

1	Omar:	Let's start with the topic sentence ... this you write "the advantage of large college" ... this one is like too general ...
2	Matrodi:	Ah, okay, how can I write?
3	Omar:	So, to be correct, you must say "large colleges has many advantages" ... so that you will mention the advantages of large college.
4	Matrodi:	Ah ... like large colleges has ...
5	Omar:	has many advantage ...
6	Matrodi:	Can you write line just here?
7	Omar:	Yeah. After that you have to put ...
8	Matrodi:	Point.
9	Omar:	Yeah, period and then start the new sentence.
10	Matrodi:	So, I should write capital?
11	Omar:	Yes ... capital letter. and then "large colleges has many different section" ... also here ... you start a new sentence.

Other stances that were found in the data were not as frequent nor as stable across the feedback sessions. For example, Gosairy, a feedback receiver, was responsive in three sessions, and defensive in three other sessions, depending on who he was paired with.

Excerpt 6 shows how Gosairy interacted with Majeed who assumed an authoritative stance as a feedback giver. As shown in the excerpt, Majeed attempts to direct Gosairy's attention to the incorrect use of a verb form with the pronoun "I", telling Gosairy that the verb form "were" should be used rather than "was" (Turn 19). Gosairy rejects Majeed's suggestion (Turn 20), and what follows is a long series of turns where the two reject each other's suggestions, insisting on their viewpoint. Gosairy also suggests that they ask the teacher to resolve the disagreement (Turns 24, 27).

Excerpt 6

19	*Majeed*:	One minute ... one minute ... another mistake ... I ... you don't write was ... he she it ... write was ... I they you we write ... were ...
20	Gosairy:	no ... I was ...
21	*Majeed*:	no ... I were ...
22	Gosairy:	no no ... I was ...
23	*Majeed*:	I sure ...
24	Gosairy:	are you sure? let me ask the teacher ...
25	*Majeed*:	after ...
26	Gosairy:	no no ... I will ... believe me ... when you say something ... I was engineer ... he she it and I ... they all take was ...
27	*Majeed*:	We will talk with the teacher after ...
28	Gosairy:	Are you sure?
29	*Majeed*:	Yes ... like ... I were liked .. here not write liked ... like ... just like ... not the past ... just ...
30	Gosairy:	You're mistake.

A closer examination of the pre and post-test results showed that givers who adopted an authoritative stance consistently across all the feedback sessions had higher gain scores than those whose stances varied across the sessions. In the case of the receivers, all showed gains in their post-test scores, with the exception of the few who adopted a passive stance (for more details see Aldossary 2017).

Data elicited from the retrospective interviews can help explain why learners adopted such distinct stances in the peer response activities. Interviews conducted with feedback givers showed that those who adopted an authoritative stance shared a view about their perceived role in this activity. Most likened their role to that of a teacher with a responsibility to assist their peers. Their goal was to improve their peers' writing. For example, Omar admitted that the responsibility to provide correct feedback encouraged him to prepare for the task, to look up vocabulary and review grammar rules:

> *Being a giver ... makes you control ... And like ... you are the ... leader ... it makes you responsible ... the receiver will listen to you ... and put what you say ... [learn] a lot of vocabulary ... and also try to learn as many grammar as I can ... can try to correct as you can.* (Omar, interview)

The authoritative manner in which these students provided feedback seemed to reflect the teacher centered EFL classes in Saudi Arabia (see Assalahi 2013). In such classes, the teacher is viewed as the ultimate expert whose authority and expertise are not questioned. The focus of the feedback the givers provided, despite the checklist, was predominantly WCF (on language and mechanical errors) which is typical of the type of feedback learners in EFL classes in Saudi Arabia tend to receive on their writing (e.g., Shahrani & Storch 2014).

The responsive receivers' comments in the interviews indicated that their behavior was also goal driven and situational. They were driven by their desire to improve their writing, and thus accepted most of the feedback provided and expressed gratitude for the help given. For example, in his interview Matrodi commented that discussions with his feedback givers were "interesting and very helpful" as they helped him "get better and better [with] grammar... [and] ideas".

What seemed to make the activity enjoyable for these responsive learners was the opportunity to seek clarification and confirmation and to receive additional explanations — opportunities absent in their regular EFL classes. For example, Eid, another consistently responsive receiver, noted in the interview that the activity provided him with opportunities to "discuss about why this is wrong or why this is right." and that it was "good like that". In other words, these negotiations provided both givers and receivers language learning opportunities. This perhaps explains why most learners showed language learning gains in the post tests.

However, when learners formed an authoritative/defensive relationship, the receiver's stance shows the importance of the relational dimension of agency. It depended on how they evaluated the giver's language proficiency in relation to their own proficiency. In the interview, Gosairy said that he benefited from "some of them [the givers]" because "sometimes you know better than him [the giver]", and thus "I didn't believe in them [some givers' feedback]". Gosairy mentioned that after the sessions in which he adopted a defensive stance he sought assistance from other sources "search[ing] about it on the Internet ... ask[ing] my family about it." Clearly Gosairy's actions were also driven by a desire to improve his writing but when he mistrusted the feedback the peer gave him, he sought help elsewhere. In authoritative/defensive interactions, there were fewer language learning opportunities as the feedback was disputed and rejected (see Excerpt 6).

Again, we can explain the distinct behavior associated with these giver and receiver stances using the construct of agency and the framework provided by activity theory. The key elements in this activity are highlighted (bolded) in Figure 4. The givers, most of whom adopted an authoritative stance, seemed driven by a sense of responsibility and a desire to help their peers produce a better draft. The receivers had complementary goals – a desire to improve their writing. The behavior of authoritative givers and responsive receivers to some extent imitated the behavior of the teachers in their EFL classes (community), but the lack of explicit power hierarchies in this activity meant that the receivers could question and seek further clarification. In the case of defensive (and probing) receivers, the power hierarchies were related to how the learners evaluated their own proficiency in comparison to that of their peers. Learners were expected to participate in the activity as part of their regular classwork, but their participation was not assessed. Hence, and as indicated in Figure 4, the learners' capacity to exercise their agency was largely volitional, driven predominantly by the desire to improve their writing.

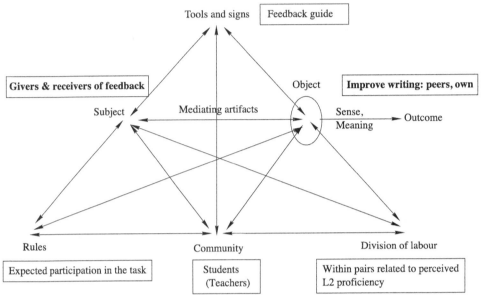

Figure 4. Learners' stances in a peer feedback activity as an enactment of their agency

6. Discussion and Recommendations

The extracts presented in this paper show adult language learners enact their agency in various ways to achieve their goals in teacher and peer response activities. Learners' agency in these activities was shown to be largely volitional, driven by individual goals. However, it was also relational — as learners interacted with others in a particular context: researchers, teacher, peers. What these extracts also show is that agency is situated. Factors such as power hierarchies and expected norms of behavior in particular contexts mediate learners' ability to exercise their agency.

In the classroom, when the teacher provides feedback, power hierarchies and expected norms of behavior curtail learners' ability to exercise their agency. Learners may simply accept the feedback provided, regardless of whether they agree or understand it. In peer feedback activities, although learners who provide peer feedback may emulate teacher behavior, feedback receivers have the capacity to exercise their agency, accepting, questioning or rejecting the feedback given. Similarly, in experimental studies, the relationship with the feedback provider (usually a researcher) is short lived and insignificant to the participants — affording them greater capacity to exercise their agency.

Learners' ability to enact their agency is important, as it seems to have implications for language learning opportunities. In the experimental study, learners deliberated about the feedback provided (particularly indirect feedback) even if ultimately they decided to reject it. Similarly, in the peer feedback activities, learners sought additional clarifications and were able to reject feedback when they questioned its veracity. This explains the mainly positive views about the activity in the interviews. In contrast, in the classroom some students may seek additional clarifications, as in the case of Diane, but as illustrated in the case of Katherine and reported in other studies (Lee 2014; Zhao 2010), learners often simply comply with teacher feedback even if they do not understand or agree with it. Such compliance is unlikely to result in language learning. It is also more likely to lead to a sense of frustration and confusion.

Using activity theory can provide us with a better understanding of learners' agentive behavior when responding to teacher or peer feedback. However, as Lantolf and Thorne (2006) point out, the application of activity theory should go beyond description and analysis, it should lead to transformation. In other words, the purpose of research should go beyond gaining a better understanding of learners' enactment of their agency. Rather, it should lead to positive interventions that can enable learners to engage more fully and effectively as agents in their language learning activity, taking advantage of the learning opportunities that certain tasks can offer them and thereby a greater sense of achievement. Thus in what follows, I describe two activities, one related to teacher feedback provision the other to peer feedback activities, that may go some way to achieve these aims.

One way to promote learner agency in response to teacher feedback on their writing is perhaps to encourage learners to take a greater lead in the feedback process (see also Maas 2017). The strategy I (and my colleagues) have adopted in our EAP classes to achieve this aim is the use of annotations. Annotations simply involve learners in identifying areas of concern or uncertainty in their drafts. Figure 5 shows an example of an annotated excerpt from a student's writing. The student has underlined and numbered her areas of concern with related questions or comments in the margins.

Annotated text	Annotations
Table 1 displays Australia's postgraduate employment outcomes by study area in 2015 and 2018.[1] Compared with the[2] data in 2015, the percentile scores of employment outcomes in 2018 show a significantly[3] increasing trend. Among the above listed study areas, Science & Mathematics presents[4] the most dramatic growth from 48.3 to 85.6. Meanwhile, majors such as Computing & Information Systems, Engineering, Teaching as well as Creative arts have also been proved to gain obvious higher employment rates which have generally risen by more than 20 percent in 2018. Whereas, the outcome percentage of Tourism, hospitality, sport and recreation has witnessed[5] a slight decline from 93.8 to 91.8.	1. Should I use another way to summarize the main idea? I think this is similar to chart title. 2. "the" necessary? 3. I'm confused about significant & significantly 4. Simple present or present perfect? 5. Is this word suitable?

Figure 5. Example of an annotated student text

Annotations not only encourage learners to reflect about their own writing but can also guide the teacher when giving feedback. The teacher responds to the annotations, providing both positive (reassurance) and negative (corrective) feedback. Where a number of annotations deal with the same type of error (e.g., the use of articles or choice of verb tense), the teacher can provide a simple explanation or refer the student to an appropriate reference. This makes the feedback more tailored to the student's expressed needs. The teacher usually also provides feedback on other weaknesses in the drafts that may not have been identified by the learners. Learners are encouraged to review all the feedback received and keep a log of their errors to guide their annotations in subsequent writing tasks. Our research (Storch & Tapper 1997) has shown that the system is particularly suitable for intermediate – advanced learners. In our EAP classes, we strongly encourage students to annotate their assignments but we do not mandate it. Although we have implemented the system only on drafts submitted for teacher feedback, the system could equally be used in peer feedback activities.

The other activity I have recently implemented in one of my EAP subjects is a peer response activity that replicates the peer review process implemented by academic journals. Here, too, the aim is to encourage learners to be agentive, particularly when responding to peer feedback. The activity has multiple stages. In the first stage, learners submit a draft of their writing, and the drafts are allocated to peers for feedback, with each learner required to provide feedback on two texts. Each learner then receives written peer feedback from two anonymous peers. In the next stage, the learners respond to the feedback, writing brief explanations as to why a reviewer's specific suggestion (when provided) was accepted or rejected. Figure 6 provides an example of student responses to the feedback received on their writing from their two anonymous peers.

Relevant text	Reviewer A's suggestion	Review B's suggestion	Decision and explanation
Learning <u>was</u> considered as an inherent skill for a long time	Has been	Had been	Reject A & Accept B. Action happened in past & ended → need past perfect not present perfect
An American researcher Watson <u>found</u> the Behaviorist theory.	Established	—	Accept A. Established = more academic word
Habit formation is widely used in other fields to explain behavior, for example in the field of education.	—	including the field of education.	Reject B. The suggestion changes the meaning of my sentence.

Figure 6. Example of a student's response to anonymized peer feedback

In the final stage of this activity, students submit their revised text to the teacher. Both the provision and response to the peer feedback are graded to encourage students to invest in both activities. Informal student feedback suggests that the students found this activity challenging but rewarding. They comment that the need to engage critically with peer feedback is novel but that it encouraged them to look up resources and process the feedback received much more deeply than when they were engaging in peer feedback activities in other language classes.

The suggested activities were implemented with adult learners of intermediate to advanced L2 (English) proficiency. Clearly there is a need to consider whether and how they can be implemented with learners in different contexts, and with lower proficiency levels. Such studies need to be classroom based and longitudinal, investigating the potential impact of such activities on not only learners' language development but also their ability to become autonomous language learners.

7. Conclusion

Gao (2013) argues that teachers should consider what kind of strategies can assist learners to become reflective agents. I would like to conclude by suggesting that teachers also need to become reflective agents. We need to reflect periodically on whether our teaching practices enable learners to behave as agentive learners in our L2 writing classes. For example, we need to reflect on the kind of feedback comments we provide, on whether we encourage students and give them sufficient opportunities to seek clarification of feedback received, and what kind of expectations we communicate to our students regarding their response to the feedback.

References

Ahearn, L. M. 2001. Language and agency [J]. *Annual Review of Anthropology* 30: 109-137.

Aldossary, M. 2017. Peer feedback and the L2 writing of givers and receivers: A quantitative and qualitative longitudinal study involving Saudi students [D]. PhD dissertation. University of Melbourne.

Assalahi, H. M. 2013. Why is the grammar-translation method still alive in the Arab world? Teacher beliefs and its implications for EFL teacher education [J]. *Theory and Practice in Language Studies* 3(4): 589-599.

Bitchener, J. 2019. The intersection between SLA and feedback research [A]. In K. Hyland & F. Hyland (eds.). *Feedback in Second Language Writing: Contexts and Issues* (2nd ed.) [C]. Cambridge: Cambridge University Press. 85-105.

Bitchener, J. & N. Storch. 2016. *Written Corrective Feedback for L2 Development* [M]. Bristol, UK: Multilingual Matters.

Brooks, L. & M. Swain. 2009. Languaging in collaborative writing: Creation of and response to expertise [A]. In A. Mackey & C. Polio (eds.). *Multiple Perspectives on Interaction in SLA* [C]. Mahwah, NJ: Lawrence Erlbaum Associates. 58-89.

Chomsky, N. 1975. *Reflections on Language* [M]. London: Temple Smith.

Deters, P., X. Gao, E. R. Miller & G. Vitanova (eds.). 2015. *Theorizing and Analyzing Agency in Second Language Learning* [C]. Bristol, UK: Multilingual Matters.

Douglas Fir Group. 2016. A transdisciplinary framework for SLA in a multilingual world [J]. *Modern*

Language Journal 100(Supplement): 19-47.

Duff, P. 2012. Identity, agency, and second language acquisition [A]. In S. Gass & A. Mackey (eds.). *The Routledge Handbook of Second Language Acquisition* [C]. London: Routledge. 410-426.

Ellis, R. 2010. A framework for investigating oral and written corrective feedback [J]. *Studies in Second Language Acquisition* 32(2): 335-349.

Engeström, Y. 2001. Expansive learning at work: Toward an activity theoretical reconceptualization [J]. *Journal of Education and Work* 14(1): 133-156.

Ferris, D. & K. Kurzer. 2019. Does error feedback help L2 writers? Latest evidence on the efficacy of written corrective feedback [A]. In K. Hyland & F. Hyland (eds.). *Feedback in Second Language Writing: Contexts and Issues* (2nd ed.) [C]. Cambridge: Cambridge University Press. 106-124.

Gao, X. 2010. *Strategic Language Learning: The Roles of Agency and Context* [M]. Bristol, UK: Multilingual Matters.

Gao, X. 2013. Reflexive and reflective thinking: A crucial link between agency and autonomy [J]. *Innovation in Language Learning and Teaching* 7: 226-237.

Gass, S. 1997. *Input, Interaction and the Second Language Learner* [M]. Mahwah, NJ: Lawrence Erlbaum Associates.

Han, Y. & Y. Xu. 2019. Student feedback literacy and engagement with feedback: A case study of Chinese undergraduate students [J]. *Teaching in Higher Education* 26(2): 181-196.

Lantolf, J. P. & A. Pavlenko. 2001. (S)econd (L)anguage (A)ctivity theory: Understanding second language learners as people [A]. In M. Breen (ed.). *Learner Contributions to Language Learning: New Directions in Research* [C]. London: Pearson Education. 141-158.

Lantolf, J. P. & S. Thorne. 2006. *Sociocultural Theory and the Genesis of Second Language Development* [M]. Oxford: Oxford University Press.

Larsen-Freeman, D. 2019. On language learner agency: A complex dynamic systems theory perspective [J]. *The Modern Language Journal* 103(supplement): 61-79.

Lee, I. 2014. Revisiting teacher feedback in EFL writing from sociocultural perspectives [J]. *TESOL Quarterly* 48(1): 201-213.

Leow, R. P. 2015. *Explicit Learning in L2 Classroom: A Student-centred Approach* [M]. New York: Routledge.

Liu, K. & N. Storch. Under review. Second language learners' engagement with written feedback.

Lockhart, C. & P. Ng. 1995. Analyzing talk in ESL peer response groups: Stances, functions, and content [J]. *Language Learning* 45(4): 605-651.

Maas, C. 2017. Receptivity to learner-driven feedback in EAP [J]. *ELT Journal* 71: 127-140.

Matsuda, P. K. 2015. Identity in written discourse [J]. *Annual Review of Applied Linguistics* 35(1): 140-159.

Morton, J. & N. Storch. 2019. Developing an authorial voice in PhD multilingual student writing: The reader's perspective [J]. *Journal of Second Language Writing* 43(1): 15-23.

Pavlenko, A. & J. Lantolf. 2000. Second language learning as participation and the (re)construction of selves [A]. In J. Lantolf (ed.). *Sociocultural Theory and Second Language Learning: Recent Advances* [C]. Oxford: Oxford University Press. 155-177.

Sachs, R. & C. Polio. 2007. Learners' uses of two types of written feedback on an L2 writing revision task [J]. *Studies in Second Language Acquisition* 29: 67-100.

Shahrani, A. & N. Storch. 2014. Investigating teachers' written corrective feedback practices in a Saudi EFL context: How do they align with their beliefs, institutional guidelines, and students' preferences? [J]. *Australian Review of Applied Linguistics* 37: 101-122.

Smith, B. E., M. B. Pacheco & C. Rossato de Almedia. 2017. Multimodal codemeshing: Bilingual adolescents' processes composing across modes and languages [J]. *Journal of Second Langauge Writing* 36: 6-22.

Storch, N. & M. Aldossary. 2019. Peer feedback: An activity theory perspective on givers and receivers' stances [A]. In M. Sato & S. Loewen (eds.). *Evidence-based Second Language Pedagogy: A Collection of Instructed Second Language Acquisition Studies* [C]. New York: Routledge. 123-144.

Storch, N. & J. Tapper. 1997. Student annotations and writing conferences: What NESB and NS students say about their own writing [J]. *Journal of Second Language Writing* 6(3): 245-264.

Storch, N. & G. Wigglesworth. 2010a. Students' engagement with feedback on writing: The role of learner agency/beliefs [A]. In R. Batstone (ed.). *Sociocognitive Perspectives on Language Use and Language Learning* [C]. Oxford: Oxford University Press. 166-185.

Storch, N. & G. Wigglesworth. 2010b. Learners' processing, uptake, and retention of corrective feedback on writing [J]. *Studies in Second Language Acquisition* 32(2): 303-334.

Vygotsky, L. S. 1978. *Mind in Society: The Development of Higher Psychological Processes* [M]. Cambridge, MA: Harvard University Press.

Wigglesworth, G. & N. Storch. 2012. Feedback and writing development through collaboration: A socio-cultural approach [A]. In R. Manchon (ed.). *L2 Writing Development: Multiple Perspectives* [C]. Boston: de Gruyter. 69-100.

Yu, S. & I. Lee. 2015. Understanding EFL students' participation in group peer feedback of L2 writing: A case study from an activity theory perspective [J]. *Language Teaching Research* 19(5): 572-593.

Yu, S. & I. Lee. 2016. Peer feedback in second language writing (2005-2014) [J]. *Language Teaching* 49: 461-193.

Zhang, Z. V. & K. Hyland. 2018. Student engagement with teacher and automated feedback on L2 writing [J]. *Assessing Writing* 36: 90-102.

Zhao, H. 2010. Investigating learners' use and understanding of peer and teacher feedback on writing: A comparative study in a Chinese English writing classroom [J]. *Assessing Writing* 15(1): 3-17.

Zheng, Y. & S. Yu. 2018. Student engagement with teacher written corrective feedback in EFL writing: A case study of Chinese lower-proficiency students [J]. *Assessing Writing* 37: 13-24.

About the Author

Neomy STORCH is an Associate Professor in ESL and Applied Linguistics and the convenor of the ESL Program at the School of Languages & Linguistics, the University of Melbourne, Australia. Her research interests include collaborative writing, feedback on writing, assessing writing development, and authorial voice in the writing of multilingual doctoral students. Email: neomys@unimelb.edu.au

A Corpus-based Analysis of Noun Phrase Complexity in English Dissertations Written by L1 English and L1 Arabic Students

Hani ALBELIHI[1]　Ge LAN[2]

[1]Qassim University, Saudi Arabia
[2]City University of Hong Kong, China

Abstract: This corpus-based study sought to investigate the association between noun phrase complexity and language background in the introductory sections of English dissertations written by L1 English and L1 Arabic doctoral students. A corpus was built based on 100 dissertations, including 50 dissertations for each group. Based on the index of writing complexity features in Biber et al. (2011), 11 noun modifiers were extracted to represent noun phrase complexity in the writings of the two groups. A Chi-square test and residual analysis were then applied to explore how language background influenced the 11 noun modifiers. The results show that language background largely influences four specific noun modifiers: premodifying nouns, PPs (other), prepositions followed by *-ing* clauses, and infinitive clauses. More specifically, the L1 students used premodifying nouns more frequently to construct compressed noun phrases in their dissertations, whereas the L2 students produced more diverse patterns of noun phrases based on prepositional phrases (other), prepositions followed by *-ing* clauses, and infinitive clauses. Finally, pedagogical implications are provided, such as the suggestion that online corpora be used to teach noun phrases in graduate writing classrooms.

Keywords: corpus analysis; academic writing; grammatical complexity; noun phrases; second language writing

1. Introduction

A strong publication record is an indispensable goal for doctoral students who want to secure a faculty career, rank, and awards, and being well-versed in academic writing is fundamental to academic accomplishment (Aitchison & Guerin 2014). Accordingly, academic writing development is of paramount concern in higher education (Staples et al. 2016). Universities are committed to helping students foster the development of their academic writing during both undergraduate and graduate studies. One important area of writing development is *grammatical complexity,* which has received increasing attention in writing studies. Indeed, this construct has been considered one of the three important dimensions (i.e., complexity, accuracy, and fluency) used to benchmark language development, performance, and proficiency (Ellis 2003; Housen et al. 2012; Norris & Ortega 2009; Ortega 2015; Wolfe-Quintero et al. 1998).

Grammatical complexity has been primarily researched based on clausal structures (e.g., subordinate clauses) at early studies based on T-units (Bulté & Housen 2012); however, studies in the 2010s demonstrated the importance of integrating phrasal structures into grammatical complexity to represent the construct comprehensively (Lan et al. 2019b). Among phrasal features, it is particularly critical to investigate noun phrases (NPs) in academic writing, for many large-scale corpus analyses on academic writing have demonstrated the high frequency of NPs in this register (Biber et al. 1999). Furthermore, scholars have argued that advanced academic writing is often based on complex NPs (e.g., Biber et al. 2011; Parkinson & Musgrave 2014; Staples et al. 2016); thus, it is essential to explore how advanced writers (i.e., doctoral students) use NPs in their academic writing. This study aims to capture differences among NP structures in English dissertations written by L1 English and L1 Arabic doctoral students in the field of education.

Although there has been a long history of comparing L1 and L2 texts in writing studies, most previous empirical studies have primarily focused on texts from L2 writers at beginning or intermediate levels (e.g., L2 students in ESL or EAP programs). To the best of our knowledge, few studies have focused on texts of advanced writers, for instance, doctoral students. A doctoral dissertation is a critical written genre for this group of student writers; therefore, we consider it indispensable to analyze NPs in this particular genre. Furthermore, as previous research has mentioned that L1 background could affect grammatical complexity (e.g., Lu & Ai 2015; Staples & Reppen 2016), we attempt to examine such influence by focusing on doctoral students with Arabic as their L1. This language group was selected due to the fact that Arabic students constitute a large proportion of international students in higher education worldwide, including both undergraduate-level and graduate-level studies (Institute of International Education 2019). Because of the educational cooperation between China and Saudi Arabia in the past decade (2011-2020), an increasingly number of Saudi Arabic students have studied in China as exchange students, or vice versa (Muhammad 2014). Such a comparison could reveal differences that can be acknowledged and addressed by university professors to effectively enhance academic writing for diverse populations of graduate students in higher education.

2. Literature Review

2.1 Grammatical complexity as a multidimensional construct

Since the 1990s, grammatical complexity has been substantially studied in the field of L2 writing as an important research construct, and various grammatical measures have been applied in empirical studies (Ortega 2015). Grammatical complexity measures can be classified into two main categories: large-grain measures (e.g., mean length of clause) and fine-grain measures (e.g., adverbial and adjective clauses). Despite the various grammatical measures that have been used in L2 writing studies, scholars have pointed out a critical issue: grammatical complexity has been primarily represented by clausal complexity (Biber et al. 2011; Bulté & Housen 2012). Lu (2011) summarized 14 effective grammatical measures and revealed that two syntactic measures are the most frequent in L2 writing: mean length of T-unit and clauses per T-unit. As a T-unit refers to a main clause and all dependent clauses attached to the main clause, T-unit-based measures largely focus on clausal subordination (Biber et al. 2011). Bulté and Housen (2012) expressed a similar concern that the existing measures of grammatical complexity are primarily based on clausal subordination.

In the 2010s, scholars have been working on integrating phrasal complexity into grammatical complexity to make the representation of this construct complete (Lan et al. 2019b). In terms of theoretical works, Bulté and Housen (2012) proposed a model of L2 complexity, adding phrasal complexity as a dimension of linguistic complexity. In the same vein, Biber et al. (2011) built a theoretical framework of complexity features, which included dependent phrases that function as adverbial and noun modifiers as a dimension of complexity. As a result, more empirical studies on L2 writing have recently focused on the underrepresented dimension of phrasal complexity (Lan & Sun 2019). More specifically, compressed NPs, an important feature related to phrasal complexity, have been increasingly studied in L2 writing in the recent years (e.g., Ansarifar et al. 2018; Lan et al. 2019a; Parkinson & Musgrave 2014; Wang & Beckett 2017).

2.2 Noun Phrases (NPs) and academic writing

The definition of NPs has been consistent over time. For instance, Liberman and Sproat (1992) defined an NP as referring to "the head of noun [being] preceded by a sequence of modifiers" (p. 131). Similarly, Ni (2003) defined NPs as "strings of words with an internal structure centered around an obligatory head, which may be supplemented by determiners, premodifiers and post-modifiers" (pp. 159-160). In L2 writing, recent empirical studies have mostly adopted Biber et al.'s (1999) understanding of NP structure (e.g., Lan et al. 2019a; Parkinson & Musgrave 2014). This linguistic pattern is summarized as:

- Determiner + (pre-noun modifiers) + head noun + (post-noun modifiers and complements)

Example 1
- *The appealing definitions of NPs in the articles can give a clear conceptualization of the current study's goal.*

In more detail, the subject phrase in Example 1 includes a determiner (*the*), an attributive adjective as a premodifier (*appealing*), and a head noun (*definitions*). The sentence ends with a prepositional phrase (PP) as a postmodifier (*of NPs in the articles*). However, from a syntactic perspective, pronoun and nominal clauses can also be counted as NPs because they can appear in the positions of subject and object as well (Lan et al. 2019a). For instance, in the sentence *what he mentioned in the seminar is not expected by the group*, the nominal clause *what he mentioned* can also be considered an NP in a broad sense (Biber et al. 1999). In our study, we exclude pronoun and nominal clauses from our analysis of NPs; rather, we only applied Biber et al.'s (1999) linguistic patterns, for it is rare to identify pronouns and nominal clauses that fit the modifying relation between head nouns and modifiers (Lan et al. 2019a). Indeed, very few pronouns are used with pre- or post-noun modifiers, except for some limited cases (e.g., *something*, *nothing*), and nominal clauses do not include any modifying pattern based on nouns and modifiers.

Corpus studies have revealed that NPs often have either pre- and/or post modifiers in academic prose (Biber et al. 1999). In professional writing and research articles, phrasal modifiers (e.g., attributive adjectives, preposition phrases, appositive NPs) are often used to modify head nouns (Biber & Gray 2010). Biber and Gray (2010) summarized this style of academic writing as being one of structural compression, which means that academic writing heavily relies on the use of compressed NPs, i.e., a head noun with phrasal modifiers (see Example 2). Hyland and Jiang (2017) also mentioned that NPs with phrasal modifiers often generate a sense of formality, so these grammatical features tend to be preferred in academic writing. In addition, a wide range of studies (Halliday 1979; Halliday & Martin 1993) have demonstrated the extensive use of nominalizations as one of the most popular features in contemporary scientific prose. This involves the transformation of active processes characterized by adjectives and/or verbs into nouns (e.g., from *global* or *globalize* to *globalization*). The use of nominalizations is also based on compressed NPs, which is related to structural compression mentioned in Biber and Gray (2010).

Several scholars have argued that compressed NPs are potent tools for semantically packing meaning (e.g., Biber et al. 1999; Cullip 2000). Example 2 illustrates this potential of NPs. As shown in Example 2, the modifiers (a PP as postmodifier [*of an authority*], an infinitive clause postmodifier [*to monitor the movement*], and an *-ing* clause [*carrying waste*]) play a significant role in expanding the meaning of the head noun (i.e., *the absence*) in a highly condensed way.

Example 2

- *"The absence of an authority to monitor the movement of ships carrying waste"* (Cullip 2000: p. 85).

2.3 Empirical studies on NP complexity and writing development

Due to the important role of NPs in academic writing, scholars have empirically explored the relations between NPs and writing development. A landmark study that helped to generate this recent research trend on NPs and writing development is Biber et al. (2011), who proposed a developmental index of writing complexity features. Some scholars have extracted all the noun modifiers from the index to conduct empirical research on NPs (e.g., Ansarifar et al. 2018; Lan et al. 2019a; Parkinson & Musgrave 2014; Wang & Beckett 2017), whereas others have only included a subset of the noun modifiers in the index (e.g., Staples et al. 2016; Taguchi et al. 2013). Results from previous studies in various contexts (e.g., varied written genres, writing at different academic levels, and writing from students with distinct L1 backgrounds) have provided support for Biber et al.'s (2011) argument that the use of phrasal structures (e.g., NPs) increases with writing development.

For instance, Parkinson and Musgrave (2014) investigated noun modifiers by comparing their frequencies between EAP and TESOL MA students. The findings revealed that the MA students used more advanced noun modifiers from Biber et al.'s developmental index (i.e., PPs and appositive NPs), while EAP students used more simple noun modifiers (i.e., attributive adjectives). In another study, Staples et al. (2016) explored the development of a broad range of grammatical features across four different academic levels (i.e., first-year undergraduate, second-year undergraduate, final-year undergraduate, and graduate) in distinct writing genres (e.g., essays and literature) of varied fields (e.g., physical sciences and social sciences). They found that as the academic level advanced, the use of phrasal noun modifiers (e.g., premodifying nouns, PPs) increased for L1 students.

Most recently, Ansarifar et al. (2018) compared the frequencies of noun modifiers in 99 MA and 64 doctoral abstracts, written in English, produced by L1 Persian students with 149 abstracts written by expert writers. The results revealed that the MA students underused noun modifiers compared to the expert writers with respect to four distinct noun modifiers (i.e., premodifying nouns and PPs (*of*) and PP (other) as noun postmodifiers). In contrast, the abstracts of doctoral students did not differ significantly in the use of noun modifiers from the expert writers. In a comprehensive survey of linguistic complexity, Biber et al. (2020) claimed that these investigations regarding NPs are neither redundant nor lacking distinctiveness because they provide a direct, full representation of grammatical complexity found in academic prose. Furthermore, Biber et al. (2020) asserted that these studies provide support for the argument in Biber et al. (2011), and the authors welcomed further studies on the stages of writing development.

2.4 Comparing L1 and L2 academic writing

During the past decades, researchers conducting comparative analyses between L1 and L2 students' written texts have attempted to address differences in a wide range of lexico-grammatical features. Hinkel (2003) compared L1 and L2 college student writing and found that the latter used significantly more simplistic syntactic features than the former, such as sentences with copula verbs (e.g., *There <u>are</u> many different languages in the world*). Recently, Lu and Ai (2015) compared syntactic complexity in the academic writings of students of different L1 backgrounds (e.g., Chinese, French, English). They found that L1 English students produced significantly more complex nominal structures than L2 students with different L1 backgrounds based on two large-grained measures (i.e., complex nominals per clause and complex nominals per T-unit). In addition, Staples and Reppen (2016) analyzed the influence of L1 backgrounds (i.e., English, Chinese, Arabic) on seven grammatical features in two academic written genres (i.e., narratives and argumentative essays). They reported that the use of noun modifiers (i.e., premodifying nouns, nouns+that clauses) differed significantly among the three groups of students. Furthermore, in the writings of Arabic and Chinese students, Staples and Reppen (2016) found repetition of certain lexico-grammatical features, such as premodifying nouns (e.g., *online video games*). Thus, the existing empirical evidence suggests that language background influences the use of lexico-grammatical features, including NPs.

Although NP complexity has been studied based on different variables (e.g., writing proficiency, academic levels), few scholars have compared the use of NPs between L1 and L2 writing with a comprehensive set of noun modifiers. To the best of our knowledge, few studies have particularly focused on graduate academic writing regarding the use of NPs. As NPs are an important and highly frequent grammatical feature in academic writing, it is important to empirically study how NP complexity is influenced by L1 background in graduate academic writing. Such research can assist in providing grammatical instruction on the use of NPs to help graduate students become better writers and write in ways that will meet the expectations of their academic communities. To bridge this gap, we investigate NP complexity in dissertations written by L1 English and L1 Arabic doctoral students based on the 11 noun modifiers proposed in Biber et al.'s (2011) index. In this study, we address the following research questions:

1. Is there an association between NP complexity and L1 backgrounds in the introduction of dissertations?
2. Which specific grammatical features make large contributions to this association?

3. Methods

3.1 Corpus

The corpus collected for the current study consists of 100 introduction sections of dissertations (50 for L1 English students and 50 for L1 Arabic students) from the field of education, which includes a wide range of sub-majors such as special education, educational leadership, applied linguistics, linguistics, teaching English as second language / TESOL, and sport management. We chose education as the foremost field in the current study for two reasons. First, this will enable us to draw connections between our results and previous studies. For instance, Parkinson and Musgrave (2014) focus on students enrolled in an MA TESOL program, part of the broader field of education. Furthermore, Ansarifar et al. (2018) focus on the discipline of applied linguistics, which is also part of the field of education. Second, both of the two researchers' backgrounds in the current study are related to the field of education; therefore, this allows for a more in-depth analysis of the writings in this field than for others (e.g., medicine and chemistry).

The dissertations were collected using two different search engines: 1) using ProQuest[1] to build the L1 corpus with randomly sampled dissertations written by native English-speaking students and 2) using the Saudi Digital Library[2] to build the L2 corpus with randomly sampled dissertations written by Saudi Arabian students. With respect to identifying texts in the L1 corpus, an email was sent to each writer asking if they spoke English as a first language. The texts in the two sub-corpora are both based on recent dissertations, from 2011 to 2019. To minimize the effect of disciplinary variation, we

---

1 ProQuest is a large database that stores multiple academic works around the world.

2 The Saudi Digital Library (SDL) is a free database for Saudi students and scholars. It requires users to gain approval from the Ministry of Education in Saudi Arabia. All Saudi graduate students worldwide must upload their dissertations and theses via SDL; it now has more than 27,000 dissertations stored in its digital repository.

chose the discipline of education. Regarding the two sub-corpora's dissertation topics, the majority were related to applied linguistics, special education, and sport management. The two sub-corpora in our study have nearly the same number of tokens (see Table 1). The L1 corpus consists of 50 introduction sections of dissertations with 51,606 tokens; similarly, the L2 corpus consists of 50 introduction sections of dissertations with 51,382 tokens.

Table 1. Number of entire tokens in the corpora

Corpus	File No.	Tokens
L1 English	50	51,606
L2 Arabic	50	51,382

It is necessary to mention three reasons that drove us to opt for examining introductory sections. Our motivation on the introduction of dissertation aligns with the recent publication Lu et al. (2021). They argue that the introductions of research articles are a vital part-genre, which includes a rich use of p-frames associated with NP patterns (e.g., the NOUN of). The uses of these p-frames are related to multiple rhetorical moves and steps in the introductions of research articles, such as establishing a research territory, presenting research purposes and claiming values of research area. To a large extent, there is a similarity between dissertations and research articles, NPs are worth exploring in the introductions in the dissertations as well.

3.2 Grammatical features of interest

As mentioned in the previous section, the current research is based on a subset of Biber et al.'s (2011) developmental index of writing complexity features. Biber et al.'s index is based on three different linguistic functions: adverbials, complements, and noun modifiers. In this study, we extracted linguistic features functioning as noun modifiers (see Table 2). Noun modifiers can be classified into the following types: (1) attributive adjectives, (2) relative clauses, (3) nouns as modifiers, (4) PPs (*of*), (5) PPs[3] (other), (6) *-ing* clauses, (7) *-ed* clauses, (8) infinitive clauses, (9) prepositions followed by *-ing* clauses, (10) noun complement clauses, and (11) appositive NPs. These noun modifiers are distributed in Biber et al.'s index beginning from stage two to stage five (stage one is omitted because there are no noun modifiers in this stage). Stage two, for example, only includes the attributive adjectives; stage three includes premodifying nouns and relative clauses; stage four includes *-ing* clauses, *-ed* clauses, PPs (*of*), and PPs (others). In contrast, stage five includes prepositions + *-ing* clauses, noun complement clauses, infinitive clauses, and appositive noun clauses. Two out of the 11 noun modifiers are positioned as pre-noun modifiers (attributive adjectives and premodifying nouns), while others are positioned as post-noun modifiers. Concerning the types of noun modifiers, five noun modifiers are phrasal (e.g., PPs, appositive NPs), and the remaining are clausal

---

3 According to Biber et al. (2011), PPs are divided into two categories, namely, PPs that begin with *of* and those that begin with other prepositions (e.g., *to*, *with*, *on*, etc.).

modifiers (e.g., relative clauses, noun complement clauses).

Table 2. Noun modifiers in Biber et al.'s (2011) index

Stage	Noun modifiers	Position	Type	Example[4]
2	Attributive adjectives	Pre	phrasal	holy city
3	Premodifying nouns	pre	phrasal	vocabulary knowledge
	Relative clauses	post	clausal	movements that have made up the discipline of English
4	*-ing* clauses	post	clausal	the possibility of joining intensive English language programs
	-ed clauses	post	clausal	methods applied in the study
	PPs (*of*)	post	phrasal	the pleasure of comic relief
	PPs (other)	post	phrasal	their current studies within English studies
5	Prepositions + *-ing* clauses	post	phrasal	the importance of augmenting the presence of Black faculty
	Noun complement clauses	post	clausal	the idea that writing does not end needs to be theorized
	Infinitive clauses	post	clausal	a leadership style to build community support
	Appositive noun phrases	post	phrasal	instructor–student conferencing pedagogy (ISC)

3.3 Tagging and processing

The two sub-corpora of the study were tagged by applying the Biber Tagger.[5] The Biber Tagger can tag part-of-speech (e.g., nouns, adjectives, and adverbs) and a broad range of lexico-grammatical features (e.g., complement clauses and relative clauses). Generally, the Biber Tagger is designed to be applied to studies that focus on linguistic variation in texts and genres. In terms of the Biber Tagger's accuracy, it is considered an accurate tagger with precision and recall rates of over 90% for both L1 and L2 writings (Biber & Gray 2013a, 2013b). To ensure tagging accuracy, we conducted tag checking on eight grammatical features related to the 11 noun modifiers (i.e., attributive adjectives, nouns, prepositions, relative clauses, *-ing* clauses as modifiers, *-ed* clauses as modifiers,

---

4 The examples are taken from the current dissertation corpus.
5 The researchers contacted one of the Biber Tagger teams to ask for help in tagging the corpora.

infinitive clauses, and noun complement clauses). Five of the eight features had F-scores greater than 90%. We then worked on fixing tags for the remaining three features, which were *-ing* clauses as modifiers, *-ed* clauses as modifiers, and noun complement clauses (see Appendix A for the report of the F-scores).

3.4 Extraction of the noun modifiers

After the two sub-corpora were tagged, we extracted the noun modifiers by dividing the processing of the two sub-corpora into two parts: automated and manual processing. For automated processing, a Python program was used, developed by one of the authors, to extract the noun modifiers from each sub-corpus. Example 3 demonstrates the output of the Python program (a concordance line with the specific noun modifiers). It depicts the concordance line for an attributive adjective (<<<educational systems>>>). Angle brackets are used to mark the target noun modifier (*educational*) and the head noun (*system*).

Example 3

- *Degree in English from the two totally different <<<educational systems>>> of these two countries*

It should be pointed out that there are two types of automated processing—direct extraction and indirect extraction — which were first documented by Lan and Sun (2019). Direct extraction means that the program extracts the noun modifiers whose grammatical functions can be tagged by the Biber Tagger. Thus, direct extraction in this study was based on the part-of-speech (POS) tags. The Biber Tagger can directly tag the grammatical function of five noun modifiers: attributive adjectives, relative clauses, *-ing* clauses, *-ed* clauses, and noun complement clauses (see Appendix B for more information on the POS tags). On the other hand, indirect extraction means that, based on chunking patterns,[6] the program extracts the potential cases of noun modifiers whose grammatical function cannot be tagged. For instance, the program extracts all potential cases of infinitive clauses as noun modifiers based on the chunking pattern of "Nouns + Infinitive Marker TO" as in *the plan to build a database*. While chunking patterns are not as accurate as direct extraction, there is no better automated procedure for identifying potential cases of interest. The noun modifiers targeted by indirect extraction include premodifying nouns, PPs (*of*), PPs (other), prepositions followed by *-ing* clauses, and infinitive clauses.

Example 4

- *A study, which correlates language with users and <<<communities to>>> understand language in contexts.*

A unique case is appositive NPs, which are extracted based on four patterns. Two patterns are considered highly frequent in academic texts according to Biber et al. (1999),

---

6 *Chunking* refers to a group of words that lead to a meaningful input of language chunks (Bird et al. 2009).

namely, appositive NPs separated by parentheses, as in *a predominant language test (i.e., TOEFL)*, and appositive NPs separated by commas, as in *task-based instruction, an important teaching method*. We also added two other patterns to extract this modifier after qualitatively checking 20 randomly selected files: appositive NPs separated by square brackets, as in *the author [Prof. Burnham]*, and those separated by a hyphen (or dashes), as in *quantitative research method — a commonly used method*.

Next, in terms of the manual processing, we manually adjusted all the concordance lines to increase the accuracy of the extracted noun modifiers as much as possible. Our manual checking of the concordance lines ensured the elimination of inaccurate cases from the program. Example 4 provides an example of a potential case identified by the infinitive clause chunking pattern (i.e., *communities to*). We removed this case from the concordance lines because the infinitive clause (*to understand language in context*) is an adverbial instead of a modifier for the head noun (*communities*). For uncertain cases, we consulted two doctoral candidates from applied linguistic field to reach a final decision on each unsure case (see Appendix C).

3.5 Numerical data and statistical analysis

A data set was built based on the manually adjusted frequencies of the 11 noun modifiers in the two sub-corpora. As the sub-corpora in this study have different sizes (i.e., 51,606 and 51,382), we normalized the frequencies of the noun modifiers to 50,000 words (close to the corpora sizes) to eliminate the effect of text length in the statistical analysis. Then, to answer the first research question, a Chi-square test was run to investigate the influence of language background on the use of NPs in SPSS. The effect size (i.e., Cramer's V) was also reported together with the Chi-square value. Furthermore, a Chi-square value is omnibus, so with this value alone we could not demonstrate which specific noun modifiers largely contributed to the influence of language background on NPs. Thus, to answer the second research question, we calculated standardized residuals in SPSS to illustrate the contributions of the individual noun modifiers to the omnibus Chi-square value. The standardized residuals helped us identify how specific noun modifiers contributed to the influence of language background on NPs.

4. Results

4.1 The association between language background and the 11 noun modifiers

The result of the Chi-square test demonstrates an association between language background and NP complexity in our corpus. The observed χ^2 value is 198.184, which is greater than the critical χ^2 value, 23.209 (degrees of freedom = 10, alpha level = 0.01). Therefore, these two variables are not independent from each other. In other words, NP complexity in the two sub-corpora is influenced by language background (i.e., English vs. Arabic). However, it is also necessary to report the value of Cramer's V to demonstrate the strength of association between language background and NP complexity. Cramer's V was calculated to be 0.096. This value indicates a weak strength of association between language background and NP complexity.

Table 3. Chi-square Test and Cramer's V

Observed χ^2	Critical χ^2	*p* value	Cramer's V
198.184	23.209	*p*<0.01	0.096

Note. The degrees of freedom = 10, and the alpha level is 0.01.

4.2 Four noun modifiers out of 11 contributed to the association the most

The standardized residuals illustrate the contributions of individual noun modifiers used by the two groups of students to the association between language background and NP complexity. The greater the absolute value of a standardized residual, the greater the contribution the corresponding noun modifier makes to the association (Lan et al. 2019a). Thus, based on Table 4, four noun modifiers used by both groups of students largely contribute to the association: premodifying nouns (|6.935|, |-7.098|), PPs (other) (|-3.957|, |4.050|), prepositions followed by -*ing* clauses (|-4.344|, |4.447|), and infinitive clauses (|-3.115|, |3.188|). In other words, language background influences NP complexity in the two sub-corpora of dissertation introductions primarily because of the influence of these four specific noun modifiers.

Table 4. Standardized residuals of the 11 noun modifiers

	L1 English	L2 Arabic
Attributive adjectives	-0.333	0.341
Premodifying nouns*	6.935	-7.098
Relative clauses	0.325	-0.332
PPs (*of*)	0.549	-0.562
PPs (other)*	-3.957	4.050
-*ing* clauses	-0.353	0.361
-*ed* clauses	-0.747	0.764
prepositions + -*ing* clauses*	-4.344	4.447
Infinitive clauses*	-3.115	3.188
Noun complement clauses (that)	0.211	-0.216
Appositive NPs	-1.123	1.149

Note. The noun modifiers with significant standardized residuals are marked with asterisks.

The standardized residuals can be categorized into positive and negative values. A positive standardized residual suggests that the observed value in a cell is used more than its expected value, whereas a negative standardized residual indicates that the observed value in a cell is used less than its expected value (Sharpe 2015). Therefore, among the four noun modifiers with the greatest contribution to the association, it can be concluded that: (1) Premodifying nouns are used more than expected in the L1 sub-corpus, and the other three modifiers are used less than expected; (2) in contrast, in the L2 sub-corpus, PPs (other), prepositions + -*ing* clauses, and infinitive clauses are used more than expected, whereas premodifying nouns are used less than expected.

5. Discussion

5.1 Association between NP complexity and L1 background in the introductions of dissertations

The association between language background and NP complexity indicates that the use of the noun modifiers is influenced by language background (i.e., English vs. Arabic) in doctoral dissertations. Our finding is generally consistent with previous studies on grammatical complexity in other research contexts, such as ESL/EAP writing, first-year undergraduate writing, and general academic writing in college (e.g., Eckstein & Ferris 2018; Hinkel 2003; Lu & Ai 2015; Staples & Reppen 2016). Although previous studies have revealed that language background influences the use of NPs and noun modifiers, our study investigated this influence from a different statistical perspective. Thus, this finding adds a piece of evidence to the growing body of existing literature on the topic. With respect to the Cramer's V value, the weak association of language background (English vs. Arabic) with NP complexity is not surprising. As far as we are aware, Lan et al. (2019a) is the only empirical study on NP complexity that is statistically similar to this study. This study also found a weak association between writing proficiency and NP complexity. We agree with Lan et al. (2019a) that a weak association should be expected in research based on fine-grained grammatical features. This study only included the 11 noun modifiers proposed in Biber et al.'s (2011) hypothesized index of writing complexity features. Although the 11 noun modifiers are a comprehensive set of features for analyzing NP complexity, they only constitute a small set of grammatical features in general. Cramer's V is a type of effect size, and large effect size is often based on an accumulation of a series of variables. In this research context, the influence of language background on academic writing should be related to a cumulation of linguistic features, semantic features, discoursal features (e.g., coherence, cohesion), and content in academic writing (Lan et al. 2019a). Therefore, we are not surprised by the weak strength of the association due to the nature of the fine-grained analysis in this study.

5.2 Grammatical features making large contributions to this association

The residual analysis pinpoints four noun modifiers that largely contribute to the influence of language background (i.e., English vs. Arabic) on NP complexity in doctoral dissertations, namely, premodifying nouns, PPs (other), prepositions followed by -ing clauses, and infinitive clauses. We then conducted a qualitative analysis based on 10 randomly selected excerpts from the two corpora, respectively, which helped us have an interpretation of how L1 English and L1 Arabic students produce NP patterns in their dissertations' introductions.

First, the L1 English doctoral students tended to effectively use premodifying nouns to construct a wide range of noun-noun sequences in their dissertations. The relationship between premodifying nouns and head nouns is less explicit but more complex than the relationship between other modifiers, such as attributive adjectives and relative clauses. As Biber et al. (1999) mentioned, while noun-noun sequences can pack intensive information, "they result in extreme reliance on implicit meaning, requiring addressees to infer the intended logical relationship between the modifying noun and head noun" (p.

590). Biber et al. (1999) then summarized multiple logical relationships within noun-noun sequences, such as composition (e.g., *zinc supplement*), identity (e.g., *exam paper*), and content (e.g., *credit agreement*), among others. Compared to the L1 English students, the L2 English students were likely to have greater difficulties in using and interpreting the logical relationships of noun-noun sequences or multiple noun sequences. The qualitative analysis triangulates the results of the residual analysis. Taking a close look at the corpus, we noticed that both L1 and L2 students produced a number of technical terms (e.g., *sport management*, *speech acts*), which are related to their dissertation topics. This is consistent with previous studies related to grammatical complexity or NP complexity in undergraduate academic writing, and scholars mentioned the repeated cases of noun-noun sequences in L2 writing, including academic writing from Arabic students (e.g., Lan et al. 2019b; Staples & Reppen 2016). Having said this, L1 English students also produced a wide range of noun-noun sequences based on fixed-collocations (e.g., *research centers*, *language learners*, *curriculum design*) and multiple noun sequences (e.g., *minority student enrollment*, *language management policies*). These patterns are not common in the introductions of doctoral dissertation from Arabic students. Thus, L1 English students demonstrate varied use of premodifying nouns in their dissertations.

Excerpt 1

- [Policy] makers **to develop** professional programs **in teaching** reading subject at <elementary> [school] level *that may influence the efficacy **of teaching** reading*. With the development lofl the <global> economy, English is seen as a <worldwide> language, and it plays a <crucial> role in most aspects lofl our lives. Researchers linl education want to offer some insights into the process lofl learning.

Excerpt 2

- <Organizational> justice is defined as the perception lofl how fairly teachers believe they are treated. [Faculty] trust linl principal and colleagues had <significant> <independent> effects on <organizational> justice. When trust is evident, there is a <high> level lofl <organizational> justice. <High> levels lofl <organizational> justice lead to <favorable> [teacher] behaviors.

Second, the L2 students tended to produce more diverse NP patterns in their dissertations. The L2 students used PPs (other), prepositions followed by -*ing* clauses, and infinitive clauses more than expected in their dissertations. Excerpt 1 demonstrates the NPs produced by the L2 students. It shows the use of frequent noun modifiers (e.g., attributive adjectives, PPs [*of*]) in English academic writing in general (Parkison & Musgrave 2014; Lan & Sun 2019). Also, modifiers that made large contribution to the association can be seen: (1) a clausal feature: an infinitive clause as a modifier (*to develop professional programs*); (2) a phrasal-clausal mixed feature: prepositions followed by

-*ing* clauses (e.g., *programs in teaching reading*); (3) a phrasal feature: PPs (other) (e.g., *researchers in language education*). In contrast, the NPs in the dissertations of L1 English students tended to be less diverse (see Excerpt 2). Excerpt 2 illustrates three phrasal modifiers: two highly frequent phrasal modifiers (i.e., attributive adjectives, PPs [*of*]), one instance of PPs (other) (*faculty trust in principal and colleagues*), and premodifying nouns (e.g., *teacher behaviors*). In terms of the L1 students, the results are mostly consistent with a general claim that when students become academically advanced, they produce more compressed NPs based on phrasal noun modifiers in academic writing. In particular, Staples et al. (2016) found that L1 English students produced more compressed NPs from undergraduate to graduate levels across different written genres in multiple disciplines. However, for the Arabic students, our findings do not align with previous studies in other L2 writing contexts. For instance, Parkinson and Musgrave (2014) argued that L2 MA TESOL students tended to produce more compressed NPs in their graduate-level studies. Ansarifar et al. (2018) also found that Persian PhD students in applied linguistics produced phrasal modifiers to build compressed NPs with no significant differences compared to expert writing (i.e., journal articles). Therefore, we consider there to be a potential to raise Arabic students' awareness of using phrasal modifiers to further support their academic writing development at the advanced academic stage (i.e., PhD level).

6. Conclusion and Pedagogical Implications

In this study, the aim was to investigate the influence of language background on the use of NP complexity in the introductions of English dissertations written by L1 English and L1 Arabic students. The results show an influence of language background on NP complexity, and this influence is mainly contributed to by four noun modifiers: premodifying nouns, PPs (other), prepositions followed by *-ing* clauses, and infinitive clauses. L1 English and L1 Arabic doctoral students used these modifiers differently in their dissertations' introductions. Several limitations need to be noted regarding the present study. One major limitation is the small size of the two sub-corpora: 50 dissertations for each sub-corpus. Although small corpora can, in many cases, provide valid results if robust corpus techniques are used (Sinclair 2004), a larger corpus will more effectively represent doctoral dissertations in general. Furthermore, in terms of academic disciplines, the dissertations in our corpus are confined to the field of education. We would have more effective findings if we could include dissertations from other disciplines.

From a linguistic perspective, this study provides new understandings of the differences between L1 and L2 English doctoral writing. Based on these insights, pedagogical implications can be proposed. Doctoral students, either L1 or L2 English, study to become scholars in the academic community in different fields. They need to acquire the ability to use compressed NP structures to meet the writing expectations of their respective communities. Writing workshops can be held for doctoral students to provide instruction on dissertation writing. This is especially important for L1 Arabic doctoral students. Without a doubt, L1 Arabic doctoral students can be considered advanced academic writers who are proficient enough to handle different grammatical structures in their writing. However, it is still necessary to enhance their awareness of building compressed NPs to pack intensive information in compact spaces. For example, professors can prepare samples of academic texts (e.g., research articles) that include a wide range of compressed NPs and then ask students (individually or collaboratively) to identify the high-frequency grammatical features in these texts. Moreover, particular instructional focus could be placed upon premodifying nouns. Because L1 Arabic doctoral students may not use these as diversely as their L1 counterparts, we suggest using specific examples of noun-noun sequences to illustrate different logical relationships between premodifying nouns and head nouns. Examples can be efficiently extracted from online corpora, including the academic written register of the Corpus of Contemporary American English, the Michigan Corpus of Upper-Level Student Papers, and the British Academic Written English Corpus.

References

Aitchison, C. & C. Guerin. 2014. Writing groups, pedagogy, theory and practice [A]. In C. Aitchison & C. Guerin (eds.). *Writing Groups for Doctoral Education and Beyond: Innovations in Practice and Theory* [C]. London: Routledge. 3-17.

Ansarifar, A., H. Shahriari & R. Pishghadam. 2018. Phrasal complexity in academic writing: A comparison of abstracts written by graduate students and expert writers in applied linguistics [J]. *Journal of English for Academic Purposes* 31: 58-71.

Biber, D. & B. Gray. 2010. Challenging stereotypes about academic writing: Complexity, elaboration, explicitness [J]. *Journal of English for Academic Purposes* 9(1): 2-20.

Biber, D. & B. Gray. 2013a. Discourse characteristics of writing and speaking task types on the TOEFL iBT® test: A lexico-grammatical analysis [J]. *ETS Research Report Series* 1: i-128.

Biber, D. & B. Gray. 2013b. Being specific about historical change: The influence of sub-register [J]. *Journal of English Linguistics* 41(2): 104-134.

Biber, D., B. Gray & K. Poonpon. 2011. Should we use characteristics of conversation to measure grammatical complexity in L2 writing development? [J]. *TESOL Quarterly* 45(1): 5-35.

Biber, D., B. Gray, S. Staples & J. Egbert. 2020. Investigating grammatical complexity in L2 English writing research: Linguistic description versus predictive measurement [J]. *Journal of English for Academic Purposes* 46: 2-14.

Biber, D., S. Johansson, G. Leech, S. Conrad & E. Finegan. 1999. *Longman Grammar of Spoken and Written English* [M]. London: Longman.

Bird, S., E. Klein & E. Loper. 2009. *Natural Language Processing with Python* [M]. Oreilly Media.

Bulté, B. & A. Housen. 2012. Defining and operationalising L2 complexity [A]. In A. Housen, F. Kuiken & I. Vedder (eds.). *Dimensions of L2 Performance and Proficiency: Complexity, Accuracy and Fluency in SLA* [C]. Amsterdam: John Benjamins. 21-46.

Cullip, P. 2000. Text technology: The power-tool of grammatical metaphor [J]. *RELC Journal* 31: 76-104.

Eckstein, G. & D. Ferris. 2018. Comparing L1 and L2 texts and writers in first-year Composition [J]. *TESOL Quarterly* 52(1): 137-162.

Ellis, R. 2003. *Task-based Language Learning and Teaching* [M]. Oxford: Oxford University Press.

Halliday, F. 1979. Theses on the Iranian revolution [J]. *Race & Class* 21(1): 81-90.

Halliday, M. A. & J. R. Martin. 1993. *Writing Science: Literacy and Discursive Power* [M]. London: Routledge.

Hinkel, E. 2003. Simplicity without elegance: Features of sentences in L1 and L2 academic texts [J]. *TESOL Quarterly* 37(2): 275-301.

Housen, A., F. Kuiken & I. Vedder (eds.). 2012. *Dimensions of L2 Performance and Proficiency: Complexity, Accuracy and Fluency in SLA* (Vol. 32) [C]. Amsterdam: John Benjamins.

Hyland, K. & F. K. Jiang. 2017. Is academic writing becoming more informal? [J]. *English for Specific Purposes* 45: 40-51.

Institute of International Education. [OL] (accessed 18/11/2019). *Number of international students in the United States hits all-time high.* https://www.iie.org/Why-IIE/Announcements/2019/11/Number-of-International-Students-in-the-United-States-Hits-All-Time-High

Lan, G. & Y. Sun. 2019. A corpus-based investigation of noun phrase complexity in the L2 writings of a first-year composition course [J]. *Journal of English for Academic Purposes* 38: 14-24.

Lan, G., K. Lucas & Y. Sun. 2019a. Does L2 writing proficiency influence noun phrase complexity? A case analysis of argumentative essays written by Chinese students in a first-year composition course [J]. *System* 85: 102-116.

Lan, G., Q. Liu & S. Staples. 2019b. Grammatical complexity: 'What Does It Mean' and 'So What' for L2 writing classrooms? [J]. *Journal of Second Language Writing* 46: 100-673.

Liberman, M. & R. Sproat. 1992. Modified noun phrases in English [J]. *Lexical Matters* 24: 131.

Lu, X. 2011. A corpus-based evaluation of syntactic complexity measures as indices of college level ESL writers' language development [J]. *TESOL Quarterly* 45(1): 36-62.

Lu, X. & H. Ai. 2015. Syntactic complexity in college-level English writing: Difference among writers with diverse L1 backgrounds [J]. *Journal of Second Language Writing* 29: 16-27.

Lu, X., J. Yoon & O. Kisselev. 2021. Matching phrase-frames to rhetorical moves in social science research article introductions [J]. *English for Specific Purposes* 61: 63-83.

Muhammad, T. 2014. China and Saudi Arabia: Strengthening ties through education [N]. *Daily Sabah*, 2014-4-14.

Ni, Y. 2003. Noun phrases in media texts: A quantificational approach [A]. In J. Aitchison & D. M. Lewis (eds.). *New Media Language* [C]. London: Routledge. 159-168.

Norris, J. M. & L. Ortega. 2009. Towards an organic approach to investigating CAF in instructed SLA: The case of complexity [J]. *Applied Linguistics* 30(4): 555-578.

Ortega, L. 2015. Syntactic complexity in L2 writing: Progress and expansion [J]. *Journal of Second Language Writing* 29: 82-94.

Parkinson, J. & J. Musgrave. 2014. Development of noun phrase complexity in the writing of English for Academic Purposes students [J]. *Journal of English for Academic Purposes* 14: 48-59.

Sinclair, R. 2004. Participation in practice: Making it meaningful, effective and sustainable [J]. *Children and Society* 18: 106-118.

Sharpe, D. 2015. Your chi-square test is statistically significant: Now what? [J]. *Practical Assessment, Research and Evaluation* 20(8): 1-10.

Staples, S. & R. Reppen. 2016. Understanding first-year L2 writing: A lexico-grammatical analysis across L1s, genres, and language ratings [J]. *Journal of Second Language Writing* 32: 17-35.

Staples, S., J. Egbert, D. Biber & B. Gray. 2016. Academic writing development at the university level: Phrasal and clausal complexity across level of study, discipline, and genre [J]. *Written Communication* 33(2): 149-183.

Taguchi, N., W. Wetzel & D. Zawodny. 2013. What linguistic features are indicative of writing quality? A case of argumentative essays in a college composition program [J]. *TESOL Quarterly* 47(2): 420-430.

Wang, S. & G. Beckett. 2017. "My excellent college entrance examination achievement" noun phrase use of Chinese EFL students' writing [J]. *Journal of Language Teaching and Research* 8(2): 271-277.

Wolfe-Quintero, K., S. Inagaki & H. -Y. Kim. 1998. *Second Language Development in Writing: Measures of Fluency, Accuracy and Complexity* [M]. National Foreign Language Resource Center.

Appendix A. *Precisions, recalls, and F-scores of the targeted features for tag checking*

Noun Modifier	Precision	Recall	F-score
attributive adjective	96.54%	93.17%	94.83%
noun	95.89%	97.62%	96.75%
relative clause	90.91	95.31%	93.06%
PP	97.64%	97.99%	97.72%
-ing clause	51.32%	85.72%	64.20%
-ed clause	85.71%	62.50%	72.29%
infinitive (to)	89.34%	97.83%	93.39%
noun complement clause	77.50%	100%	87.32%

Appendix B. *The two types of automatic extraction*

Noun Modifier	Tags in Biber Tagger	Chunking Patterns	Extraction
attributive adjective	Jj+atrb+++ Jjr+atrb+++ Jjt+atrb+++	N/A	POS tag
relative clause	Tht+rel+++ Whp+rel+++	N/A	POS tag
noun as modifier	N/A	Noun + noun	Chunking
PP (*of*)	N/A	Noun + prep (of)	Chunking
PP (other)	N/A	Noun + prep (other)	Chunking
***-ing* clause**	Vwbn+++xvbg+	N/A	POS tag
***-ed* clause**	Vwbn+++xvbn+	N/A	POS tag
infinitive clause	N/A	Noun + infinitive-to	Chunking
Preposition + ing clause	N/A	Noun + prep + *-ing* verb	Chunking
noun complement clause	Thtþ+ncmp+++	N/A	POS tag
appositive noun phrase	N/A	Regular expressions	Chucking

Note. Appositive noun phrases cannot be tagged by the Biber tagger, so regular expressions were used to extract patterns in Biber et al. (1999). (Adopted from Lan and Sun 2019, p. 23).

Appendix C. *Accuracy rates of manual processing*

Noun Modifier	Categories of Accuracy Rates	Accuracy Rate after Qualitative Check
attributive adjective	POS Tag	99.80%
Relative clause	POS Tag	99.22%
Noun as modifier	Chunking	95.36%
PP (*of*)	Chunking	96.67%
PP (other)	Chucking	93.78%
-ing clause	POS Tag	97.55%
-ed clause	POS Tag	99.48%
Infinitive clause	Chunking	95.77%
preposition + *-ing* clause	Chunking	94.17%
Noun complement clause	POS Tag	98.14%
Appositive noun phrase	Chunking	98.47%

Note. (1) "Low" suggests that the accuracy rates are lower than 50%, because the chunking patterns do not extract the modifiers effectively; (2) after the qualitative check, all of the incorrect cases were excluded. The accuracy rates after the qualitative check were calculated by dividing the number of unsure/inconsistent cases from the two coders by the total cases, namely, the intercoder reliability. The unsure/inconsistent cases were further coded by a third coder (Lan et al. 2019b, p. 23).

About the Authors

Hani ALBELIHI is an Assistant Professor of Language Literacy and Sociocultural Studies, College of Arts and Sciences, Methnab, Qassim University, Saudi Arabia. His research interests include corpus-related issues of linguistics, second language writing and writing across the curriculum.

Ge LAN (corresponding author) is an Assistant Professor in the Department of English at City University of Hong Kong, China. His research interests include corpus linguistics, second language writing, English for academic purposes, functional linguistics, syntax, and natural language processing. Email: gelan4@cityu.edu.hk

学科对比视角下的学术语篇中作者立场构建研究[*]

刘　烨[1]　董记华[2]

[1] 齐鲁师范学院　　[2] 山东大学

提要：本研究以自建的工学和语言学学术语篇语料库为基础，从知识性立场、态度性立场和作者显现标记三个维度对上述两个学科语料库中的立场构建特征进行对比分析。分析显示，工学和语言学学术语篇中立场构建均具有建立客观权威形象的倾向，但在具体立场话语使用方面存在显著差异。本研究的发现有助于我们深入了解不同学科学术语篇的立场构建和知识传达中的学科特征和规约性。研究结果可以帮助作者和学生掌握学科规约表达、进行恰当的立场构建并实现与读者之间的有效交流，同时可以为学术英语写作等相关课程的内容设计、课程组织和教学安排提供实证参考。

关键词：学术语篇；立场构建；学科间差异

1. 引言

　　学术语篇具有交际性和社会性特征（Bakhtin 1981），因而该文体的构建一般要求作者以一种符合学术规约的方式进行知识构建和传达，以获取读者的认同和学术界的认可（Recski 2005；Swales 1990）。学术语篇中的立场构建是作者实现知识传递、命题构建和开展与读者有效交流的重要方式（徐昉 2015）。

　　立场主要是指作者在语篇中所展现的自身态度、对命题的判断以及对自我和他人话语的评价（Biber 2006）。由于作者在写作过程中需要考虑读者的不同期望，立场构建不仅是学术语篇互动性的重要体现，也是学科规范的直接反映（Hyland & Jiang 2016）。学科对比视角的分析有助于揭示不同学科群体中的学术规约，有助于深入挖掘不同学科群体在知识背景、思维方式和观点论证等方面存在的特征和差异（Hammouda 2008；Prelli 1989）。

　　基于学科对比视角的立场表达研究逐渐成为语言学的一个热点话题，并引起国内外学者的关注和重视（Bruce 2016；Charles 2003；Kim & Crosthwaite 2019；Samraj 2005）。例如，Charles（2003）对比了国际关系和材料科学学术语篇中的立场标记语，发现国际关系论文中的立场名词使用更加频繁，两个学科在知识构建和立场表达方面存在显著差异；Dong 和 Buckingham（2018）发现立场短语在农学和经济学领域存在不同的搭配网络，并指出立场短语搭配既构成了学科群体规范，又受其制约，二者相互影响。国内学者对学术语篇中的立场构建同样给予了较多关

---

[*] 本研究系山东大学教育教学改革项目（2021Y068）和陕西省社科基金项目（2020K025）的阶段性成果。

注。徐宏亮（2011）对比了中国学者与英语母语学者的学术语篇中的立场标记语，发现中国学者具有较强的立场标记语的使用意识，但在立场标记语的使用频数方面低于英语本族语作者，并且所使用的立场构建方式较为直接。徐昉（2015）通过对比已发表的国际期刊论文和国内英语专业本硕博论文中立场标记语的特征，发现我国二语学习者所使用的立场标记语显著少于国际期刊论文，并指出二语写作者需要平衡不同类型的立场构建，以有效进行命题知识的评价和个人情感态度表达，从而实现作者与读者的有效交流和科学的学术语篇构建。

上述研究表明，不同学科作者一般在各自学科规约的指导下有效地进行知识的传递和与读者的交流。然而，现有关于学科间语篇分析中的立场特征主要集中于特定的立场名词、短语搭配和句式结构等语法层面，而且研究对比的学科门类较为有限，仍需进一步拓展深入，以为更为全面的学科立场建构范式提供实证参考和借鉴。

本研究以工学和语言学为例，通过分析两个学科的立场构建特点，深入挖掘学科间的差异。工学分支较多、研究范围较广，覆盖如土木工程、计算机工程、电气电子与通信工程等专业（李战国、王斌锐 2013）。工科论文一般需要较强的专业知识背景作为支撑，突出客观性并强调对实验数据和条件的描述（王芙蓉、王宏俐 2015）。而语言学论文研究范式一般包含定量研究、定性研究以及混合研究等不同范式（Farsani et al. 2021）。通过对比工学和语言学，可为两门学科的学术写作教学提供更为具体的理论指导，帮助学生了解学科间认识论、研究范式、立场构建、语言表达等方面的特征。因此，本研究将以立场构建为切入点，对比分析工学和语言学学术语篇中的立场构建所存在的学科共性与差异。本文将回答以下两个问题：

（1）工学和语言学论文的立场构建方式和标记语使用特征有何差异？

（2）工学和语言学作者在立场标记语的具体类别中存在哪些学科间的异同？

2. 理论框架

在立场标记语的理论框架方面，本研究参考了徐昉（2015）根据 Hyland（2005）的立场分类模型修订的分类框架。该框架以学术语篇分析为基础，具有较强的互动性，并已在前期研究中被广泛使用（如 Qiu & Jiang 2021；Ramoroka 2017；Yoon 2017）。其内容包括知识性立场标记、态度性立场标记和作者显现标记三个维度。知识性立场标记主要是针对"知识命题"的立场表达，包括模糊语（hedges）和加强词（boosters）两类。其中，模糊语弱化作者对命题的责任，使读者可以参与到对话中（Hyland 2008）；相反，加强词表达作者对话语的肯定，强调共同信息和言语背后的群体身份，该类表达使读者更易于接受（Hyland 2005）。这两种立场标记展示了客观信息的确定性和不确定性，以及与读者之间的协商程度等方面（Hyland 1998）。态度性立场是对命题的直观评价，体现了对作者立场观点的直接介入（Hyland & Jiang 2016）。态度标记词的使用允许作者在表达自身立场的同时，与学科导向的价值保持一致（Hyland 2008）。作者显现标记则指作者在文章中出现的显现度（Hyland & Jiang 2016）。自我指称语（self-mention）代表了论文写作者的不同角色定位；作者在指代自己时除了使用I之外，还会使用其他与其文中身份相关的the author、the researcher等自我指称语。具体立场标记语分类详见表1。

表1 立场标记语分类

立场组成	立场标记语	阐释	例子
知识性立场标记	加强词	表达言语的确定性并与读者保持一致	actually、always、certain、clearly、evident、in fact
	模糊语	将话语保守表达为一种观点而非既定事实	about、argue、around、claim、doubt、may
态度性立场标记	态度标记词	表达作者的主观情感态度而非认知性立场	agree、disappointed、fortunate、hopeful、prefer
作者显现标记	自我指称语	使用第一人称等指代词指向自己	I、me、the author、the researcher

3. 研究方法

3.1 数据收集

本研究通过检索全球最大、覆盖学科最全的综合性学术信息资源库（Web of Science）建立工学和语言学学术期刊论文语料库。笔者选取研究性学术论文作为语料的主要原因是研究性论文是一种主要的学术文体，并且该类论文具有较高的综合性，研究设计更为完整，更能体现作者的立场构建特征（Shirazizadeh & Amirfazlian 2021）。

为了确保语料的权威性、规范性和代表性，本研究在听取专家推荐并参考期刊影响因子的基础上，选取工学和语言学领域各10本影响力较高的SCI或SSCI期刊作为自建语料库的语料来源（所选期刊见附录）。其中，工学语料库期刊2020年的平均影响因子为6.351，语言学的平均影响因子为2.33。可见，所选取的期刊能够较好代表两个学科研究论文的水平。

为了确保两个语料库的可比性，本研究将语料的检索时间限定为1970至2020。最终检索语料共780篇，共9,139,797字符，其中工学语料库包含390篇文章，3,541,316字符，语言学语料库包含390篇文章，5,598,481字符。此外，为了更好地展示学术语篇中作者立场构建的特征，本研究删除了论文中的致谢、参考文献和附录部分。

3.2 数据处理

本研究的数据处理分为三步。首先，笔者使用MAXQDA软件，依据本研究使用的立场分类框架，随机抽取语料库中30%的语料进行人工标注，并根据标注的结果确立立场标记语的标注。在得到结果后，运用MAXQDA软件的自动赋码功能对完整语料库进行标注。

其次，由于部分检索项在不同语境中具有不同含义，在自动检索完成后，笔者对检索结果进一步筛选和标注，通过上下文语境检测具有多重语义的表达，人工剔除不属于立场表达的检索项。为保证语料标注的信度和效度，本研究的另一位作者随机选取了10%的语料进行标注，两次标注的内容通过Cohen Kappa一致性检验，一致性系数为0.901（p=0.00），这表明本研究的标注具有较高的一致性。最后，为避免对比语料间规模大小对结果的影响，本研究采用百万词频数对统计数据进行分析，并用卡方检验工具（梁茂成 2010）测算两个学科间立场构建话语中的差异。

4. 结果与讨论

4.1 立场标记语的总体分布

从立场标记语的总体使用来看，学术语篇中模糊语占比最高（总体标准化频数：20245.19每百万词，工学：7119.67，语言学：13125.52），其次是加强词和自我指称语，使用最少的是态度标记词（详见图1）。这说明两个学科在学术语篇构建中均较多地融入知识性立场表达，以构建客观和权威的形象，这与Biber（2006）的关于知识性立场标记使用频数高于态度性立场标记的结论一致。

在具体的立场类别中，知识性立场标记语中的模糊语使用频数最高，每百万词20245.19词（工学：7119.67，语言学：13125.52）。根据Lewin（2005），模糊语为作者提供了阐述暂定为真实的命题及供读者评判的空间。同样，两个学科作者所使用的加强词使用总频数位居第二（总频数为19042.41，工学：8701.57，语言学：10340.84）。加强词表示作者对论据的信心，并试图说服读者接受观点。两类知识性立场标记语的高频使用表明两个学科的学术写作者具有较强的读者互动意识。

自我指称语总体使用频数位居第三，其总体标准化频数为8087.74每百万词（工学：3831.05，语言学：4256.69）。自我指称语既可以传达作者在语篇构建中的参与度又能更好地体现作者的观点，该类标记语的使用频数较低说明两个学科作者均倾向于采用一种较为隐含的方式来凸显作者在语篇中的身份。

态度标记语是立场话语中出现频数最低的标记语（总体标准化频数：4538.80，工学：1769.12，语言学：2769.68）。态度标记语的低频使用与Biber et al.（1999）的研究发现一致。该类标记语是表达作者评价的直接方式，其低频使用说明两个学科的作者尽量避免对所述命题的态度性评价，这与学术语篇客观中立的特征相符合（Martin & White 2005）。出现这一现象的原因可能是由于学术语篇中的情感类表达需符合学术规范，并围绕研究目的对命题或观点价值评价，所以可供论文写作者选择的情感类词汇受限。

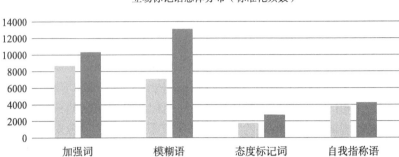

图 1　学术语篇中立场标记语总体分布

4.2 立场表达的学科间差异

表 2 展示了工学与语言学之间立场标记语的总体特征。由该表可见，工学语料库中的具体立场构建话语的使用频数均显著低于语言学语料库。该结论与 Hyland 和 Jiang（2018）互动式元话语研究中应用语言学与电子工程的对比数据有相似之处，即应用语言学在立场标记语中的使用频数均高于电子工程。该发现表明不同学科作者在自身定位、言语确定性和态度表达方面均存在显著的学科规约性。

表 2　立场标记语总体频数分布

立场分类	立场标记语	工学		语言学		卡方检验	p 值
		总频数	标准化频数（每百万词）	总频数	标准化频数（每百万词）		
知识性立场标记	加强词	30815	8701.57	57893	10340.84	606.47	0.00
	模糊语	25213	7119.67	73483	13125.52	7324.88	0.00
态度性立场标记	态度标记词	6265	1769.12	15506	2769.68	913.86	0.00
作者显现标记	自我指称语	13567	3831.05	23831	4256.69	96.43	0.00
总计		75860	21412.38	170713	30492.73	6799.98	0.00

在立场标记语的具体类别中，语言学语料库中所使用的知识性立场标记语的数量显著高于工学语料库（工学：15821.24，语言学：23466.36，p=0.00）。这反映出语言学作者更倾向于通过对命题的评判来实现立场构建。产生上述现象的一个可能的原因为语言学作者在论文中使用较多解释性和推理性语言，而工学作者会相对直接地呈现研究数据（Hyland 2008）。

具体而言，语言学中模糊语的出现频数显著高于工学（p=0.00），这说明语言学作者在论证时更倾向保留一定的对话空间，同意读者对所述话语进行协商。由于语言学中的质性研究部分容易受作者主观经验影响，易遭到读者的质疑和挑战（孙飞宇 2018），因此语言学作者一般会通过模糊语进行审慎评价，以提高表达的严谨性，避免绝对化。同样，加强词的使用频数在两门学科中存在显著性差异（p=0.00），反映出语言学作者更擅长使用加强词表达对命题的肯定和观点的陈述。造成该差异的主要原因为两个学科的学术写作特点和学术规约。工学学术论文中包含较多公式、图表等客观数据，作者可直接对数据结果进行统计描述，因而较少需要加强词支撑其研究结论。而语言学中观点的提炼和论证一般对前人文献有较强的依赖性，因此语言学作者需使用加强词强化观点论述并更好地说服读者。

态度性立场标记的对比分析显示，工学语篇中态度标记词的出现频数显著低于语言学（p=0.00），这说明工学作者在语篇构建时较少进行主观评价。但是，在高频词使用中，两个学科作者所使用的高频词却表现出明显的学科共性，前10的高频词主要围绕以下几方面展开：是否具有研究意义（如important、essential）、对前人研究是否认同（如agree、disagree、prefer）、结果是否达到预期（如expected、interesting）等，这反映出两个学科学术语篇中态度标记词的使用类别方面具有一定的趋同性特征。

同时，在自我指称语的使用方面，语言学作者更倾向于通过显现的自我指称语言介入到文本和语篇的构建中（p=0.00）。前期研究表明，作者一般拥有不同的角色定位，如"写作者（writer）""研究者（researcher）""论证者（arguer）""评价者（evaluator）"等（Bondi 2012；Dontcheva-Navratilova 2012；Fløttum 2010；Ivanič 1998）。为了更好地展示自我指称语的使用特征，本研究进一步分析了工学和语言学中所使用的具体自我指称语，研究结果见表3。由该表可见，两个学科在所使用的五种自我指称表达方面均存在显著的学科差异，这体现两个学科的作者在直接介入文本以及以何种身份介入语篇表达方面存在不同的学科规约性。该发现证实了Kuo（1999）和Bondi（2006）关于作者自我呈现和构建方式的学科差异性的发现。

表3 自我指称语学科分布（标准化频数）

作者显现标记	自我指称语	工学	语言学	卡方检验	p值
写作者	the author/writer	6.21	18.93	25.1	0.00
研究者	the researcher	0	20.90	74.0	0.00
论文或研究	this paper/research	293.96	182.19	120.2	0.00
第一人称单数	I/my/me	9.03	599.81	2041.8	0.00
第一人称复数	we/our/us	3521.85	3434.86	4.77	0.03

在自我指称语的具体使用方面，语言学中所使用的第一人称单数显著高于工学语篇（p=0.00），这说明语言学作者倾向于使用最为直接的第一人称来表达自身观点，构建其在文本中的直接介入，以增强文章的说服力。同时，语言学论文中也表现出显著较多的关于研究者（the researcher）和写作者（the author/writer）的身份，

这说明和工学相比，语言学作者也较为倾向于一种相对较为隐含的方式来展现作者在文本中的呈现和表达方式。

相反，工学学术语篇中this paper/research的使用频数显著高于语言学（p=0.00）。这体现出工学作者倾向于从论文或研究的角度进行实验步骤或结论的描述，以研究或论文的方式来呈现自己，避免以施动者的形象出现在论文中。同时，工学中第一人称复数（we）的出现频数也显著高于语言学（p=0.03），该现象可能是由于工学研究一般由多名研究人员合作开展，因此作者多使用研究团队的形式进行语篇中的观点陈述和内容构建。

5. 结论

本研究以工学和语言学两个学科的学术语料库为研究对象，深入对比分析了学术语篇中作者立场构建的学科差异。研究表明，两个学科的论文中知识性立场标记的出现频数均高于态度性立场标记，这说明两个学科的作者更倾向于从客观性维度进行立场构建。同时，本研究也进一步揭示了语言学和工学在知识性立场标记、态度性立场标记及作者显现标记中均存在不同的学科规约性。工学作者在论文中倾向于弱化作者存在，突出知识的客观性；语言学作者较多使用态度性立场表达，以获得读者认同。上述差异可归因于学科间不同的认识论和社会惯例。工学学科的实证主义认识论和知识累积结构促使其以数据和事实为导向构建权威，而语言学中的思辨与逻辑特征均需通过语言描述和阐释达到自我立场构建及寻求读者认同的目的。

本研究希望能为科研人员和学生作者提供学术语篇立场构建方面的学科规约及学术规范参考，帮助其掌握不同学科在学术语篇构建和知识传达过程中的认知和情态等方面的倾向性和学科差异性，以实现有效的立场构建和表达。本研究建议国内英语学术写作等相关课程针对不同学科学术语言特点制定课程目标、课堂内容及教学活动，融入立场标记语教学，帮助学生掌握不同学科立场构建的特点和要求。同时需要指出，本研究只分析了工学和语言学两个学科，未来研究有必要将研究范围扩充至其他学科及其分支学科，从而更全面地分析学科间立场构建和学科规约的差异性。

参考文献

Bakhtin, M. 1981. *The Dialogic Imagination: Four Essays* [M]. Austin: University of Texas Press.

Biber, D. 2006. *University Language: A Corpus-based Study of Spoken and Written Registers* [M]. Amsterdam: John Benjamins.

Biber, D., S. Johansson, G. Leech, S. Conrad, E. Finegan & R. Quirk. 1999. *Longman Grammar of Spoken and Written English* [M]. London: Pearson Education.

Bondi, M. 2006. A case in point: Signals of narrative development in business and economics [A]. In K. Hyland & M. Bondi (eds.). *Academic Discourse Across Disciplines* [C]. Frankfurt: Peter Lang. 47-72.

Bondi, M. 2012. Voice in textbooks: Between exposition and argument [A]. In K. Hyland & C. S. Guinda (eds.). *Stance and Voice in Written Academic Genres* [C]. New York: Palgrave Macmillan. 101-115.

Bruce, I. 2016. Constructing critical stance in university essays in English literature and sociology [J]. *English for Specific Purposes* 42: 13-25.

Charles, M. 2003. 'This mystery...': A corpus-based study of the use of nouns to construct stance in theses from two contrasting disciplines [J]. *Journal of English for Academic Purposes* 2(4): 313-326.

Dong, J. & L. Buckingham. 2018. The textual colligation of stance phraseology in cross-disciplinary academic discourse [J]. *International Journal of Corpus Linguistics* 23(4): 408-436.

Dontcheva-Navratilova, O. 2012. Cross-cultural differences in the construal of authorial voice in the genre of diploma theses [J]. *Linguistic Insights — Studies in Language and Communication* 160: 301-328.

Farsani, M. A., H. Jamali, M. Beikmohammadi, B. D. Ghorbani & L. Soleimani. 2021. Methodological orientations, academic citations, and scientific collaboration in applied linguistics: What do research synthesis and bibliometrics indicate [J]. *System* 100(3): 1-17.

Fløttum, K. 2010. Linguistically marked cultural identity in research articles [J]. *Linguistic Insights — Studies in Language and Communication* 125: 267-280.

Hammouda, D. D. 2008. From novice to disciplinary expert: Disciplinary identity and genre mastery [J]. *English for Specific Purposes* 27(2): 233-252.

Hyland, K. 1998. Boosting, hedging and the negotiation of academic knowledge [J]. *Text & Talk* 18(3): 349-382.

Hyland, K. 2005. Stance and engagement: A model of interaction in academic discourse [J]. *Discourse Studies* 7(2): 173-192.

Hyland, K. 2008. Disciplinary voices: Interactions in research writing [J]. *English Text Construction* 1(1): 5-22.

Hyland, K. & F. Jiang. 2016. Change of attitude? A diachronic study of stance [J]. *Written Communication* 33(3): 251-274.

Hyland, K. & F. Jiang. 2018. In this paper we suggest: Changing patterns of disciplinary metadiscourse [J]. *English for Specific Purposes* 51: 18-30.

Ivanič, R. 1998. *Writing and Identity: The Discoursal Construction of Identity in Academic Writing* [M]. Amsterdam: John Benjamins.

Kim, C. H. & P. Crosthwaite. 2019. Disciplinary differences in the use of evaluative that: Expression of stance via that-clauses in business and medicine [J]. *Journal of English for Academic Purposes* 41: 100775.

Kuo, C. 1999. The use of personal pronouns: Role relationships in scientific journal articles [J]. *English for Specific Purposes* 18(2): 121-138.

Lewin, B. 2005. Hedging: An exploratory study of authors' and readers' identification of 'toning down' in scientific texts [J]. *Journal of English for Academic Purposes* 4(2): 163-178.

Martin, J. R. & P. White. 2005. *The Language of Evaluation: Appraisal in English* [M]. Basingstoke: Palgrave Macmillan.

Prelli, L. J. 1989. *A Rhetoric of Science: Inventing Scientific Discourse* [M]. Los Angeles: University of

South Carolina Press.

Qiu, X. & F. Jiang. 2021. Stance and engagement in 3MT presentations: How students communicate disciplinary knowledge to a wide audience [J]. *Journal of English for Academic Purpose* 51: 100976.

Ramoroka, B. T. 2017. The use of interactional metadiscourse features to present a textual voice: A case study of undergraduate writing in two departments at the University of Botswana [J]. *Reading & Writing* 8(1): 1-11.

Recski, L. 2005. Interpersonal engagement in academic spoken discourse: A functional account of dissertation defenses [J]. *English for Specific Purposes* 24(1): 5-23.

Samraj, B. 2005. An exploration of genre set: Research article abstracts and introductions in disciplines [J]. *English for Specific Purposes* 24(2): 141-156.

Shirazizadeh, M. & R. Amirfazlian. 2021. Lexical bundles in theses, articles and textbooks of applied linguistics: Investigating intradisciplinary uniformity and variation [J]. *Journal of English for Academic Purpose* 49: 1-13.

Swales, J. 1990. *Genre Analysis: English in Academic and Research Settings* [M]. Cambridge: Cambridge University Press.

Yoon, H. 2017. Textual voice elements and voice strength in EFL argumentative writing [J]. *Assessing Writing* 32: 72-84.

李战国、王斌锐, 2013, 美国高校工学学科结构变动的特点及成因分析 [J],《中国高教研究》(5): 50-56。

梁茂成, 2010, 卡方检验和对数似然率计算工具 [CP], https://m.x-mol.com/faculty/detail/226589 (2021 年 11 月 28 日读取)。

孙飞宇, 2018, 社会科学的质性研究与意义的发现 [J],《公共管理评论》(3): 3-11。

徐宏亮, 2011, 中国高级英语学习者学术语篇中的作者立场标记语的使用特点———一项基于语料库的对比研究 [J],《外语教学》(6): 44-48。

徐昉, 2015, 二语学术语篇中的作者立场标记研究 [J],《外语与外语教学》(5): 1-7。

王芙蓉、王宏俐, 2015, 基于语料库的语言学和工科学术英语词块比较研究 [J],《外语界》(2): 16-24。

附录：工学语料库和语言学语料库中选取的全部期刊及 2020 年影响因子

工学（10本）:

Progress in Energy and Combustion Science（影响因子：28.938）

Information Science（影响因子：5.910）

IEEE Transactions on Automatic Control（影响因子：5.625）

Arabian Journal of Chemistry（影响因子：4.762）

IEEE Transactions on Antennas and Propagation（影响因子：4.371）

IEEE Transactions on Aerospace and Electronic Systems（影响因子：3.672）

International Journal of Electronics and Communications（影响因子：3.510）

IEEE Journal of Quantum Electronics（影响因子：2.384）

IEEE Transactions on Magnetics（影响因子：1.626）

IEEE Transactions on Computers（影响因子：2.711）

语言学（10本）

Applied Linguistics（影响因子：4.286）

The Modern Language Journal（影响因子：3.538）

Language Learning（影响因子：3.408）

Studies in Second Language Acquisition（影响因子：2.838）

Foreign Language Annals（影响因子：2.198）

TESOL Quarterly（影响因子：2.071）

System（影响因子：1.979）

Journal of Pragmatics（影响因子：1.350）

International Journal of Applied Linguistics（影响因子：1.000）

Lingua（影响因子：0.643）

作者简介：

刘烨，齐鲁师范学院外国语学院助教。主要研究领域：语篇分析、语料库语言学。

董记华（通信作者），山东大学外国语学院教授、博导。主要研究领域：语料库语言学、学术英语写作、专门用途英语等。电子邮箱：dongjihua@sdu.edu.cn

中国学生英语硕士论文中转述动词使用研究*

刘应亮[1]　魏　依[2]

[1] 武汉理工大学　[2] 湖北省仙桃中学

提要：转述动词是学术写作中的一种常见引用方式，不仅可以引出他人观点，还可以用来表达语篇作者对转述信息的态度和立场。本文基于中国学生英语硕士论文语料，参照期刊论文中转述动词的使用特点，研究中国学生在学术语篇中转述动词的使用情况。研究发现，相对于期刊论文专家作者，中国学生偏好使用少数几个转述动词，频繁使用 Think 动词，不恰当使用消极动词（如 claim、believe）。该研究有利于发现英语学习者转述动词的使用特点，指导学习者在学术写作中恰当使用转述动词。

关键词：学术写作；转述动词；语料库；立场

1. 引言

文献引用是学术语篇中不可缺少的部分，引用他人研究观点有利于增强自己论证的可信度和说服力（Charles 2006a；Hyland 1999；娄宝翠 2011）。近年来学术英语写作研究表明，文献引用不仅用来传达他人的研究观点和结果，还融合了作者对引用内容的看法和态度，用于解释或组织语篇信息，使语篇达到交际目的（Hunston 1993；Hyland 2002；娄宝翠 2011）。文献引用形式、引用句式结构、词汇和时态的选择能表明作者的不同态度立场（Shaw 1992；Swales 1990；唐青叶 2004；徐昉 2012），这种复杂性给二语学习者带来了一定困难。研究发现，二语学习者对于引用句式和词汇的选择比较单一，不能恰当使用转述动词表达立场态度（孙迎晖 2009；余国良 2007）。鉴于此，本研究参照英语期刊论文，分析中国英语学习者学术写作文本，以更好了解学习者转述动词的使用特点。

2. 文献回顾

转述动词作为立场表达的一种重要修辞手段，不仅体现引用内容的性质，还体现语篇作者对引用内容的态度。学者们根据转述动词在引用中的不同功能对转述动词进行了不同分类。Thompson 和 Ye（1991）根据转述行为中被引用作者言语行为的评价意义，将转述动词分为三种：（1）积极意义动词，即语篇作者对引用内容持支持态度，如 point out、state、hold；（2）消极意义动词，即对引用内容持批评质疑态度，如 suggest、oppose、attack；（3）中性立场动词，即客观转述引用内容，

---

*　本研究系国家社科基金项目"中国学习者议论文论证能力发展特征研究"（编号：19BYY229）的阶段性成果。

如say、write、examine。该分类表明作者通过使用不同的转述动词来表达自己对引用信息的不同态度，从而体现作者的立场。根据转述行为中的符号意义，Thompson和Ye（1991）进一步将转述动词分为三类：（1）话语动词，用来描述语篇中言语表达过程，如state、write；（2）心理动词，用来描述心理过程，如believe、think；（3）研究动词，用来描述具体研究过程，如find、discover。这种分类方式被广泛运用到后来的研究中，如Thomas和Hawes（1994）、Hyland（2002）和Luzón（2018）。另一方面，Charles（2006b）基于动词的语法结构，提出转述动词语义分类，将转述动词分为四类：（1）Argue动词，即用于指引用观点，如argue、suggest、propose；（2）Show动词，即用于指转述客观事实，如show、demonstrate、reveal；（3）Find动词，即用于转述发现、了解或记得的信息，如find、discover、observe；（4）Think动词，即用于指带有主观感情色彩的引用信息，如think、assume、hope。Charles（2006b）也提出，这个分类方式和Thompson和Ye（1991）提出的按转述动词符号意义进行的分类有相似之处，即Argue动词类似于话语（文本）动词，Show动词和Find动词类似于研究动词，Think动词类似于心理动词。该分类方式将作者立场态度和转述动词的语义和语法系统地联系起来，更精确地分析了转述动词的修辞功能和所体现的作者立场。后来的研究多使用该分类法（如Friginal 2013；Kwon et al. 2018；Marti et al. 2019）。

转述动词不仅表达作者的立场，而且是联系读者的重要手段；转述动词的选择受到学科和社会文化因素影响（Hyland 2005）。首先，不同学科论文中转述动词的特点不尽相同（Charles 2006a，2006b；Hyland 2000，2002；Thomas & Hawes 1994）。人文学科作者偏好用话语动词，如argue、suggest、study，而自然科学和医学作者更偏好研究动词，如report、describe、show（Charles 2006b；Hyland 2002；Thomas & Hawes 1994）。另一方面，不同社会文化背景的作者在转述动词的选择上也有一定差异。Luzón（2018）发现，相对于英语母语作者，西班牙语母语作者更多使用话语动词，通过引用其他作者的思想和解释来支持自己的观点。英语母语作者则常常通过研究动词委婉地批评前人的研究（张立茵、陈新仁 2020）。张军民（2012）通过对比国际学者，发现中国学者更偏向使用中立、怀疑态度的转述动词，避免直接表达个人观点，这符合中国人推崇的中庸之道。

对于新手学术写作者（如硕、博士生），特别是二语写作者而言，如何正确使用转述动词来增强语篇互动性并表达作者的立场是学术写作中的难点。有研究显示，新手作者偏好Show动词，而专家作者更多使用Argue动词（Friginal 2013；Marti et al. 2019）。而Liardét和Black（2019）则发现，二语作者多用suggest指引观点，而专家作者多用show和find表示赞同命题。造成不同研究结果的原因是写作体裁的不同，前者分析的是研究论文的语料，而后者分析的是文献综述报告和议论文。相同的转述动词在这些体裁中的功能有所不同。相关研究还发现，中国英语学习者在转述动词使用上存在一定问题，如使用类型单一（胡志清、蒋岳春 2007），且存在误用不同评价意义的转述动词的现象（娄宝翠 2011，2013）。

目前，英语学术写作研究更多关注句子层面的引用形式，鲜有针对转述动词及其立场态度的研究。为更全面地了解学习者学术写作中转述动词的使用特点，本文基于学习者语料，参照期刊论文中转述动词的使用情况，研究学习者转述动词的使用频率和评价意义及语义分布特点。本文拟回答以下研究问题：

（1）我国英语学习者在硕士论文中使用的高频转述动词有哪些？

（2）相较于专家作者，我国英语学习者在转述动词的评价意义分布和语义分布方面有何特点？

3. 研究方法

本研究的分析语料来源于两个自建小型语料库：学习者语料库和专家语料库。前者包括近五年《中国优秀硕士学位论文全文数据库》收录的10所重点高校的30篇英语语言学专业硕士毕业论文，均为实证研究论文。后者为参考语料库，包括国际语言学期刊（如 *Annual Review of Applied Linguistics*、*Journal of Second Language Writing*、*Language Teaching*）近十年30篇实证研究论文。每篇文章的摘要、目录、致谢、标注、参考文献和附录等部分已被清理，只保留论文题目和正文。经统计，学习者语料总计523,620词，专家语料总计264,278词。

根据限定性转述从句的特点，转述从句中都保留that一词（Hyland 1999；娄宝翠 2011）。我们利用AntConc 3.4.3检索出每篇文章中包含that的索引行，然后人工识别出动词引导的从句。识别标准如下：（1）文中有明确的引文出处标注；（2）文献原作者是他人，或是其他机构组织，若是某个学派，应出现代表人物；（3）转述动词主语包括作者姓名和机构名称、人称代词、相关词组（如 ***'s study，***'s research，***'s paper 等）或it。

我们统计了两个语料库中所有转述动词后，参照Thompson和Ye（1991）的评价意义分类方式，将转述动词分为积极意义动词（如point out、state）、消极意义动词（如believe、claim）和中性动词（如say、write）（举例见表1）。参照Charles（2006a：318）和Friginal（2013：212）的语义分类方式，将转述动词分为Argue动词（包括argue、suggest、assert等32个动词）、Show动词（包括show、illustrate、indicate、demonstrate、confirm、mean和reveal）、Find动词（包括find、realize、observe、discover、establish、infer、recognize、identify和note）和Think动词（包括think、hold、assume、feel、hope和know）（举例见表2）。最后，我们结合转述动词出现的上下文语境，分析作者意图、研究所使用转述动词的评价意义和语义分布特点。

表1 不同评价意义转述动词举例

	举例
积极动词	• Peng Xuanwei (2011: 69-81) analyzes the esthetic stance of the history of Western literary criticism according to the categories of Appraisal Theory, and **states** that the so-called 'literariness' in criticism is indeed of appraisal (Thesis-1).
	• Duchêne, Moyer, and Roberts (2013) **point out** that while "the discourses of globalization and neoliberalism are ones of 'mobility,' 'flows,' 'flexibility' and 'de-regulation,' many of the practices entailed in globalization are of control and regimentation" (p. 9) (Article-1).
消极动词	• Dance and Zak-Dance **claimed** "public speeches are the act of using spoken language to communicate with many individuals at the same time." [38] (Thesis-4)
	• In doing so, Irvine was following Hymes (1974) in **suggesting** that while linguistic forms no doubt denote and index relations of production and socioeconomic differentiations and inequalities, 'they may also be among those forces, and they may be objects of economic activity' (Irvine 1989: 255) (Article-3).
中性动词	• Odlin (1989) **said** transfer can occur in all levels of linguistic system, including the lexical level, suggesting the acquisition of words is also never immune to L1 transfer (Thesis-2).
	• Goodman **writes** that a thing's dispositions are 'no less important to us than its overt behavior, but they strike us by comparison as rather ethereal. And so we are moved to inquire whether we can bring them down to earth' (Goodman 1954, p. 40) (Article-13).

表2 转述动词语义分类举例

	举例
Argue 动词	• Cummins (1979) **proposes** a "dual-iceberg" analogy to describe the transfer of bilingual learners, first language to the second language (Thesis-7).
	• He encourages critical reflexivity among researchers, whatever their approach, in confronting their biases, and **suggests** that the risks of unacknowledged subjectivity are no greater in case study than in other work (Article-7).
Show 动词	• The study of Neff et al. (2003) **showed** that EFL writers used modal verbs inappropriately when compared with native writers, for example, they will either avoidance or overused modal verbs (Thesis-3).
	• Williams (1981), for example, has **demonstrated** that readers tend to overlook obvious errors in articles that are published in a prestigious journal (Article-9).
Find 动词	• Tarone et al. studied the voice of academic writings in 1981 and **found** that the "we + active verb" structure was used as frequently as passive structures (Thesis-5).
	• Esmaeili (2002), when investigating writing strategies through a questionnaire taken after writing two reading–writing tasks, **discovered** that reading played a critical role for writers (Article-29).
Think 动词	• Tyler (2001, p. 109) **holds** that amongst the most polysemous words in English, and in other languages, are prepositions (Thesis-25).
	• Brogaard, Balcerak Jackson, and Hofweber **assume** that (17) is an unambiguous identity statement (Article-14).

4. 研究结果和讨论

4.1 高频转述动词

我们首先统计了硕士论文和期刊论文两个语料库中所有带 that 的限定性转述从句，并计算出原始频次和标准化频次（每 10 万词）。卡方检验统计分析结果显示，学习者使用动词引导的限定性转述从句比专家使用的频率更高，差异显著（$p<0.05$），两个语料库中限定性转述从句见表 3。

表 3　限定性转述从句频次

	转述从句频率	标准化频率（每 10 万词）
硕士论文	940*	179.5
期刊论文	292	110.4

注：*$p<0.05$

总体而言，学习者使用动词引导的限定性转述从句频率较高。在本研究分析的 30 篇硕士论文中，只有两篇使用频率较低。硕士论文中限定性转述从句的高频使用，一方面从一定程度上说明英语学习者具有文献引用意识；大量引用他人研究观点，体现了学习者对该领域了解的广度和深度（马蓉、秦晓晴 2014）。另一方面，学习者更倾向使用动词引导的限定性转述从句，而专家在引用过程中更多使用非融入式引用，这一发现也印证了前人的研究结果（徐昉 2012）。大多数学习者过度依赖动词支配的转述形式，可能是因为学习者对引用语言形式认识不足，缺乏文献引用、转述信息等学术写作技巧的指导和训练。其次，由于学习者不会使用复杂的名词性短语或名词性词组转述他人观点，因此过度依赖动词支配的转述从句。

研究发现，两个语料库中部分转述动词的出现频率占所使用转述动词的一半以上，而其他转述动词出现频率极低，因此，我们统计了两个语料库中使用频率最高的 10 个转述动词以做进一步分析（见表 4）。

表 4　硕士论文和期刊论文中高频转述动词

硕士论文高频转述动词			期刊论文高频转述动词		
高频词汇	原始频率（523,620 词）	标准化频次（每 10 万字）	高频词汇	原始频率（264,278 词）	标准化频次（每 10 万字）
find	115	22.0	argue	59	22.3
point out	79	15.1	find	35	13.2
show	79	15.1	show	30	11.4
hold	59	11.3	suggest	19	7.2
believe	49	9.4	note	19	7.2

（待续）

（续表）

硕士论文高频转述动词			期刊论文高频转述动词		
高频词汇	原始频率 （523,620词）	标准化频次 （每10万字）	高频词汇	原始频率 （264,278词）	标准化频次 （每10万字）
indicate	48	9.2	conclude	13	4.9
state	46	8.8	point out	10	3.8
claim	45	0.86	state	10	3.8
suggest	41	0.78	claim	9	3.4
propose	35	0.67	observe	8	3.0
合计	596	113.8	合计	212	80.2

如表4所示，硕士论文中出现频率最高的是find，而期刊论文中出现频率最高的argue不在硕士论文高频转述动词之列。两个语料库中find、point out、show、state、claim、suggest出现的频率都较高，但硕士论文出现频率较高的hold和believe等词在期刊论文中仅出现了一次。进一步分析发现，在期刊论文语料的292个转述从句中，专家使用了88个不同的转述动词；而在硕士论文语料的940个转述从句中，学习者只使用了73个不同转述动词。

硕士论文中出现的高频转述动词和娄宝翠（2011）统计的结果基本一致。hold和believe属于心理动词，带有较强的主观感情色彩，通常出现在日常对话交流中，在学术语篇中出现频率较低，过多使用此类词会导致学术语篇口语化（Kwon et al. 2018；吴格奇 2019）。学习者过多使用hold和believe，可能是因为学习者不了解这些转述动词的使用语境，将口头语常用的动词用在学术写作中，说明学生对学术写作这一正式语体的特点认识不足。另外，与专家作者相比，学习者使用的转述动词缺乏多样性，重复使用有限的转述动词，说明学生集中使用他们熟悉的转述动词（胡志清、蒋岳春 2007；孙迎晖 2009）。

4.2 转述动词的评价意义

根据Thompson和Ye（1991）对转述动词的分类，硕士论文中的高频转述动词包括四个表示积极意义的动词（find、hold、point out、state）、四个表示消极意义的动词（believe、claim、propose、suggest）和两个表示中性意义的动词（indicate、show）。期刊论文中的高频转述动词包括五个积极动词（argue、find、note、point out、state）、两个消极动词（claim、suggest）和三个中性动词（conclude、observe、show）。如表5所示，专家和学习者语料中使用频率最高的都是积极动词，占比超过一半。在期刊论文中排列第二位的是中性动词，消极动词占比最少，只有13.21%；而硕士论文中消极动词的比例超过中性动词，达到28%，与期刊论文中消极动词的使用频率差异显著（$p<0.05$）。

表5　高频转述动词评价意义分布

	硕士论文		期刊论文	
	标准化频次（每10万字）	所占比例	标准化频次（每10万字）	所占比例
积极动词	57.1	50.17%	50.3	62.74%
消极动词	32.5*	28.52%	10.6	13.21%
中性动词	24.3	21.30%	19.3	24.06%

注：*p<0.05

消极意义转述动词的使用代表对转述信息的不确定、怀疑或否定。在学术论文中，"CLAIM + that clause"结构中的claim倾向于消极意义，上下文语境会出现表达质疑否定的态度的文字（娄宝翠 2011）。另外，believe的使用显示被引用者判断的主观性和不确定性，通常用来表达不同观点之间的冲突（Hunston 1995）。这说明仅依靠观察索引行并不能确定词汇的评价意义，需要结合上下文语境，了解作者真正想要表达的态度立场。在期刊论文语料中，claim和believe等消极意义转述动词出现时，上下文语境中一般会出现表示转折意义的连词（如but、however）。

例1

　　This view however has been challenged by Mohan and Lo (1985). They argued that the eight-legged essay is outdated, and could not represent the actual contemporary Chinese rhetoric. Kirkpatrick (1997) shared a similar view with Mohan and Lo (1985) when he *claimed* that the two traditional Chinese text styles have very little influence on contemporary Chinese writing (Article-22).

如例1所示，作者在上文介绍了与Mohan和Lo（1985）相反的观点，在本段开始用however引出Mohan和Lo（1985）的论点，并对Kirkpatrick（1997）的观点持怀疑态度。

学习者比专家使用消极动词的频率更高，这一发现与前人研究结果相悖。前人研究发现学习者很少使用消极意义转述动词（余国良 2007；孙迎晖 2009）。学习者一般不直接表达对转述信息的不确定、怀疑或否定的态度，更多使用比较委婉含蓄的表达方式（Hunston 1993）。鉴于此，我们结合学习者语料中消极转述动词出现的上下文语境，对消极转述动词的使用进行了具体分析。分析发现，硕士论文中存在不少转述动词的误用现象，即作者不清楚转述动词的立场态度，在表达支持认同态度和立场时，却选择了believe、claim等消极动词。

例2

　　Selinker (1972) *believes* it is hardly acceptable not to place individual differences into the central position of second language acquisition. Therefore the study of individual differences is a very important section in second language acquisition (Thesis-13).

例3

Scholars put forward various opinions about categorizations of individual difference factors from different theoretical perspectives and research needs. Skehan (1989) *believes* that individual differences shall involve four variables: language aptitude; motivation; learning strategy; cognitive and affective factors (Thesis-2).

例4

Besides, some researchers also *claimed* that the prototype effects came up in nonlinguistic structures as well as in linguistic conceptual structures, like coping with semantic phenomena (Thesis-5).

上述三个例句均选自学习者语料，作者本意是通过引用来支持自己的论述，却误用了claim、believe等词。在例2中，作者的观点是强调个人差异在二语习得中的重要性，引用信息主要强调个人差异在二语习得中的地位。由此可见，作者的真实意图是引用Selinker的观点来证实自己的论述，强调个人差异在二语习得中的重要性，却使用了具有消极意义和不确定性的转述动词believe。例3中，作者通过引用信息介绍个人差异的四个变量，为研究提供了理论背景知识，也不恰当地使用了believe。例4中，从前文连接词besides，我们可以发现引用信息起到了补充说明的作用，作者的本意不是对转述信息进行质疑或批判，却误用了消极意义转述动词claim。学习者语料中出现误用转述动词的现象，可能是因为学习者不了解看似客观的转述动词隐含了作者的态度立场，且对转述动词表达的态度立场不甚明确。这不仅会在阅读文献时容易错误理解他人立场，还会在学术写作中使用不当，给读者造成误解。

4.3 转述动词的语义分布

我们根据Charles（2006a）的分类方式统计了硕士论文中四类动词出现的频次，结果见表6。

表6 硕士论文和期刊论文转述动词分布情况

	硕士论文		期刊论文	
	标准化频次 （每 10 万字）	所占比例	标准化频次 （每 10 万字）	所占比例
Argue 动词	78.5*	48.43%	59.4	54.98%
Think 动词	16.8*	11.07%	8.0	2.95%
Show 动词	30.4*	20.00%	16.6	16.24%
Find 动词	28.8	20.38%	23.5	25.83%

注：*$p<0.05$

　　如表6所示，在硕士论文和期刊论文中，转述动词频率从高到低的顺序一样，都是Argue动词（如argue、suggest、propose）、Find动词（如find、discover、observe）、Show动词（如show、demonstrate、reveal）和Think动词（如think、assume、hope）。Argue动词在两个库出现的频率最高，占所有转述动词的一半左右；Think动词在两个语料库中使用频率都最少。除了Find动词，其他三类转述动词在硕士论文中的出现频率显著高于期刊论文（$p<0.05$）。

　　该结果与Charles（2006a）的结论一致，Argue动词在政治学和材料学论文中的使用频率最高。Argue动词用于交际，主要用于转述文本信息（Charles 2006a）。Think动词用于转述个人观点，带有强烈主观感情色彩。硕士论文中过多使用表达主观感情色彩的转述动词，不利于塑造学术身份。Think动词多分布在学习者语料中，如例5和例6所示：

例5

　　He thinks that the behavior is mostly developed through sociological experiences and encounters (Thesis-7).

例6

　　He holds that both structural elements and factors of experiences can contribute to the unsuccessful expressing caused by CS (Thesis-17).

　　在例5和例6中，作者分别用了think和hold转述他人观点，给读者留下该观点缺乏客观有力的证据的印象。我们发现，think一词在学习者语料中共出现24次，在专家语料中只出现了一次。学习者倾向使用Think动词的现象与Kwon et al.（2018）的研究结果一致，他们的本科生二语学习者语料中Think动词的比例高达24.35%，高于本研究硕士学习者语料中该类动词的比例（11%）。这进一步证实学习者将口语中常用的转述动词用于学术语篇，同时也说明随着学习者进入更高的阶段，语体意识增强，能够运用其他类转述动词。

5. 结语

　　本文通过比较学习者学术写作语料和期刊论文语料，发现学习者使用转述动词的总体频率高于专家作者，这说明学习者能够意识到文献引用的重要性，能在学术写作中大量引用前人研究观点，但是引用形式单一，过度依赖动词支配的转述从句，未能灵活使用文献引用的不同语言形式。在转述动词评价意义分布特点上，学习者能较好地运用积极转述动词和中性转述动词表达不同立场，但存在误用消极动词的现象；在转述动词语义分布方面，学习者使用Argue动词、Find动词和Show动词的频率与专家作者相当，但过多使用主观色彩较强的Think动词，使语篇显得口语化，而且重复有限的转述动词，缺乏多样性。这说明学习者对不同转述动词的使用语境和所包含的态度立场认识不足，对学术写作语体缺乏深入了解。

在学术写作教学中，教师可以结合期刊论文中的实例，向学生介绍讲解转述动词的不同意义和功能，让学生意识到转述动词不只是简单转述文献信息，也是体现作者的评价立场并辅助构建作者观点的工具。教师还可以用语料库辅助教学，展示转述动词的频次和分布特点，并辅以改错等针对性练习（Friginal 2013）。教师也可设计任务引导学生分析期刊论文中不同引用形式、语言特点和转述动词表达的态度立场，以增强学生的体裁意识和立场意识。

本研究通过参照期刊论文语料中转述动词的使用特点，分析学习者使用转述动词的特点，并发现学习者在这一方面存在的问题和不足，以期为教学提供更多启示。本研究只分析了学习者文本，未能对学习者进行访谈以了解其对转述动词的认识以及使用转述动词的真正意图。今后的研究可以结合文本分析和刺激回访来考察影响学习者文献引用行为的因素。

参考文献

Charles, M. 2006a. Phraseological patterns in reporting clauses used in citation: A corpus-based study of theses in two disciplines [J]. *English for Specific Purposes* 25: 310-331.

Charles, M. 2006b. The construction of stance in reporting clauses: A cross-disciplinary study of theses [J]. *Applied Linguistics* 27(3): 492-518.

Friginal, E. 2013. Developing research report writing skills using corpora [J]. *English for Specific Purposes* 32: 208-220.

Hunston, S. 1993. Professional conflict: Disagreement in academic discourse [A]. In M. Baker, G. Francis & E. Tognini-Bonelli (eds.). *Text and Technology: In Honour of John Sinclair* [C]. Amsterdam: John Benjamins. 115-136.

Hunston, S. 1995. A corpus study of some English verbs of attribution [J]. *Functions of Language* 2: 133-158.

Hyland, K. 1999. Academic attribution: Citation and the construction of disciplinary knowledge [J]. *Applied Linguistics* 20(3): 341-367.

Hyland, K. 2000. *Disciplinary Discourses: Social Interactions in Academic Writing* [M]. London: Longman.

Hyland, K. 2002. Activity and evaluation: Reporting practices in academic writing [A]. In J. Flowerdew (ed.). *Academic Discourse* [C]. Harlow: Pearson Education. 115-130.

Hyland, K. 2005. Stance and engagement: A model of interaction in academic discourse [J]. *Discourse Studies* 7: 173-292.

Kwon, M. H., S. Staples & R. S. Partridge. 2018. Source work in the first-year L2 writing classroom: Undergraduate L2 writers' use of reporting verbs [J]. *Journal of English for Academic Purposes* 34: 86-96.

Liardét, C. L. & S. Black. 2019. "So and so" says, states and argues: A corpus-assisted engagement analysis of reporting verbs [J]. *Journal of Second Language Writing* 44: 37-50.

Luzón, M. 2018. Variation in academic writing practices: The case of reporting verbs in English-medium research articles [J]. *Ibérica* 36: 171-194.

Marti, L., S. Yilmaz & Y. Bayyurt. 2019. Reporting research in applied linguistics: The role of nativeness and expertise [J]. *Journal of English for Academic Purposes* 40: 98-114.

Shaw, P. 1992. Reasons for the correlation of voice, tense and sentence functioning in reporting verbs [J]. *Applied Linguistics* 13: 302-319.

Swales, J. M. 1990. *Genre Analysis* [M]. Cambridge: Cambridge University Press.

Thomas, S. & T. P. Hawes. 1994. Reporting verbs in medical journal articles [J]. *Journal of English for Academic Purposes* 13(2): 129-148.

Thompson, G. & Y. Ye. 1991. Evaluation in the reporting verbs used in academic papers [J]. *Applied Linguistics* 12(4): 365-382.

胡志清、蒋岳春，2007，中外英语硕士论文转述动词对比研究[J]，《语言研究》（3）：123-126。

娄宝翠，2011，学习者英语硕士论文中的转述动词[J]，《解放军外国语学院学报》（5）：64-68。

娄宝翠，2013，中英大学生学术论文中转述动词及立场表达对比分析[J]，《山东外语教学》（2）：50-55。

马蓉、秦晓晴，2014，二语学术写作中的引用特征及与写作质量的关系[J]，《外语电化教学》（5）：57-62。

孙迎晖，2009，中国学生英语硕士论文引言部分转述语使用情况的语类分析[J]，《外语教学》（1）：53-57。

唐青叶，2004，学术语篇中的转述现象[J]，《外语与外语教学》（2）：3-6。

吴格奇，2019，合法化语码理论的专门性及其在学术论文分析中的应用[J]，《外国语言与文化》（1）：136-146。

徐昉，2012，实证类英语学术研究话语中的文献引用特征[J]，《外国语》（6）：60-68。

余国良，2007，文献引用行为中批判性思维的个案研究[J]，《外语学刊》（5）：124-128。

张军民，2012，基于语料库的英语学术语篇转述动词研究[J]，《河南师范大学学报（哲学社会科学版）》（3）：246-249。

张立茵、陈新仁，2020，专家作为评价者的引用行为研究[J]，《外语与外语教学》（6）：121-130。

作者简介：

刘应亮（通信作者），武汉理工大学外国语学院副教授，硕士生导师。主要研究方向为二语写作、学术写作。电子邮箱：yliu@whut.edu.cn

魏依，湖北省仙桃中学教师，主要研究方向为二语写作、学术写作。

英语专业高年级学生人物记叙语篇中话语转述性词块运用复杂性研究[*]

于万锁　　郝　媛

太原理工大学

提要：转述人物话语是人物记叙语篇中塑造人物的重要手段。然而，有关引出人物话语转述性词块的前人研究相对缺乏。本文通过自建英语专业高年级在校学生人物记叙语篇语料库并对比美国大学生的人物记叙语篇语料库，考察英语专业高年级学生与美国大学生人物记叙语篇中话语转述性词块运用的复杂性差异，然后通过对原作者进行访谈来探寻造成差异的深层原因。研究结果表明：（1）与美国大学生相比，中国英语专业高年级学生人物记叙语篇中使用的话语转述性词块的中心词多为高频词。虽然这类学生具有产出多种词块的意识，但其词块使用总量少于美国大学生，其词块中最难词也多为高频词。（2）英语专业高年级学生在人物记叙语篇写作中倾向于使用词数较少的、短小的话语转述性词块，且词块结构相对单一，种类远远少于美国大学生，词块的多样性和复杂性不够。该研究发现对人物记叙语篇写作中的话语转述性词块教学具有一定的启示意义。

关键词：英语专业高年级学生；人物记叙语篇；话语转述性词块；词块复杂性

1. 引言

在以人物刻画为核心的人物记叙语篇中，话语是刻画人物的重要手段之一。叙述者常用人物的言语来塑造人物，推动情节发展（申丹 1991）。而人物话语的引出主要靠话语转述语，其在转述人物话语和塑造人物性格中起着不可替代的作用。话语转述语指在人物记叙语篇直接引语中，引导出人物话的词语；同时，它也可能涉及副语言特征的描写，还可能是对引语的补充、说明、阐释等（贾中恒 2000）。话语转述语具有预示和支配语篇意义的语用功能，是转述的核心（徐赳赳 1996），从结构上可分为单个话语转述动词与多词组成的话语转述性词块，这类词块由转述性动词及其修饰语构成。

话语转述性词块通过对人物说话时的声音强调以及对肢体动作和说话方式的描绘，再现了说话者说话时的真实情景。转述语不仅发挥着诠释人物话语的功能，而且对塑造人物形象助益良多（Ruano San Segundo 2016）。学界最先关注此类语言现象的是贾中恒（2000）。他基于英、汉文学作品首次对转述语进行了界定，并从形

---

[*] 本研究为山西省软科学研究一般项目"工科博士生英语科技论文构篇词语运用的丰富性研究"（编号：2019041055-1）和山西省教育厅研究生优秀教材建设项目"英语硕士学位论文语篇构建理论与实践"（编号：2021YJJG072）的阶段性成果。

式、语义和语用三个层面分析其特征。文献梳理发现，话语转述性词块目前尚未引起学界的足够重视。不过，国内外学者对二语学习者写作词块的研究成果颇丰，这些研究主要有三大路径。一是二语学习者词块使用的发展性特征研究（如胡元江2015；黄开胜、周新平 2016；戚焱 2010）。二是二语词块使用与语言水平的相关性研究（如丁言仁、戚焱 2005；戚焱、夏珺 2016）。三是词块使用的特点研究。此类研究包括：（1）不同母语背景、英语水平学习者词块使用对比；（2）不同学科之间的词块特征对比（如 Cortes 2004；Hyland 2008）；（3）不同语类的词块使用对比（如王立非、张岩 2006）；（4）不同语域的词块使用对比（如黄开胜 2018）。其中，不同母语背景、英语水平学习者的词块使用对比研究成果最为丰富。研究结果表明，中国二语学习者词块产出意识较强，词块使用量明显多于本族语者；中、高级学习者词块丰富性显著高于初学者。但中国二语学习者比本族语者选词更加宽泛模糊，使用较多的衔接性词块，并且在常用词块的结构和功能上与本族语者相比差异明显，口笔语交际中使用偏好也存在差异（如 Chen & Baker 2010；Staples et al. 2013；胡元江等 2017；李梦骁、刘永兵 2017；刘应亮等 2020；杨滢滢 2015；张会平 2020；张霞 2010）。毫无疑问，前人对于词块的探索为我们研究英语专业高年级学生人物记叙语篇中话语转述性词块运用的复杂性特征提供了借鉴，其研究思路对我们的研究设计及分析框架具有很大启发意义。不过，前人对词块使用特征的研究主要集中于使用频率、使用偏好、结构与功能分布和准确性等方面，尚未触及英语专业高年级学生人物记叙语篇中话语转述性词块运用的复杂性特征。而对英语专业高年级学生人物记叙语篇中话语转述性词块的复杂性进行研究，有助于英语专业教师了解学生话语转述性词块的使用特征，继而针对该特征设计出更加有效的教学方案，以提升英语专业学生人物记叙语篇写作的整体水平。

鉴于此，本研究基于自建英语专业高年级在校学生人物记叙语篇语料库，对比美国大学生人物记叙语篇语料库，考察英语专业高年级学生与美国大学生人物记叙语篇中话语转述性词块运用的复杂性差异，之后对原作者进行访谈，分析造成该差异的深层原因。具体研究问题包括：

（1）英语专业高年级学生人物记叙语篇中话语转述性词块复杂性有何特点？

（2）英语专业高年级学生话语转述性词块运用复杂性同美国大学生相比是否有差异？若有，差异在何处？有何原因？

2. 词块复杂性评价维度

本研究参照刘黎岗和缪海涛（2018）的词汇复杂性与语法复杂性理论分析框架，创造性地提出了词块复杂性的评价维度。词块复杂性由词块难度和词块复杂度构成。

词块难度包括词块中心词的词汇难度、词块中低频词的数量和词块中最难词的词汇难度。词汇难度通过判断该词是否为低频词来测量。对低频词的鉴定，基于

"词汇频率概貌"（Lexical Frequency Profile, LFP）（Laufer & Nation 1995）来进行。词块中心词和词块中最难的词越难，代表词块越复杂；词块中低频词的数量越多，代表该词块越复杂。

词块复杂度包括词块长度、词块类别及其结构复杂度。词块越长，代表该词块越复杂。对于词块种类和结构复杂度的测量，本研究参照了《英文写作常见问题与对策》（于万锁、朱婷 2008）一书中所整理的各种人物话语转述性词块。该书中列举了作者几十年搜集整理的大量典型话语转述性词块。我们将书中所有转述性词块提取出来，根据其结构进行了分类。然后，对不同类别的转述性词块作了难度等级排序处理。为确保词块难度分级的针对性和准确性，我们随机选取了10名英语专业学生进行访谈。访谈要求受访者基于自己的话语转述词块知识，对转述性词块进行难度等级排序。最后，结合学生的访谈结果，我们对之前所做的转述性词块难度分级框架作了微调，形成了最终的难度等级排序表（见表1）。

表1　话语转述性词块分类及难度等级排序

词块类别			难度等级
动词 + 状语	动词 + 副词		1/ 低等难度
	动词 + 代词		
	动词 + 副词 + 介词短语		
	动词 + 介词短语	动词 + 介词 in + ...	2/ 中等难度
		动词 + 介词 with + ...	
		动词 + 介词 through/like/under/from/at/ ... + ...	
	动词 + 名词短语		3/ 高等难度
	动词 + 非谓语结构		
动词 + 从句			
介词短语			

3. 研究设计

本研究使用AntConc软件，抽取英语专业学生人物记叙语篇语料库与美国大学生语料库中话语转述性词块；采用Range软件，分析词汇复杂度，对比两个语料库中话语转述性词块难度和复杂度的差异。研究过程大致可分三个步骤：

首先，确定研究语料。本研究所用的观察语料库是随机挑选的46篇国内某理工院校英语专业本科三年级在校学生考场所写的人物记叙语篇，作文主要围绕"My Father in Celebration of the Spring Festival"这一主题，词容为22,389个形符。

参照语料库选自《美国大学生作文荟萃》和《美国大学生作文选》中所选取的50篇人物记叙语篇，写作主题主要是身边的人，词容为48,010个形符。

其次，搜集处理话语转述性词块。研究人员先对观察语料库和参照语料库中的话语转述性词块进行赋码，借助文本分析软件AntConc进行检索，提取出了语料库中所有赋码的话语转述性词块。然后，统计了两个语料库中转述性词块的中心词、低频词以及词块中最难词，利用Range软件，分析了词块中心词和词块中最难词的难度等级；统计了两个语料库中转述性词块的长度，并将词块按照结构进行了分类，以考察其结构特征。

接着，检验话语转述性词块的差异显著性。使用卡方检验计算工具对两个语料库中话语转述性词块出现的频率进行了差异性检验，观察其差异的显著性。

最后，针对差异性检验结果，我们选取了三名具有代表性的原作者（学生）进行了深度访谈，以探明造成英语专业高年级学生与美国大学生话语转述性词块运用复杂性差异的深层原因。

4. 研究结果与讨论

4.1 话语转述性词块难度对比分析

如前文所述，"话语转述性词块"在结构上是由转述动词加上其修饰语构成的，所以话语转述性词块的中心词就是指词块中的转述动词。表2显示，英语专业学生话语转述性词块的中心词在常用1000词表中的频数远大于其他三个词表中的频数之和，其占比达到了81.58%；其他三个词表的占比分别为13.16%、2.63%、2.63%。美国大学生的中心词占比最高的虽然也是常用1000词，但其占比（73.13%）相对于英语专业学生的81.58%而言，少了8.45%。而美国大学生低频词的使用比例（17.91%）远大于英语专业学生的（5.26%）。为了进一步摸清两个群体在话语转述性词块中心词运用上是否存在显著性差异，我们进行了差异显著性检验。结果发现，除次常用1000词外（$p_{次常用1000词}=0.405>0.05$），英语专业学生和美国大学生话语转述性词块中心词在常用1000词和低频词上都存在显著性差异。

表2 英语专业学生和美国大学生话语转述性词块中心词难度对比

		英语专业学生		美国大学生		p 值
		频数	占比（％）	频数	占比（％）	
高频词	常用 1000 词	31	81.58	98	73.13	0.000*
	次常用 1000 词	5	13.16	12	8.96	0.405
低频词	学术词表	1	2.63	7	5.22	0.034*
	表外词	1	2.63	17	12.69	0.000*

注：*$p<0.05$

由上述量化分析可知，英语专业学生较之美国大学生，其人物记叙语篇所产出的话语转述性词块的中心词往往是为数众多的高频词，而低频词的数量远远小于美国大学生，两个群体在常用词的使用上存在显著性差异。产出性词汇总量较小，可能迫使英语专业学生在引述人物话语时不得不重复使用某些高频话语转述动词，从而造成了话语转述性词块复杂度偏低。这一发现验证了刘东虹（2004）的研究结论：产出性词汇量的大小直接影响二语写作中用词的复杂度。例如：

例1：

But she *said coldly*, "you must take it, if you don't take it, how can you find a good job? Do you want to do some heavy and exhausting jobs, I don't allow." （英语专业学生）

例2：

"Play! Start playing," John *pleaded again in hushed tones*.（美国大学生）

英语专业学生话语转述性词块中常用较简单、高频的转述动词，如said（例1），而美国大学生在转述话语时，会用到plead（例2）这样的低频词。此外，英语专业学生在用话语转述性词块转述人物话语时，常选用一些较宽泛、模糊的转述动词，如例1中"said coldly"（冷冷地说道），这就会导致学生在转述人物话语时，细节描写不到位，不能像美国大学生写作中的plead again in hushed tones（例2）那样精准地描绘出John压低声音再次祈求对方的说话方式所包含的丰富内容：John已经恳求过对方一次了。

表3　英语专业学生和美国大学生话语转述性词块中低频词总量对比

		英语专业学生	美国大学生	*p* 值
词块中低频词	数量	10	79	0.000*
	占比（%）	9.90	15.74	

注：*$p<0.05$

表4　英语专业学生和美国大学生话语转述性词块中最难词难度等级对比

		英语专业学生		美国大学生		*p* 值
		数量	占比（%）	数量	占比（%）	
高频词	常用 1000 词	26	68.42	78	58.21	0.000*
	次常用 1000 词	9	23.69	17	12.68	0.117
低频词	学术词	1	2.63	4	2.99	0.180
	表外词	2	5.26	35	26.12	0.000*

注：*$p<0.05$

由表3和表4可知，英语专业学生词块中低频词数量较为有限，占比（9.90%）小于美国大学生的15.74%，且两者存在显著差异（$p=0.000<0.05$）。就词块中最难词的难度等级而言，英语专业学生所使用的高频词占比（92.11%）比美国大学生的70.89%高出21.22%，二者差异显著。在高频词当中，次常用词的占比（23.69%）却高出美国大学生的11.01%。虽然差异不显著，但足以说明，随着英语写作能力的提高，英语专业学生词块产出意识逐渐增强，其使用的词块难度等级也在增大。不过，他们却难以跨越高频词和低频词之间存在的障碍性瓶颈。这一结论也表现在低频词的使用上。英语专业学生低频词的占比（7.89%）远远小于美国大学生（29.11%），最难词在其中的表外词上同样也存在着显著性差异。

数据分析发现，英语专业学生在人物记叙语篇写作中，话语转述性词块所用的词语多为简单的高频词，低频词占比远小于美国大学生，但次常用词的占比却比较高。这一"反常"现象表明，英语专业学生在高年级阶段通过专业知识学习和大量阅读训练，其语言输入量增大，词块总量也随之增加。该"异常现象"也反映出英语专业学生在学习过程中话语转述性词块输入以高频词为主，他们对低频词的重视程度不够，习得水平低，难以自如运用这类词汇；这可能削弱了他们低频词的产出愿望和产出总量。这一猜测一定程度上与徐翠芹（2019）的研究结论不谋而合：二语学习者写作词汇总体上偏简单化，与写作者的智力水平和认知能力不匹配。譬如：

例3：

"I've bought you two new clothes in my bag. Try them on later and consider the size." He *said with a low and slight voice*. （英语专业学生）

例4：

"Yeah," he *replied in a nonchalant tone of voice*. （美国大学生）

综上，英语专业学生在人物记叙语篇写作中话语转述性词块所用的高频词过多，且重复率高，低频词使用不足，产出词块较为简单，词块难度偏低的现象较为普遍。究其原因，可能与英语专业学生产出性词汇总量有关。访谈结果表明，英语专业学生表示他们有关话语转述性词块的积累不足，在写作中不能瞬时提取出大脑里储存的表达有关概念的词语，因此不得不重复使用自己已知的转述词汇，忽视了概念表达的准确性。已有研究发现，英语学习者缺乏运用低频词的动机（卢敏 2008）。他们在日常写作中抱有求稳心态，尽量使用熟悉和简单的词语，力避运用生疏词（秦晓晴、文秋芳 2007）。这在某种程度上反映出在中国英语教学中，教师过度要求学生语言的正确性，致使学生采用"回避"和"迂回表达"策略，不敢使用没有把握的低频词汇，在写作过程中只能反复依靠一些高频词汇表达思想，不能变换使用同义词或近义词以增加作文的词汇变化性（朱慧敏、王俊菊 2013）。

4.2 话语转述性词块结构复杂度对比分析

表5 英语专业学生和美国大学生话语转述性词块长度对比

词块长度		英语专业学生		美国大学生		p 值
		数量	占比（%）	数量	占比（%）	
词数	2	29	76.32	60	44.78	0.001*
	3	2	5.26	14	10.45	0.003*
	4	1	2.63	19	14.18	0.000*
	5	4	10.53	16	11.94	0.007*
	6	1	2.63	11	8.21	0.004*
	7	1	2.63	5	3.73	0.102
	8	-	-	3	2.24	-
	9	-	-	4	2.99	-
	11	-	-	1	0.75	-
	12	-	-	1	0.75	-

注：*$p<0.05$

表6 英语专业学生转述性词块结构

序号	转述结构		频数	占比（%）	难度等级
1	动词 + 副词		26	76.47	1
2	动词 + 介词	with...	4	23.53	2
3		in..	4		

表7 美国大学生转述性词块结构

序号	转述结构		频数	占比（%）	难度等级
1	动词 + 副词		23	27.92	1
2	动词 + 代词		23		
3	动词 + 介词	in...	12	39.58	2
4		with...	9		
5		from...	7		
6		like...	3		
7		by...	2	38	
8		at...	1		
9		behind...	1		
10		through...	1		
11		under...	1		
12		without...	1		
13	动词 + 非谓语		9	12.5	3
14	动词 + 从句		3		

表5显示，英语专业学生所使用的话语转述性词块按词块中的词语数量分类，

共有六类。六类中，二词词块占比最高，达76.32%；其次是五词词块（10.53%）；三词词块出现两次，占5.26%；四词、六词和七词词块分别仅出现一次，各占2.63%。与此不同的是，美国大学生使用了十类词块。其中，二词词块使用频率最高，占比44.78%，大大低于英语专业学生的76.32%，近乎为中国英语专业学生的一半；三词、四词、五词、六词和七词词块的使用占比均高于英语专业学生。在五类词块的运用上，两个群体存在显著性差异。除此之外，美国大学生人物记叙语篇中还出现了八词、九词、十一词和十二词等四类超长词块。

由表6和表7的对比数据可知，英语专业学生使用的话语转述性词块在结构上主要有三种。其中，使用频率最高的转述性词块为低等难度的动词加副词结构，占76.47%；其余为中等难度的动词加介词结构，占23.53%；没有使用高等难度的话语转述性词块。而美国大学生的转述性词块结构多达14种。其中，绝大多数美国学生使用的转述性词块为中等难度的动词加介词结构，占39.58%；其次是低等难度的动词加副词和动词加代词结构；高等难度的动词加非谓语和动词加从句结构使用量最少。

通过对比英语专业学生和美国大学生人物记叙语篇中话语转述性词块的结构复杂度，我们不难发现，英语专业学生在话语转述性词块的运用上倾向使用动词加副词结构。动词加介词结构中的介词主要为with和in，其他介词使用很少。与美国大学生相比，其词块长度偏短，转述性词块难度偏低，且词块结构单一、语义简单。访谈发现，造成英语专业高年级学生与美国大学生话语转述性词块结构复杂度差异的深层原因主要有四：一是英语专业学生对人物记叙语篇的构建理论掌握不足。英语专业学生还不太熟悉在人物记叙语篇写作中借助人物对话来塑造人物个性的写作手法，因而无法准确、生动地还原人物话语，再现人物的真实意图。有同学坦言："平时阅读中不太重视转述词块，没有认识到转述词块的重要性。"他们不知道通过话语转述词块来描写人物说话的丰富细节，所掌握的话语转述词块总量不够。二是英语专业学生不了解本族语者刻画人物时所使用的各类话语转述性词块，不能准确描写说话人的各种声音，伴随的面部表情、手势及其他体态动作等能体现人物性格的细节。三是他们的转述性词块和其他转述词语积累不足，使其在写作中只能重复使用自己很有把握的话语转述词语，从而导致其对人物话语的刻画单调乏味，缺乏生动性，且有整体趋同的倾向性。四是受汉语表达习惯和中国文化固有的思维定式的负迁移影响，致使其在写作中倾向于使用长度短小的词块来转述人物话语。譬如，有学生表示，受中文思维的影响，他们能想到的表达最多就是"XX地说"，英语中对应的就是"say"后面加副词，也不知道其他的表达。这种推测一定程度上验证了Dewaele和Pavlenko（2003）的研究结论：文化差异对词语运用的丰富性也会产生较大影响。

5. 结语

本研究考察了英语专业高年级学生和美国大学生两个群体在人物记叙语篇中所运用的话语转述性词块的复杂性维度特征。结果发现，在词块难度上，与美国大学生相比，英语专业高年级学生人物记叙语篇中使用的话语转述性词块的中心词多为高频词。虽然他们具有产出多种词块的意识和愿望，但因其词块运用能力不足而导致所用的词块总量明显少于美国大学生。其词块中最难词也多为高频词，低频词的用量不足。在词块复杂度上，英语专业高年级学生在人物记叙语篇写作中倾向于使用长度短小的话语转述性词块，极少使用六、七词词块，更未触及八词以上的超长词块。在词块结构上，英语专业学生所使用的话语转述性词块多为难度偏低的动词加副词结构，别的结构类别的使用远远少于美国大学生，有的甚至存在着"真空地带"。在高频话语转述性词块和低频话语转述性词块之间似乎存在着难以逾越的"关卡"，极易造成高原期的石化现象。总体而言，英语专业高年级学生在话语转述性词块运用的复杂度和难度上都不尽如人意，体现不出高年级学生在高级英语写作中所应该展现出的"高级别"特征。

鉴于上述研究发现，英语专业高年级写作教师应该针对学生话语转述性词块运用复杂性不够这一问题，在记叙文语篇教学中积极引导学生系统地分类积累话语转述性词块，采取多种措施，鼓励学生在人物话语刻画中尝试使用有难度的、结构复杂的话语转述性词块。同时加强对话语转述性词块中低频词的训练，鼓励学生大胆使用低频词汇，不要怕出错。鉴于英语专业高年级学生在高频话语转述性词块和低频话语转述性词块之间存在着"高原期现象"，英语写作教师应该采用"声音强化法"在内的多种教学方法，长期地、高频次地、互动式地、学以致用地对学生进行刺激，以使低频话语转述性词块在学生脑海中深深扎根，达到"整存整取""想用即用""想用能用"的最高写作目的。

需要特别指出的是，本研究也存在一定的局限性。比如，目前学界尚未系统地提出话语转述性词块复杂性分类框架和维度测量方法，本研究所采用的分类框架和复杂性维度测量方法或许还存在着主观性。另外，由于研究所抽取的样本容量不够大，地域分布不够广，研究结果可能无法揭示我国英语专业高年级学生所用的话语转述性词块复杂维度的真实特征。以后的相关研究还需加大研究规模，全面系统地探讨不同地域、不同层次的外语院校英语学习者英语记叙语篇中话语转述性词块的运用特征，提出更加理想的分类框架和测量方法，尽快摸清我国英语专业高年级学生在话语转述性词块的运用和习得上所存在的困难、问题及规律，为我国二语写作词块研究作出理论和方法上的贡献。

参考文献

Chen, Y. & P. Baker. 2010. Lexical bundles in L1 and L2 academic writing [J]. *Language Learning and Technology* 2: 30-49.

Cortes, V. 2004. Lexical bundles in published and student disciplinary writing: Examples from history and biology [J]. *English for Specific Purposes* 4: 397-423.

Dewaele. J. M. & A. Pavlenko. 2003. *Effects of the Second Language on the First* [M]. Clevedon: Multilingual Matters.

Hyland, K. 2008. Writing theories and writing pedagogies [J]. *Indonesian Journal of English Language Teaching* 2: 91-110.

Laufer, B. & P. Nation. 1995. Vocabulary size and use: Lexical richness in L2 written production [J]. *Applied Linguistics* 16: 307-322.

Ruano San Segundo, P. 2016. A corpus-stylistic approach to Dickens' use of speech verbs: Beyond mere reporting [J]. *Language and Literature* 2: 113-129.

Staples, S., J. Egbert, D. Biber & A. McClair. 2013. Formulaic sequences and EAP writing development: Lexical bundles in the TOEFL iBT writing section [J]. *Journal of English for Academic Purposes* 3: 214-225.

丁言仁、戚焱，2005，词块运用于英语口语和写作水平的相关性研究[J]，《解放军外国语学院学报》（3）：49-53。

胡元江，2015，基于语料库的英语专业高年级学生口语词块结构特征研究[J]，《外语研究》（5）：26-30。

胡元江、石海漫、季萍，2017，英语学习者与本族语者议论文词块的结构与功能特征——基于语料库的对比研究[J]，《外语研究》34（4）：58-62。

黄开胜，2018，中国英语专业学习者词块输出的语体特征对比研究[J]，《外语界》（5）：71-79。

黄开胜、周新平，2016，基于语料库的中国英语学习者词块输出能力的趋势研究[J]，《外语界》（4）：27-34。

贾中恒，2000，转述语及其语用功能初探[J]，《外国语》（2）：35-41。

李梦骁、刘永兵，2017，中国学习者英语学术论文结论语步的词块特征研究[J]，《外语教学》（1）：34-38。

刘东虹，2004，写作策略与产出性词汇量对写作质量的影响[J]，《现代外语》（3）：302-310+330。

刘黎岗、缪海涛，2018，语言复杂度的理论与测量[J]，《外语研究》（1）：52-55。

刘应亮、郭晓凤、连丽萍，2020，高中生英语写作词块使用研究[J]，《二语写作》（1）：62-69+152。

卢敏，2008，产出性词汇知识广度的发展特征——基于英语专业学生书面语的研究[J]，《外语教学理论与实践》（2）：10-15。

戚焱，2010，英语专业学生口语中词块使用情况的跟踪研究[J]，《外语界》（5）：34-41。

戚焱、夏珺，2016，背诵词块对英语写作和口语水平的影响[J]，《解放军外国语学院学报》（1）：96-103。

秦晓晴、文秋芳，2007，中国大学生英语写作能力发展规律与特点研究 [M]。北京：中国社会科学出版社。

申丹，1991，小说中人物话语的不同表达方式 [J]，《外语教学与研究》（1）：13-18+79。

王立非、张岩，2006，基于语料库的大学生英语议论文中的语块使用模式研究 [J]，《外语电化教学》（4）：36-41。

徐翠芹，2019，从写作停顿看体裁差异对中国英语学习者写作认知加工过程的影响 [J]，《解放军外国语学院学报》（4）：103-110+160。

徐赳赳，1996，叙述文中直接引语分析 [J]，《语言教学与研究》（1）：52-66。

杨滢滢，2015，中美大学生同一主题作文词汇和词块运用特征对比研究 [J]，《外语界》（3）：51-58+75。

于万锁、朱婷，2008，英文写作常见问题与对策 [M]。上海：上海科学技术出版社。

张会平，2020，中国英语初学者写作词块使用特征研究 [J]，《解放军外国语学院学报》（4）：19-25+86+160。

张霞，2010，基于语料库的中国高级英语学习者词块使用研究 [J]，《外语界》（5）：48-57。

朱慧敏、王俊菊，2013，英语写作的词汇丰富性发展特征———一项基于自建语料库的纵贯研究 [J]，《外语界》（6）：77-86。

作者简介：

于万锁（通信作者），太原理工大学外国语学院，教授，硕士生导师。主要研究领域：二语写作、学术英语写作、语篇语言学、二语习得。电子邮箱：ywstyut@163.com

郝媛，太原理工大学外国语学院，主要研究领域：英语写作。

国外英语议论文论证发展研究：回顾与展望

牛瑞英

广东外语外贸大学

提要：英语议论文写作是英语学习者的必备技能，教授该技能的关键在于培养学生的论证能力。然而，无论是英语母语者还是二语学习者的议论文写作，都存在论证不充分的问题。本文旨在从研究文献寻求解决该问题的路径。为此，本文在定义论证和论证能力、阐释议论文论证发展研究理论视角的基础上，综述目前关于英语议论文论证发展的实证研究。结果发现：现有研究主要采用心理认知视角，考察各种教学方法和策略、写作标准以及学生主导的活动对议论文论证发展的影响，采纳社会文化理论视角和探讨学习过程的研究较少；关于二语学习者的研究少于涉及英语母语者的研究，基于课堂教学的研究尤为不足。针对上述现状，本文指出英语议论文论证发展研究的未来方向。

关键词：英语议论文写作；论证；理论视角；研究关注点；研究方向

1. 引言

英语议论文写作是英语学习者的必备技能。比如美国2010年颁布的英语课程共同核心州立标准（Common Core State Standards）规定，6至12年级的学生必须具备议论文读写能力；同时，相关学者（如Newell et al. 2011；Newell & Bloom 2017）指出，议论文写作有助于大学生培养逻辑思辨能力，取得学业成功和就业机会。议论文写作在我国外语教学中同样占据重要地位。英语议论文写作是大学生的必修课程，各种英语水平考试都利用议论文测量学生的写作水平。良好的议论文写作能力是学生撰写英语学术论文的基础。与议论文写作的重要性相呼应，教育部最新颁布的《普通高等学校本科外国语言文学类专业教学指南》（2020：2）明确提出，英语专业学生应具备"良好的思辨能力"，包括思辨写作能力。鉴于议论文和思辨能力的紧密关系，培养议论文写作能力无疑是外语教学的重要组成部分。

然而，对于议论文写作，英语母语和二语写作者都存在论证不充分的问题。2012年美国中学生写作评估报告显示，仅有25%的12年级高中生的议论文包含充分的理由和实例支撑，达到议论文的质量要求；美国大学生的议论文同样存在论证元素缺失和观点偏颇的问题（Ferretti & Fan 2016；Ferretti & Lewis 2019；Song & Ferretti 2013）。关于我国的外语写作，研究发现，英语专业大学生的议论文缺少驳论（Qin & Karabacak 2010），存在使用论据种类和数量不足的问题（Zhang 2018）。

鉴于议论文的重要性和学生在论证方面的问题，有必要探讨如何有效提升学生的议论文论证水平。本文拟综述关于英语议论文论证发展的实证研究，揭示文献关注的提升学生议论文论证的教学方法和策略，梳理当前研究主题，明确未来研究方向，为提升学生议论文论证水平提供借鉴。

2. 论证与论证发展

教学中，英语写作通常服务于"学习写作"和"以写促学"两大目的（Manchón 2011）。与此相对应，英语写作中的论证表现为推理型论证（Toulmin 1958）和探索型论证（Kuhn et al. 2016）两种形式。前者体现为英语课的议论文写作，目的是通过写作学习论证；后者体现为跨课程写作，旨在通过论证学习学科知识（Newell et al. 2015）。本文主要关注英语课堂议论文写作中推理型论证的研究。

推理型论证的核心为构建符合逻辑、令人信服的论证。对论证的关注聚焦于以图尔敏模型（Toulmin 1958）为框架的论证结构。根据图尔敏模型，连贯的论证涵盖以下元素：论点（对有争议事件所持的观点或立场）、论据（实证或实验性的证据）、保证（论据支持论点的推理，如人们普遍同意的假设、规则和原理）、支撑（对保证的支持，如事实、例子和实验数据等）、修饰语（调节论点强度的用语，如may、might等情态动词）和反驳（对反面观点的回应）。如图1所示，各元素间的关系为："论点"为论证的核心，"论据"通过"保证"支持论点，"支撑"为"保证"提供支持，同时，运用"修饰语"调整论点的强度，并"反驳"反面观点，增强论证的说服力。因此，论证就是运用论据支撑论点，并对反面观点予以有力反驳的推理过程。

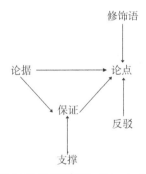

图1　图尔敏论证模型（Toulmin 1958）

图尔敏模型基于逻辑和推理原则构建，已被广泛应用于五段式作文和课程论文等各种议论文的教学和评估（Hirvela 2017；Qin & Karabacak 2010）。本文综述的关于学生议论文论证发展的研究，主要把该模型作为教学干预和作文分析的依据和框架。在所综述研究中，"议论文论证发展"指一段时期内学生所写议论文论证质量的变化，包括从作文初稿到修改稿以及从学期初到学期末作文的变化。

3. 议论文论证发展研究理论视角

论证是议论文的核心。与议论文写作研究一致，议论文论证发展研究主要遵循心理认知视角和社会文化理论视角（Ferretti & Graham 2019；Newell et al. 2011）。两个视角的学习观、对议论文写作教学的看法、聚焦的研究问题以及采用的研究方法都不尽相同。

心理认知视角认为，学习是在信息处理系统内解决问题的过程。由于写作能力和信息资源有限，学生必须接受写作策略和写作模式训练（Bereiter & Scardamalia 1987；Flower & Hayes 1981），把策略和模式迁移到写作中（Reznitskaya et al. 2007）才能学会写作。具体到议论文写作，学生通过接受示范或者支架性帮助，获取完成具体任务的策略知识，学会撰写议论文（Newell et al. 2011）。相关研究通常聚焦影响学生议论文写作的因素，通过实验方法检验教学或者训练的效果。

与心理认知视角不同，社会文化视角认为人的认知发展通过社会互动的调节实现（Vygotsky 1978）。学生通过参与社会互动和实践获取议论文写作能力（Newell et al. 2011）。具体说，议论文写作是学生在社会活动中通过实践学会的，其社会活动受到为实现修辞目标而设计的各种读写工具（如体裁分析）的调节（Newell et al. 2011）。相关研究通常采用质性方法，考察学生写作的环境以及环境对学生实现修辞目标的影响（Ferretti & Graham 2019）。

鉴于"认知过程总是人们社会互动的一部分"（Newell et al. 2011：280），两种理论视角对议论文写作教学的理解实为互相补充。然而，学者们通常采纳一种理论视角开展实证研究。

4. 英语议论文论证发展研究回顾

考察学生议论文论证水平提升的研究可以追溯到20世纪九十年代中期。据笔者统计，至2020年底，各类英文期刊发表相关实证研究论文共33篇[1]。根据主题，33篇论文可以归结为三类，分别探讨教学方法和策略、写作目标以及学生主导的活动对议论文论证发展的影响。

4.1 教学方法和策略对议论文论证发展的影响

聚焦教学方法和策略的研究可进一步分为三类，分别考察各种教学方法、系列教学策略以及自我调节策略发展（self-regulated strategy development，SRSD）教学模式对学生议论文论证发展的影响。第一类研究考察的教学方法包括图尔敏模型教学、过程写作法、作文结构教学、驳论教学等。此类中各个研究之间相对独立，关注议论文教学的不同侧面，探讨不同教学方法的效果，普遍得到积极发现。具体而言，图尔敏模型是议论文论证教学的依据和指导性框架，研究发现把该模型融入教学能够提升学生的论证能力。Yeh（1998）以美国七年级少数族裔学生为考察对象，

---

1 笔者搜索期间的中文期刊，没有发现直接相关的研究，故此统计没有包括中文期刊在内。

发现在对论证发展的影响方面，基于图尔敏模型的教学模式要优于过程教学法。Kathpalia 和 See（2016）通过分析教授图尔敏模型前后的新加坡大学生的博客，发现超过一半学生的论证结构和质量都取得进步。

　　始于20世纪七八十年代的过程写作法已成为写作教学的常态，有研究考察并证实过程写作法对提升学生论证能力的作用。MacArthur 和 Lembo（2009）采用过程写作法为三名非裔美国成年学生进行一对一议论文写作训练，训练内容包括结构讲解和示范、撰写作文、依据标准评估和修改作文、单独辅导等。结果发现，学生的作文质量和结构以及反面观点处理能力都得到提高。

　　议论文的结构有助于厘清论证的结构，所以作文结构教学是议论文教学的重点。研究发现，写作阶段和修改阶段的作文结构教学都能够提升论证的质量。例如，Midgette 和 Haria（2016）要求两组美国八年级学生分别接受作文结构教学和作文结构修改教学，前者包括计划策略和作文修改清单，后者在计划阶段增加自由写作，修改阶段增加步骤说明；前后测显示，两组议论文的整体质量和结构都有显著改进。

　　驳论能增强议论文的说服力，但学生通常忽视驳论或者不知如何进行驳论。有研究探讨并证实驳论教学的积极效果。Liu 和 Stapleton（2014）考察驳论教学对125名中国大学生作文中驳论的使用以及作文质量的影响，发现驳论教学促进了学生驳论的使用，而且驳论使用与作文质量呈正相关。Liu 和 Stapleton（2020）进而从体裁教学视角，研究驳论教学对中国香港135名小学六年级学生议论文写作的影响。经过12周的教学干预，他们发现大部分学生能在作文中使用驳论。

　　第二类研究探讨系列教学策略的干预效果。与过程写作法的教学步骤不同，系列教学策略是专门针对论证的教学手段。例如，Burkhalter（1995）以小学四、六年级学生为研究对象，把学生分为实验组和对照组进行研究。实验组接受16天的议论文教学干预，包括识别表达意见的词语、提出论点、预测反面论点、辩论、把口头论证改为书面论证、识别强弱论点、支撑论点等，而对照组没有接受议论文教学干预。分析前后测作文的论点、论据和保证发现，实验组的得分高于对照组，四年级学生在后测也取得进步，从而揭示教学干预的作用，并证实：如果给予机会和恰当的教学支持，小学生也可以学会议论文写作。

　　针对不同水平的研究对象和不同特点的课程，现有研究所关注的具体教学系列策略不尽相同，但都发现教学策略的积极效应。例如，Bacha（2010）研究大学学术英语写作课的五步教学法（建立情景、剖析范文、合作写作、独立写作和关联相关文章）对四名阿拉伯语为母语的学生论证学习的影响。结果发现，学生的论证结构得到提高，论证技巧可以迁移到新的写作任务中。Campbell 和 Filimon（2018）采用单组前后测设计，研究标识阅读文本、提问、背诵、反思、总结、复习和重述等策略教学对43名美国七年级学生议论文写作的影响。经过16周的教学，发现学生在作文质量、证据和展开等方面都有显著提高。

　　第三类研究探讨 SRSD 教学模式对议论文论证发展的影响。该模式源于过程教学法对写作策略的重视，旨在帮助中小学生构思和撰写议论文的论证（De La Paz & Graham 1997）。经过多年探索，SRSD模式已经开发出三种作文构思策略和一种作文撰写策略。三种构思策略为POW（**p**ick my ideas，**o**rganize my notes，and **w**rite and say more）、STOP（**S**uspend judgment，**T**ake a side，**O**rganize ideas，and **P**lan more as you write）和DARE（**D**evelop a topic sentence，**A**dd supporting ideas，**R**eject judgment for the other side，and **E**nd with a conclusion）；撰写策略为TREE（**t**ell what you believe，give three or more **r**easons，**e**xamine each reason，and **e**nd it）。四种策略都以步骤关键词的首字母命名。

SRSD模式主要用于提升存在学习、情感或行为障碍的中小学生的议论文写作和论证，并产生积极效果。Graham et al.（2005）、Mason和Shriner（2008）分别报告了POW和TREE两种策略教学对美国小学生作文质量和长度的提升，以及在学会独立撰写五段式作文中的作用。Harris et al.（2019）和Ray et al.（2019）都发现SRSD教学对存在学习障碍或者写作困难的学生在议论文构思质量、论证要素数量和整体质量等方面有积极影响。

进行SRSD教学必须严格执行规定步骤和要求才能保证教学效果。为此，有研究（Mason et al. 2017；McKeown et al. 2019）探讨对教师进行SRSD教学培训的效果。Mason et al.（2017）研究19名教师接受SRSD培训后对学生进行SRSD教学的效果，发现所教学生在作文要素和长度方面都优于没有接受培训的教师所教的学生，证实SRSD培训的效果。相反，McKeown et al.（2019）发现25名教师接受SRSD培训后所教学生尽管在写作整体质量、分项质量和长度方面好于没有接受培训的教师所教的学生，但效应值较低，因为教师实施SRSD的信度比较低。因此，保证SRSD教学的质量至关重要。

综上表明，目前聚焦教学方法和策略的研究主要采纳心理认知视角，通过分析前后测作文考察教学效果，对教学过程关注较少。笔者发现的唯一关注教学过程的研究为VanDerHeiDe（2018）。该研究探讨教师教学话语和学生讨论与所写作文的关系。通过分析美国一位文学课教师教授写作的课堂话语以及学生作文，研究发现该教师明确指出了范文中的写作语步，通过提问启发学生在对话中使用写作语步，然后要求学生通过小组讨论学习写作语步，并将其应用到写作中。结果表明识别课堂语步对议论文写作有促进作用。

4.2 写作目标对议论文论证发展的影响

要提高写作质量，教师需要为学生设立写作目标，因为目标提供内容框架、写作动力和信息反馈（Page-Voth & Graham 1999）。写作目标分为写作阶段目标和修改阶段目标。研究发现写作阶段目标可以影响学生的议论文论证质量。Page-Voth和Graham（1999）探讨了三个写作目标（论据目标、反驳目标以及论据和反驳目标）对美国七、八年级有学习障碍或写作较弱的学生的影响，发现目标组作文比仅得到肯定反馈的无目标组的作文要长，包含较多论据和反驳，作文质量也较好。

研究还发现写作阶段目标越具体越明确，对学生的帮助越大。Ferretti et al.（2000）比较详细目标和笼统目标对美国四、六年级学生议论文的影响，发现详细目标组比笼统目标组产出更多论证要素和更有说服力的作文。Fan（2019）考察四种目标（一般目标、体裁目标、论证策略关键性问题以及体裁目标+关键性问题）对美国大学生议论文写作的影响，发现三个具体目标组的写作质量都比一般目标组的要好，体裁目标组和体裁目标+关键性问题组的作文包含较多反驳、不同观点以及对不同观点的支撑。

研究同样发现修改阶段目标对学生论证质量的提升具有影响。Midgette et al.（2008）研究聚焦于内容的修改目标和聚焦于读者意识的修改目标，与笼统目标相比，对五年级和八年级学生议论文的影响。他们分析学生的作文修改稿发现，内容目标组和内容+读者目标组都比笼统目标组的作文更具说服力，内容+读者目标组更多考虑反面论点并进行反驳。

与写作阶段的目标一样，修改阶段目标越具体越明确，学生获得的帮助越大。修改阶段目标可表现为关键性问题和论证方案，研究发现前者比后者的效果要好。如Song和Ferretti（2013）考察提出并回答关键性问题和利用论证方案两种修改策略对美国大学生写作的影响，发现关键性问题组比论证方案组的写作质量要好且包含更多驳论。Nussbaum et al.（2019）考察包含关键性问题的论证教学对论证发展的影响，发现关键性问题引发学生运用更多与之有关的反驳，这种效应可迁移到没有关键性问题的课堂写作，这表明关键性问题为学生评估论证和驳论提供结构指引。

修改目标还可采用量表和范文的形式。研究发现量表比范文的效果要好。如Latifi et al.（2020）以伊朗80名大学生为研究对象，发现在网络同伴互评环境中量表比范文能更好提高学生作文互评质量和作文质量。

4.3 学生主导的活动对议论文论证发展的影响

目前相关研究主要探讨了三种学生主导的活动：学习书面教学讲义、线上标注论证元素和学生互动。对于中小学生，教师的讲解很重要。但高年级学生（包括大学生）具有自主学习能力，应该给予机会进行自我主导的学习。有研究发现，学生学习书面教学讲义对论证有积极影响。如Butler和Britt（2011）把112名美国大学生分为四组（三个实验组和一个对照组），三个实验组分别学习论证教学讲义、宏观修改讲义，以及论证教学讲义和宏观修改讲义。对比学生初稿和修改稿发现，论证教学讲义有助于学生修改论证内容和论文结构，宏观修改讲义有助于学生作文结构的修改。

随着互联网的普及，网络平台也被用于学生议论文论证的发展。学者们开始探讨一种在线学习形式：线上论证元素标注。例如，Lu和Zhang（2013）考察了中国香港83名10年级学生运用OASIS网络工具在阅读、写作和同伴互评作文时对论证元素等进行标注和评价的学习效果。经过一年实践，研究发现学生的论证技能与其标注的数量相关，证实了网络标注和评价论证元素的促学作用。

线上标注作为学生主导的活动也被融入混合式教学，证实比传统的讲解效果更好。混合法指学生在写作文之前，除了接受教师对论证元素的讲解，还需要讨论分析范文的优劣，并在线讨论和分析写作任务，进行论证信息标注，获取师生反馈（Lam et al. 2018）。Lam et al.（2018）发现，与教师讲解相比，混合法更能显著提高学生的议论文论证技能；学生主导的活动比教师的教学更有效。

关注学生互动的研究主要采纳社会文化理论学习观，特别是以"对话塑造思想和重构知识"的理念为基础，探讨学生面对面或网络辅助互动对议论文论证发展的影响。目前考察的主要互动任务为合作推理。该任务要求学生先阅读故事，然后讨论基于阅读提出的争议性问题，最后完成写作任务。研究发现，写前合作推理有助于学生提升议论文的论证质量，丰富论证知识。如Reznitskaya et al.（2001）和Reznitskaya et al.（2007）都以美国四、五年级学生为研究对象。前者发现经过合作推理的学生作文包含更多论点、反面论点、反驳、较正式的论证手段和证据；后者通过访谈发现合作推理组对论证知识的掌握优于对照组。

除了用于写前干预，合作推理也被用作修改阶段促进学生修正论证的手段。如Wagner et al.（2017）要求美国小学四年级的12名学生先就基于阅读的争议性问题进行写作，然后对争议性问题进行合作推理讨论，最后修改作文。研究发现大部分学生能够摄取讨论中的思想，修正自己写作中的论证。

研究还发现，为了充分发挥学生互动的作用，教师应设置清晰的任务目标。Felton et al.（2015）针对学生忽视反面观点的问题，邀请142名美国大学生以结对形式，利用网络软件，围绕"死刑"这一话题进行分别以说服和以达成一致意见为目标的两项线上论证互动。分析学生对话和作文发现，以达成一致为目标的论证组更倾向于引用反面观点并调和不同观点。

学生互动中的论证水平配对也影响其论证质量和学习。Mayweg-Paus et al.（2016）把44名6至8年级的学生分为实验组和对照组，分别由不同论证水平配对和同水平配对组成，每对学生采纳对立观点，利用网络平台辩论社会问题。结果发现，实验组在论证策略方面取得更大进步，使用较多驳论、较高级的驳论和论证。

另外，互动形式也对是否能达到提升论证目的产生影响。如Salter-Dvorak（2016）考察学生在得到教师反馈后的口头展示（oral presentation）对议论文论证的影响。教师的初衷是以口头展示为手段，引起学生对论证的提问、讨论和反馈，以便提升作文论证质量。但该研究并没有得到预期效果，因为学生把口头展示看作写作评估的一部分，更注重展示的形式，很少就内容进行提问。所以，学生修改作文时更注意语言准确性而不是论证质量。

5. 英语议论文论证发展研究展望

本文通过综述相关实证研究，发现文献中探讨的提升议论文论证的方法丰富多样，既包括教师的教学方法和策略，如图尔敏模型教学、过程写作法、作文结构教学和驳论教学，也包括学生主导的学习活动，如学习书面教学讲义、线上标注论证元素和学生线下线上互动，还包括写作阶段和修改阶段的标准和要求。相关研究证实了上述方法对议论文论证发展的积极影响。这启示我们：在教学中，教师可以根据学生背景和课程特点等选择合适有效的教学方法，以提高议论文论证教学的成效。

然而，在学术层面，目前的议论文论证发展研究表现出"不平衡"的特点。第一，现有研究中，遵循心理认知视角的研究多，采纳社会文化理论视角的研究少。第二，现有研究主要考察干预效果，对学习过程关注不够。具体来说，心理认知视角的研究极少考察教学策略干预的过程；同样，社会文化理论视角的研究倾向于把学生话语看作干预，通过分析学生作文检验其对论证发展的效果，很少对学生话语进行定性分析以探讨学习过程。第三，多数研究针对英语母语学习者，针对英语外语学习者的研究数量有限。所综述的33个研究中，27个研究的受试对象为英语母语环境下的学习者（特别是美国的中小学生），仅有六个研究的考察对象为英语外语学习者（Bacha 2010；Lam et al. 2018；Latifi et al. 2020；Liu & Stapleton 2014, 2020；Lu & Zhang 2013）。第四，缺乏基于真实课堂教学的研究。在所综述研究中，绝大多数为实验或者准实验研究，基于课堂教学的研究只有一个（VanDerHeiDe 2018）。

针对上述特点，将来的研究可以加强社会文化理论视角的探究；在测量教学效果的同时，加大对学习过程的考察。另外，将来的研究也可以开展基于真实课堂教学的研究。除此以外，应该重视综述反映出的针对英语外语学习者研究的不足。这种不足与Hirvela（2017）的论断一致。Hirvela（2017）指出，英语二语议论文写作论证研究在过去的四十年一直是被忽视的领域，并做了如下论述："有大量关于论证的问题值得探索和讨论，但目前看起来我们没有明确的定位或方向，没有改变这种状况的明显趋势。论证作为一个主题占据了空间，但没有核心，即没有可以塑造这一领域的讨论焦点。相反，它处于二语写作的边缘"（pp. 69-70）。鉴于论证对写作教学和学术写作的重要性，Hirvela呼吁改变这种现状。因此，英语二语写作领域需要开展针对学生论证能力发展的系统性研究。

具体说，英语二语/外语写作领域将来可以从以下方面开展提升学生议论文论证水平的研究。第一，开展基于真实课堂教学的研究。二语学习者的议论文论证能力培养主要发生在课堂教学中，研究课堂教学有助于了解学生议论文论证发展的状况；同时，基于课堂的研究是对英语母语学习环境中相关研究的补充。第二，沿用社会文化理论视角，考察师生互动和学生互动对二语学习者议论文论证发展的影响，特别探讨互动过程，揭示影响学生议论文论证发展的机制。第三，采纳心理认知视角，借鉴现有针对英语母语环境下写作者的研究，探讨教学方法和策略以及写作标准的实施对英语二语/外语写作者议论文论证发展的影响。现有研究可以为新研究提供理论框架、研究焦点、研究框架、研究方法和分析框架，同时，新研究可以提供新证据以揭示英语二语/外语学习者议论文论证的发展特点。第四，相关研究还可以探索各种学生因素，如学生的母语论证水平、学生参与、能动性、态度和情感等，对学生议论文论证发展的影响。

参考文献

Bacha, N. N. 2010. Teaching the academic argument in a university EFL environment [J]. *Journal of English for Academic Purposes* 9(3): 229-241.

Bereiter, C. & M. Scardamalia. 1987. *The Psychology of Written Composition* [M]. Hillsdale, NJ: Lawrence Erlbaum Associates.

Burkhalter, N. 1995. A Vygotsky-based curriculum for teaching persuasive writing in the elementary grades [J]. *Language Arts* 72(3): 192-199.

Butler, J. A. & M. A. Britt. 2011. Investigating instruction for improving revision of argumentative essays [J]. *Written Communication* 28(1): 70-96.

Campbell, Y. C. & C. Filimon. 2018. Supporting the argumentative writing of students in linguistically diverse classrooms: An action research study [J]. *Research in Middle Level Education Online* 41(1): 1-10.

De La Paz, S. & S. Graham. 1997. Strategy instruction in planning: Effects on the writing performance and behavior of students with learning disabilities [J]. *Exceptional Children* 63: 167-181.

Fan, Y. 2019. The Effects of Critical Questions on Undergraduate Students' Argumentative Writing [D]. Unpublished PhD dissertation. The University of Delaware.

Felton, M., A. Crowell & T. Liu. 2015. Arguing to agree: Mitigating my-side bias through consensus-seeking dialogue [J]. *Written Communication* 32(3): 317-331.

Ferretti, R. P. & Y. Fan. 2016. Argumentative writing [A]. In C. A. MacArthur, S. Graham & J. Fitzgerald (eds.). *Handbook of Writing Research* [C]. New York: Guilford Press. 301-315.

Ferretti, R. P. & S. Graham. 2019. Argumentative writing: Theory, assessment, and instruction [J]. *Reading and Writing* 32: 1345-1357.

Ferretti, R. P. & W. E. Lewis. 2019. Argumentative writing [A]. In S. Graham, C. A. MacArthur & M. Herbert (eds.). *Best Practices in Writing Instruction* (3rd ed.) [C]. New York/London: The Guilford Press. 135-161.

Ferretti, R. P., C. A. MacArthur & N. S. Dowdy. 2000. The effects of an elaborated goal on the persuasive writing of students with learning disabilities and their normally achieving peers [J]. *Journal of Educational Psychology* 92(4): 694-702.

Flower, L. S. & J. R. Hayes. 1981. A cognitve process theory of writing [J]. *College Composition and Communication* 32: 365-387.

Graham, S., K. R. Harris & L. Mason. 2005. Improving the writing performance, knowledge, and self-efficacy of struggling young writers: The effects of self-regulated strategy development [J].

Contemporary Educational Psychology 30: 207-241.

Harris, K. R., A. Ray, S. Graham & J. Houston. 2019. Answering the challenge: SRSD instruction for close reading of text to write to persuade with 4th and 5th Grade students experiencing writing difficulties [J]. *Reading and Writing* 32: 1459-1482.

Hirvela, A. 2017. Argumentation & second language writing: Are we missing the boat [J]? *Journal of Second Language Writing* 36(1): 69-74.

Kathpalia, S. S. & E. K. See. 2016. Improving argumentation through student blogs [J]. *System* 58: 25-36.

Kuhn, D., L. Hemberger & V. Khait. 2016. *Argue with Me: Argument as a Path to Developing Students' Thinking and Writing* [M]. New York: Routledge.

Lam, Y. W., K. F. Hew & K. F. Chiu. 2018. Improving argumentative writing: Effects of a blended learning approach and gamification [J]. *Language Teaching & Technology* 22(1): 97-118.

Latifi, S., O. Noroozi & E. Talaee. 2020. Worked example or scripting? Fostering students' online argumentative peer feedback, essay writing and learning [J]. *Interactive Learning Environments* DOI: 10.1080/10494820.2020.1799032.

Liu, F. & P. Stapleton. 2014. Counterargumentation and the cultivation of critical thinking in argumentative writing: Investigating washback from a high-stakes test [J]. *System* 45: 117-128.

Liu, F. & P. Stapleton. 2020. Counterargumentation at the primary level: An intervention study investigating the argumentative writing of second language learners [J]. *System* 89: 1-15.

Lu, J. & Z. Zhang. 2013. Scaffolding argumentation in intact class: Integrating technology and pedagogy [J]. *Computer and Pedagogy* 69: 189-198.

MacArthur, C. A. & L. Lembo. 2009. Strategy instruction in writing for adult literacy learners [J]. *Reading and Writing* 22: 1021-1039.

Manchón, R. M. (ed.). 2011. *Learning-to-Write and Writing-to-Learn in an Additional Language* [C]. Amsterdam/Philadelphia: John Benjamins.

Mason, L. H., A. M. Cramer, J. D. Garwood, C. Varghese, J. Hamm & A. Murray. 2017. Efficacy of Self-Regulated Strategy Development instruction for developing writers with and without disabilities in rural schools: A randomized controlled trial [J]. *Rural Special Education Quarterly* 36(4): 168-179.

Mason, L. H. & J. G. Shriner. 2008. Self-regulated strategy development instruction for writing an opinion essay: Effects for six students with emotional/behavior disorders [J]. *Reading and Writing: An Interdisciplinary Journal* 21: 71-93.

Mayweg-Paus, E., F. Macagno & D. Kuhn. 2016. Developing argumentation strategies in electronic dialogs: Is modeling effective [J]? *Discourse Processes* 53: 280-297.

McKeown, D., E. FitzPatrick, M. Brown, M. Brindle, J. Owens & R. Hendrick. 2019. Urban teachers' implementation of SRSD for persuasive writing following practice-based professional development: Positive effects mediated by compromised fidelity [J]. *Reading and Writing* 32: 1483-1506.

Midgette, E. & P. Haria. 2016. Planning and revising written arguments: The effects of two text structure-based interventions on persuasiveness of 8th-Grade students' essays [J]. *Reading Psychology* 37(7): 1043-1075.

Midgette, E., P. Haria & C. MacArthur. 2008. The effect of content and audience awareness goals for revision on the persuasive essays of fifth- and eighth-grade students [J]. *Reading and Writing: An Interdisciplinary Journal* 21: 131-151.

Newell, G. E. & D. Bloom. 2017. Teaching and learning argumentation in high school English language arts classrooms [A]. In K. A. Hinchman & D. A. Appleman (eds.). *Adolesent Literacies: A Handbook of Practice-Based Research* [C]. New York/London: The Guilford Press. 379-397.

Newell, G. E., R. Beach, J. Smith & J. VanDerHeide. 2011. Teaching and learning argumentative reading and writing: A review of research [J]. *Reading Research Quarterly* 46(3): 273-304.

Newell, G. E., D. Bloome & A. Hirvela. 2015. *Teaching and Learning Argumentative Writing in High School English Language Arts classrooms* [M]. New York: Routledge.

Nussbaum, E. M., I. J. Dove, N. Slife, C. M. Kardash, R. Turgut & D. Vallett. 2019. Using critical questions to evaluate written and oral arguments in an undergraduate general education seminar: A quasi-experimental study [J]. *Reading and Writing* 32: 1531-1552.

Page-Voth, V. & S. Graham. 1999. Effects of goal setting and strategy use on the writing performance and self-efficacy of students with writing and learning problems [J]. *Journal of Educational Psychology* 9(2): 230-240.

Qin, J. & E. Karabacak. 2010. The analysis of Toulmin elements in Chinese EFL university argumentative writing [J]. *System* 38(3): 444-456.

Ray, A. B., S. Graham & X. Liu. 2019. Effects of SRSD college entrance essay exam instruction for high school students with disabilities or at-risk for writing difficulties [J]. *Reading and Writing* 32: 1507-1529.

Reznitskaya, A., R. C. Anderson & L. -J. Kuo. 2007. Teaching and learning argumentation [J]. *The Elementary School Journal* 107(5): 449-472.

Reznitskaya, A., R. C. Anderson, B. McNurlen, K. Nguyen-Jahiel, A. Archodidou & S. -Y. Kim. 2001. Influence of oral discussion on written argument [J]. *Discourse Processes* 32: 155-175.

Salter-Dvorak, H. 2016. Learning to argue in EAP: Evaluating a curriculum innovation from the inside [J]. *Journal of English for Academic Purposes* 22(1): 19-31.

Song, Y. & R. P. Ferretti. 2013. Teaching critical questions about argumentation through the revising process: Effects of strategy instruction on college students' argumentative essays [J]. *Reading and Writing* 26: 67-90.

Toulmin, S. 1958. *The Uses of Argument* [M]. Cambridge: Cambridge University Press.

VanDerHeide, J. 2018. Classroom talk as writing instruction for learning to make writing moves in literary arguments [J]. *Reading Research Quarterly* 53(3): 323-344.

Vygotsky, L. S. 1978. *Mind in Society: The Development of Higher Psychological Processes* [M].

Cambridge, MA: Harvard University Press.

Wagner, C. J., M. O. Parra & C. P. Proctor. 2017. The interplay between student-led discussions and argumentative writing [J]. *TESOL Quarterly* 51(2): 438-449.

Yeh, S. S. 1998. Empowering education: Teaching argumentational writing to cultural minority middle-school students [J]. *Research in the Teaching of English* 33: 49-83.

Zhang, Y. 2018. An investigation into the development of structure and evidence use in argumentative writing [J]. *Theory and Practice in Language Studies* 8(11): 1441-1448.

作者简介：

牛瑞英，广东外语外贸大学教授，博士，硕士生导师。主要研究领域：二语写作教学与反馈、二语习得。电子邮箱：niuruiying@gdufs.edu.cn

A Review of L2W Journal Articles in China
(1949-2019)

Yue CHEN

Purdue University, USA

Abstract: After decades of development, L2W has become a thriving field of study in China, with many scholars publishing a good number of journal articles on this topic each year. By reviewing China's L2W articles published in major linguistics/foreign language journals between 1949 and 2019, this article identifies L2W's four developmental periods during these 70 years and nine major topics discussed in the literature. A total of 1,412 articles were reviewed and analyzed. These articles also demonstrated an increasing favor of empirical research over non-empirical research in recent years and a strong preference of undergraduate students as their discussion context.

Keywords: second language writing; numerical trend; major topics; research methods; contexts

1. Introduction

Although the teaching of L2 writing in formal foreign language schools in modern China started as early as the 1860s[1], the earliest publication on L2 writing in the People's Republic of China (PRC) did not appear until the late 1950s and the early 1960s. One of the earliest journal articles on L2W was published in 1959 by Wangdao Ding (丁往道), entitled "A brief discussion of English writing and the writing class". This article discusses important areas of English writing that need to be addressed in teaching and suggests the establishment of a separated writing course in the English curriculum. Since then, Chinese scholars have investigated various topics related to L2W in both local and global contexts.

Early work on L2W in China focuses on finding ways to improve Chinese students' writing abilities through formal education. Articles published in the 1990s started to argue that English writing should be one of the core elements in China's English education (Zhu & Ye 1996). Meanwhile, scholars began to investigate why Chinese students' English writing has been the weak link in improving their overall English proficiencies (Zhang 1998). Therefore, Chinese scholars applied Western-oriented theories and pedagogies to Chinese teaching practice in order to improve students' English writing performances (Cai 2001; Chen & Li 1999; Su & Yang 2001; Zhang 2000). Most of the early articles on L2W in China were on practical issues such as methods to improve students' L2 writing, ways to make L2 writing teaching more effective, and features of L2 written texts.

As L2W developed, Chinese scholars started to investigate and publish on other

---

1 In 1862, *Tongwen Guan* (同文馆, the Academy of Interpreters) was established under the guidance of *Zongli Yamen* (总理衙门, the Office of Foreign Affairs) to provide training in foreign languages. English was the first foreign language taught at the Academy. The establishment of *Tongwen Guan* represented the beginning of formal English education in China.

topics that are not directly related to EFL writing pedagogies. Discourse analysis, feedback, writing assessment, and corpus analysis became popular topics investigated and published by L2 scholars in China (Bai 2012; Wu 2003; Zhou et al. 2009). The diversified topics reflect the blossoming of L2W writing scholarship in China. Currently, Chinese researchers publish articles on both theoretical and pedagogical topics related to students' L2W writing performance (He 2013; Wang & Wang 2004; Xu 2011; You 2004). As international academic exchanges have developed, it becomes more and more important for Chinese L2W scholars to bring their research to a broader audience inside and outside of China, joining the international conversation of many frontier topics with L2W scholars from all over the globe.

2. Literature Review

A number of Chinese L2W scholars have recognized the need to review existing studies not only to reflect on what is past but also to suggest future research topics. According to J. Wang (2016), there are over 100 journal articles published in China that review either one aspect of L2W (e.g., He 2018) or the overall development of the field (e.g., Zhu 2011). However, most of the reviews only investigate one aspect of L2W rather than extensively examining all related articles on L2W.

Nine existing studies (Cheng 2011; Guo 2009; He 2013; Huang & Yu 2009; Li & Li 2003; J. Wang 2016; Yan & Cui 2011; Yao & Cheng 2005; Zhu 2011) have identified "EFL writing" or "L2W" as their target context for review and synthesis, within which only two (Guo 2009; Yan & Cui 2011) extensively reviewed China's publications on L2W. Guo (2009) is the first study in China to expand beyond English writing and reviews articles on L2W in eight major linguistics journals published within a 18-year period. Table 1 shows data collection information from these nine review studies. These studies collected data from different year ranges and sources and analyzed different numbers of articles, but all of them present L2W/EFL writing as a field of study.

Table 1. Data collection in L2W/EFL writing syntheses

	Collecting period	Year range	Data sources	No. of articles	Context
Li & Li (2003)	1993-2002	10	8 major linguistics journals	127	English writing
Yao & Cheng (2005)	1980-2003	24	7 major linguistics journals	165	English writing
Huang & Yu (2009)	1993-2007	15	9 major linguistics journals	251	English writing
	2003-2007	5	17 linguistics journals	229	
Guo (2009)	1991-2008	18	8 major linguistics journals	164	L2W in China
Zhu (2011)	1980-2010	31	10 major linguistics journals	426	English writing
Cheng (2011)	2000-2009	10	9 major linguistics journals	273	English writing
Yan & Cui (2011)	2006-2010	5	9 major linguistics journals	149	L2W
He (2013)	2001-2010	10	14 major linguistics journals	402	EFL writing
Wang (2016)	1962-2015	44	1,417 journals	11,889	EFL writing

Most of these review studies draw data from major linguistics journals in China, with only one exception. J. Wang (2016) is by far the most comprehensive review study on EFL writing research in terms of time coverage and number of journal articles reviewed. She comprehensively searched the China Academic Journals Database (CAJ), the China Online Journal Database (COJ), and the Chinese Technology Periodical Database (CTP). Although J. Wang (2016) is the most inclusive review study on L2W research in China, it only reviewed articles on EFL writing and did not include research on L2 writing where the L2 is not English.

To address the need of a longitudinal review on China's L2W journal articles between 1949 and 2019, I came up with the following three questions:

    1. What is the numerical pattern of China's L2W journal articles between 1949 and 2019?

    2. What are the major topics identified in these articles?

    3. What are the features in research methods and research contexts in these articles?

3. Methods

3.1 Data sources

Data in this study are from the existing L2W articles from major linguistics/foreign language journals in China. In foreign language studies and applied linguistics, there are two general classification indexes that are widely accepted by scholars and considered the most authoritative: (1) the Chinese Core Journals Index (中文核心期刊) and (2) the Chinese Social Sciences Citation Index (中文社会科学引文索引来源期刊). Both classification indexes are updated regularly[2]. These different classification systems use slightly different criteria for inclusion, but they both cover the most distinguished journals in the field.

3.2 Data collection

The journal articles for this study were collected from China Academic Journals Full-text Database (中国期刊全文数据库). I retrieved the journal articles with three sets of topic keywords, which are " 二语 AND 写作 ", " 英语 AND 写作 " and " 外语 AND 写作 ". To retrieve all the related articles, I searched with Chinese keywords and allowed cross-language search because even though some journals include English abstracts and titles, most of them only accept and publish manuscripts that are written in Chinese.

The initial search yielded a total of 2,421 articles on L2 writing, English education, literary studies, and translation studies. I reviewed the abstract of each journal article to decide whether or not it focused specifically on L2 writing using three criteria: (1) the purpose of the article, (2) the main subject of the study, and (3) the main argument(s) in the article. I excluded literary studies that analyze the word choice or writing style of a certain author and translation studies that focus on oral translation. However, I included literary studies that compare Western and Oriental writing styles and translation studies that discuss reconstructing meaning in written translation practice. After two rounds of

---

2 At the time of my data collection, the most recent update for Chinese Core Journals Index was published in 2017, and the most recent update for Chinese Social Sciences Citation Index was in 2019.

review, I narrowed my data set to 1,412 articles.

3.3 Data analysis

After retrieving these articles, I grouped them based on their years of publication and developed coding schemes in terms of topic, research method, and context. To develop coding schemes, I applied a mixed two-step approach: (1) a top-down approach to draw codes from the existing synthesis studies, and (2) a bottom-up approach to let the codes emerge from my data. Most of the previous syntheses coded their data in terms of topics/content and research methods, and only a couple of more recent syntheses (He 2013; J. Wang 2016) have additional coding schemes. In this study, I used three types of coding schemes: a coding scheme for topics, a coding scheme for research methods, and a coding scheme for contexts.

3.3.1 Coding schemes for topics

Regarding focus of study, some previous syntheses have only several general codes (e.g., Guo 2009), and others have very detailed codes (e.g., He 2013). However, there are some common codes that appeared in multiple schemes, such as writing instruction, assessment and evaluation, written product, and influential factors.

Drawing from the existing schemes and a preliminary reading of my data, I created a coding scheme for topics with five basic codes: writing instruction, written product, writing process, writer development, and writing assessment. Four additional codes emerged as I read through the articles. Table 2 shows the codes I used in this study along with example topics under each code.

Table 2. Codes used in this study

No.	Codes	Examples
1	Writing instruction	Development and application of various pedagogies
		Problems in writing instruction
		Influential factors in writing instruction
		Curriculum development
		Teacher training
2	Written product	Rhetorical features
		Sentence structure
		Word choice and vocabulary variety
3	Writing process	Writing tasks
		Brainstorming, drafting, composing, and revising
		Editing
4	Writer development	Identity and cognition
		Struggles and difficulties
5	Writing assessment	Standardized writing tests
		Teacher/peer feedback
		Self-evaluation
6	Genre	Academic articles, business reports, Emails

(to be continued)

(continued)

No.	Codes	Examples
7	Cross-area studies	Translation studies Reading and writing Speaking and writing
8	Interactions between L1 and L2	L1 writing versus L2 writing L1's influence on L2W L2's influence on L1W
9	Disciplinary studies	Meta-analysis and reviews Translingual writing Conference reports

3.3.2 Coding scheme for research methods

Eight out of the nine syntheses I reviewed discuss the type of methods used in the synthesized articles. Codes for research methods in the existing literature are relatively less diverse. Generally, there are two types of coding schemes for research methods: one-tier schemes and two-tier schemes. Most syntheses (He 2013; Huang & Yu 2009; Li & Li, 2003; Yan & Cui 2011; Zhu 2011) adopt one-tier coding with only two codes: Empirical and Non-empirical, and three syntheses (Cheng 2011; Guo 2009; Yao & Cheng 2005) used two-tier coding schemes with the second tier for techniques used under each research type. In this study, articles were coded as empirical studies or non-empirical studies based on the description of the research design. Empirical studies are studies involving data collection and analysis, while non-empirical studies involve no actual data collection process.

3.3.3 Coding scheme for contexts

In the syntheses I reviewed, only J. Wang (2016) analyzed the context in a section titled Subject Matter. Based on J. Wang's (2016) codes and a preliminary reading of my data, I developed a two-tier coding scheme based on writers' academic levels. Table 3 presents my coding scheme for contexts.

Table 3. Coding scheme for contexts

No.	Primary code	Secondary codes
1	K-12 L2 writing	Elementary Middle school High school
2	Undergraduate L2 writing	English majors Non-English majors
3	Graduate L2 writing	Master students Doctoral students
4	Professional L2 writing	Scientific L2 writing Medical L2 writing News L2 writing Other

4. Results

The past 70 years have witnessed a dramatic increase in the number of journal articles[3] on L2W in China, with a broader range of theoretical, pedagogical, and empirical topics from scholars both within and outside China. A total of China's 28 major linguistics/foreign language journals have published 1,412 articles on L2W topics between 1949 and 2019.

4.1 Chronological analysis of the L2W journal articles

In all of the 28 journals I surveyed, 23 journals published at least one article on L2W in the past 70 years (1949-2019). The number of L2W articles published each year has increased dramatically (See Figure 1). In June of 1957, the People's Republic of China established its first academic journal in the field of foreign language studies, *Foreign Language Teaching and Research* and since then scholars have published on related issues in these language/linguistics journals. The 70 years can be divided into four major developmental periods, reflecting the numerical trend in journal article publication: (1) Silent Period (1949-1958), (2) Slow Start (1959-1997), (3) Rapid Growth (1998-2015), and (4) Prosperous Period (2016-2019).[4]

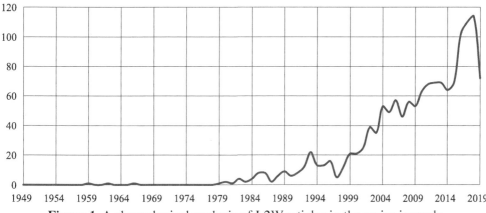

Figure 1. A chronological analysis of L2W articles in the major journals

4.1.1 Silent Period (1949-1958)

During the first 10 years (1949-1958) of the People's Republic of China, there was complete silence in journal article publication on the topic of L2W. In these silent years, China focused its national resources on economic recovery from the wars and political stability rather than academic development or educational investment. It was not until the early 1960s that English came back to higher education and was perceived as a bridge between China and the West (You 2010). This lack of academic publications shows how the beginning of L2W studies

---

3 In this section, the term "journal articles" refers journal articles in the major linguistics/foreign language journals.
4 Similar numerical trend was also identified in Wang (2016), which divided the history of L2W studies in China into three phrases of development: the early period (1961-1980), the developmental period (1981-2000), and the flourishing period (2001-2015).

in China was heavily influenced by the political environment.

Although three[5] of the 28 journals I surveyed were established during this period, none of them published anything on L2W until 1959. Early publications from these three linguistics/foreign language journals mainly discussed specific linguistic aspects of different languages (e.g., English, French, German) or analysis of western literary works. The content of these early linguistics/foreign language journal articles was strongly political. During this period, academic communications served a political purpose with regard to teaching and interacting with western language and culture.

4.1.2 Slow Start (1959-1997)

The 1959 journal article by Wangdao Ding indicates a beginning of Chinese scholars' academic publishing on L2W. The next 35 years witnessed a slow but sturdy start of L2W development. A total of 144 L2W articles were published during this period of time. Only a couple of articles appeared in the 1960s and 1970s, partially due to the political environment during that time in China. It was in the late 1970s, after the Cultural Revolution, that academic communication resumed its development. The number of L2W articles in each year increased from only a couple between the 1960s and 1980s to an average of 10 articles per year in the late 1980s and early 1990s.

Early studies in the 1960s focus on providing general suggestions on writing development (Dai 1962; Yu 1966). Dai (1962) suggests three general ways to improve students' writing ability: (1) instructors should provide students with opportunities to write on various topics and in different genres; (2) students should be writing more narratives than argumentative essays; (3) intensive reading, extensive reading, and reciting should be integrated into the teaching of writing in foreign languages. Yu (1966) summarizes his teaching experiences and provides suggestions regarding improving students' foreign language writing skills. According to Yu (1966), foreign language instructors should start with the teaching of texts in the textbook, focus on the use of newly learned vocabulary, and help students in brainstorming ideas and outlining drafts. In addition, teachers are encouraged to create extra-curricular writing opportunities for their students to practice what they had learned in class.

Another feature of this body of scholarship is the inclusion of different languages. The five languages represented in these articles are Russian (e.g., Yu 1966), English (e.g., Zhang 1979), Chinese (e.g., Yang 1982), French (e.g., Zhang 1983), and German (e.g., Feng 1995). The variety of languages addressed in the limited amount of literature shows that multiple languages were taught and studied in China as the country recovered from political disorder and prepared for economic revival. The interaction between Chinese with people from various language backgrounds reflects how the early development of L2W studies in China were heavily influenced by interactions with and studies in other cultural backgrounds.

4.1.3 Rapid Growth (1998-2015)

L2W studies started its rapid and sturdy growth in China at the end of 1990s. In the

---

5 *Zhongguo Yuwen* (《中国语文》) was founded in 1952; *Foreign Language Teaching and Research* (《外语教学与研究》) was founded in 1957; *Contemporary Linguistics* (《当代语言学》) was founded in 1961.

following 18 years, the number of L2W articles published in major journals in each year increased dramatically from 12 in 1998 to 69 in 2015. The increased annual publications resulted from the nation's open and reformed political and economic policies, as well as from the increased emphasis on international interaction and communication.

In the 869 articles published during this period, the variety of issues discussed has expanded, compared with that of the Slow Start Period. Topics presented during this period are not limited to writing instruction but start to cover writing assessment, students' written products, writer development, writing processes, cross-area studies, disciplinary studies, genre analysis, and L1 and L2 interactions.

4.1.4 Prosperous Period (2016-2019)

This four-year period is the shortest in terms of time but the most productive in terms of the number of articles. In recent years, the average number of L2W articles published reached 100 per year. The topics discussed in articles in this period are diverse and they represent the recent reform of China's educational system. All the major topics identified in this study are present in the articles published during the Prosperous Period.

4.2 Major topics

The 1,412 articles have examined L2W from various perspectives, focusing on numerous topics. Nine major topics are identified: writing instruction, features in written products, writing assessment, writer development, analysis of different genres, writing processes, disciplinary studies of L2W, cross-area studies, and interactions between L1 and L2 (See Figure 2).

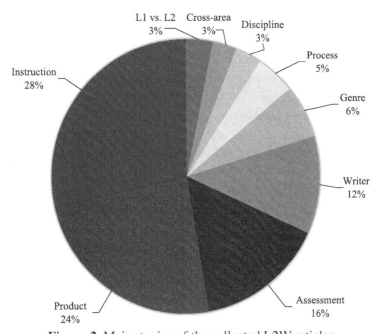

Figure 2. Major topics of the collected L2W articles

4.2.1 Writing instruction

Writing instruction is the most frequently investigated area, with 400 of the articles on the teaching of L2W, making up 28% of all L2W articles collected. The number of articles on L2 writing instruction increased gradually from 1959 to 2019. In the Slow Start Period, an average of 2.08 articles on L2W instruction were published each year, and in the Prosperous Period, the number increased to 17.75 articles per year. Although the absolute number of articles on writing instruction has increased over the years, the percentage of articles on this topic with regard to the total number of L2W articles has decreased. In the early years, most of the L2W articles collected were on writing instruction. In recent years, the percentage has declined.

The issues in these articles include general suggestions on L2 writing instruction (e.g., Dai 1962; Zhang 1992; Zhang 2006), introduction/comparison of different pedagogical approaches (e.g., Luo et al. 2011; Wang 2005; Yu & Zhang 1996), curriculum design (e.g., Sun & Chen 2009), instruction on specific linguistic aspects (e.g., Xu 1990a; Xu 1990b; Yin 2008; Zhou 1990), computer-assisted learning and teaching (e.g., Tian 2001), instruction of professional and technical writing (e.g., Luo 2002), teaching materials and textbooks (e.g., Si 2005; Yang 2007), teacher training and development (e.g., Yang 2010), instruction theories (e.g., Wang 1986), and problems and suggested solutions (e.g., Yang et al. 2009).

Another feature of articles on L2 writing instruction is the publication of translated articles in *Foreign Language Learning Theory and Practice*[6] (《外语教学理论与实践》) in the 1990s. These translated articles were originally published in venues such as *English Teaching Forum*, *Modern English Teacher*, *TESOL Quarterly*, *The Modern Language Journal*, *ELT Journal*, etc., and were translated into Chinese to be published in the Chinese journal. These translated articles introduced the Western-developed writing theories and practices to Chinese scholars and promoted cross-region academic communication in the early days.

4.2.2 Features in L2 written products

A total of 343 articles in my data are on features in L2 written products, representing 24% of the total L2W articles I analyzed. Articles on this topic emerged in the 1980s, and the average number of articles per year has increased from 0.58 in the Slow Start Period to 26.50 in the Prosperous Period, making it the most investigated topic in the Prosperous Period. This indicates an increased interest of Chinese scholars in exploring the specific features in L2 writers' products.

The specific features investigated in these articles can be divided into three categories: lexicon, sentence structure, and discourse. Articles on lexical features investigate the use of specific words (such as "this," "we," and "and") (e.g., Duanmu 1986), verb tenses (e.g., Cai 2003), lexical bundles (e.g., Xu 2012a), lexical complexity (e.g., Bao 2010), reporting verbs (e.g., Chen 2011), transition markers (e.g., Zhao 2012), pronouns (e.g., Tang 2014),

---

6 The journal's original name was *Foreign Language Teaching Abroad* (《国外外语教学》) between 1981 and 2007.

nominalizations (e.g., Xiao & Wang 2001), shell nouns (e.g., Sun 2017), modal verbs (e.g., Ma & Lv 2007), etc. Articles on sentence structure explore textual sentence stems (e.g., Zhang & Wei 2013), run-on sentences (e.g., Wang & Zhao 2017), syntactic complexity (e.g., Song & Wang 2019), yes-no questions (e.g., Ding 2006), conditional clauses (e.g., Li 2008), word order (e.g., Zheng 2014), etc. Articles on discourse structure look at adversative relations in texts (e.g., Zheng 2017), patterns of thematic progression (e.g., Lv 2009), oral features in written composition (e.g., Wen et al. 2003), correspondence effects between introduction and conclusion in empirical articles (e.g., Zheng & Jing 2017), cultural features in texts (e.g., Guo & Liu 2005), citation practice in academic writing (e.g., Xu 2012b), code-switching (e.g., Chen et al. 2016), form-meaning tangling in L2 writing (e.g., Zheng & Chang 2014), register patterns (e.g., Wen 2009), application of topic knowledge in writing (e.g., Qin & Bi 2012b), etc.

Another important feature in these articles is the reference to L1 writers when they analyze the features in L2 writers' works. For example, Li and Liu (2016) conducted a comparative corpus-based study to investigate the features of lexical bundles used in Chinese experts' academic writing in English by comparing the use of lexical bundles by Chinese and English-speaking experts' written pieces. Such reference to/comparison between two languages is not necessarily meant to suggest that one language is superior to another, but rather to provide a reference for comparison and a guideline for instruction. For example, Chen (2017) develops a corpus to compare the commenting act in Chinese and in German academic articles, and the corpus provides insights for both Chinese learners of German and German learners of Chinese.

4.2.3 Writing assessment

Writing assessment is the third most studied topic in the articles I collected. A total of 220 articles address this topic, making up 16% of the articles I examined. The topic of writing assessment first appeared in 1982 (Gao 1982), but it did not become a well-studied topic until the 2000s. Only 15 articles were published before 2000, and 93.2% of the articles on writing assessment were published in the 21st century. During the last ten years, the number of articles on writing assessment increased dramatically, from an average of 2.08 articles per year between 1982 and 2007 to an average of 13.83 articles per year between 2008 and 2019.

Articles on the topic of writing assessment are mainly about three issues: feedback, testing in general, and standardized tests. Feedback is the most discussed topic in this category, with 89 articles representing different aspects of feedback. These aspects include peer feedback versus teacher feedback (e.g., Yang 2006), written corrective feedback (e.g., Chen & Li 2009), oral feedback (e.g., Zhang & Wang 2014), grammar correction (e.g., Su 2014), and integrated human and automated writing evaluation (AWE) feedback (e.g., Huang & He 2018). Another significant number of articles are on testing in general, including topics such as rater behavior (e.g., Lin & Xiao 2018), different evaluation tools (portfolio, dynamic evaluation, teacher-student collaborative assessment, automated writing evaluation, etc.) (e.g., Chen & Ge 2008; X. Wang 2016; Zhang & Wang 2004), rating scale development (e.g., Wu et al. 2018), testing tasks (e.g., Xue 2013), how testing facilitates learning (e.g., Wang et al. 2018), validity and reliability of certain tests (e.g., Qin & Bi 2012a), and cultural aspects in testing (e.g., Liu 2016). The third most studied topic in this category is the writing elements in high stakes standardized tests, such as the Test for English Majors (TEM) (e.g., Zou & Chen 2010), the College English Test (CET) (e.g., Gu & Yang 2009), and the College Entrance Exam (e.g., Zhang et al. 2010).

4.2.4 Writer development

There are 162 articles in my data exploring various issues related to the development and improvement of L2 writers. Writer development did not draw the attention of L2 scholars in China until the 1990s, with the first articles on writer development appearing in 1993. Xi (1993) examines the grammar and writing ability of Chinese international students at Kansas University in the United States, and Wang and Li (1993) study the thinking patterns of L2 writers by examining the texts they produced. There is an obvious increase in the number of articles on this topic over the past 30 years. The average number of articles on writer development was 0.86 articles per year in the 1990s and increased to 4.1 articles per year in the 2000s and 11.5 articles per year in the 2010s.

Various specific issues related to L2 writers regarding their mental and intellectual development are addressed by articles in this category. Such issues are writer's anxiety (e.g., Ma & Dong 2018), identity (e.g., Ouyang & Tang 2006), voice (e.g., Li & Li 2013), motivation (e.g., Hui et al. 2019), creative thinking (e.g., Shang 2013), working memory (e.g., Yi & Luo 2012), thinking patterns (e.g., Wen & Liu 2006), emotional effects (e.g., Liang & Chu 2013), noticing and awareness (e.g., Zhao & Sun 2009), self-efficacy (e.g., H. Li 2017), individual differences (e.g., Li 2015), metacognition (e.g., Lu & Shi 2007), etc. These articles each provide a glimpse of the holistic development of L2 writers as human learners.

4.2.5 Analysis of different genres

The next most studied topic is the analysis of different genres, with 90 articles, making up 6% of all the L2W articles collected. With the first article on genre analysis appearing in the late 1970s, the number of articles on genre analysis did not increase much until the Prosperous Period.

Articles in this category investigate the rhetoric and language features of various genres produced by native speakers of a target language. The genres represented in my data include academic theses (e.g., Wang 2014), scientific papers (e.g., Qian 1986), tourist texts (e.g., Xiao 1986), book reviews (e.g., Hei 2010), public notice signs (e.g., M. Zhang 2006), business discourse (e.g., Wang & Li 2018), news discourse (e.g., Yang & Ran 2017), advertisement (e.g., Gao & Li 2017), legal documentary (e.g., Lin 2005), speech scripts (e.g., Hu & Zeng 2007), email messages (e.g., Zeng 2003), popular science articles (e.g., Wang 2006), Internet passages (e.g., Yuan 2017), etc. Among all these genres, the academic thesis is the most studied one. Various aspects of the academic thesis are studied, such as abstracts, acknowledgement, literature review, conclusion, move analysis, and stylistic study of academic essays.

4.2.6 Writing process

Writing processes are one of the four least studied topics in the articles I surveyed, with only 65 articles, making up 5% of the total data set. Articles on this topic first appeared in the 1990s. The numerical trend of articles on writing processes is very similar to that of articles on genre analysis, with a few articles per year prior to the Prosperous Period and a sudden increase during the Prosperous Period. The average yearly number of articles on writing processes is 1.65 between 1993 and 2015, and the number increased to 6.75 between 2016 and 2019.

The topic of writing processes covers issues related to the brainstorming, drafting, composing, and revising processes of writing. It also presents articles on various writing tasks and how different writing tasks are processed differently by L2 writers. Newly developed technology has made studies on writing processes more precise. For example, L. Wang (2016) uses keyboard recording and eye tracker to develop a program to analyze writing process in both alphabetical (e.g., English) and non-alphabetical (e.g., Chinese) languages.

4.2.7 Disciplinary studies on L2W

Disciplinary study is one of the three least represented areas, with 45 articles, making up 3% of the total articles I collected. The topic became an area of interest in the early 2000s, with the first article appearing in 2003. Li and Li (2003) analyzed articles on EFL writing published between 1993 and 2002 in eight major linguistics/foreign language journals in China to showcase the developmental situation of English writing research in China by that time. Since then, the number of articles looking at L2W as a field of study has fluctuated, with an average of 2.65 articles per year.

These articles on disciplinary studies cover three general areas, which are conference reports (e.g., Ai 2006), review studies (e.g., Huang & Yu 2009), and studies on L2W research methodology (e.g., Gui 2005). Twenty-one review studies were found in the articles I surveyed. Some of these examine one area of L2W. For example, Li and Cui (2018) surveys articles on technical writing in China and draws implications for MTI education. Some explore L2W as an independent field of study. For example, Zhu (2011) reviews articles on English writing published in major foreign language journals between 1980 and 2010 and pictures the developmental path of English writing research during that period. Others report on the development of L2W in non-Chinese contexts. For example, Qin (2017) provides a review and outlook of trends in writing studies in the United States.

4.2.8 Interactions between L1 and L2 writing

Interaction between L1 and L2 is the topic of 44 articles, making up 3% of the total articles I collected. Numerically, this topic is among the only two that have not seen an obvious increase in the number of publications over the years, with the other one being disciplinary studies. The average number of articles on L1 vs. L2 interaction published per year actually dropped in the 2010s, compared with that of the 1990s and the 2000s. The decade between 1995 and 2005 witnessed the most articles on this topic, with 2.27 articles published per year.

Three major issues are discussed in this category: the influence of L1 on L2 writing, the influence of L2 on L1 writing, and contrastive rhetoric. In the articles on L1 influencing L2, L1 literacy and L1 thinking patterns are the most studied influential factors, and in the articles on L2 affecting L1, cultural aspects and vocabulary are the most studied influential factors. In the articles on contrastive rhetoric, various features of L1 and L2 are compared, such as register variations (e.g., Zhao & Wang 2017), coreferential devices (e.g., Lu 2002), cultural aspects (e.g., Zhang & Zhao 1993), collocational frameworks (e.g., X. Li 2017), stylistic differences (e.g., Wang 2001), and discourse interactions (e.g., Gao 2018).

4.2.9 Cross-area studies

Cross-area study is the least studied topic in my data, with 42 articles, representing 3% of the total articles I surveyed. The first article on this topic appeared in the late 1980s, but the 1990s witnessed zero articles on this topic. It was not until the early 2000s that scholars resumed publishing on L2W-related cross-area studies in major linguistics/foreign language journals. The number of articles in this category fluctuated during the 2000s and early 2010s and started to increase in the Prosperous Period.

Articles in this category investigate the relationship between writing and other areas of study, such as reading, speaking, listening, translating, etc. In the articles I collected, the majority is on translation studies (34 articles), making up 81% of the total articles in this category. These translation studies cover various contexts, ranging from literature (e.g., Cai & Yu 2018), academic works (e.g., Ye 2016), and newspaper articles (e.g., Zhao 2018) to medical theses (e.g., Duan & Gu 2002), political texts (e.g., Guo 2015), and public notice signs (e.g., Li 2000).

4.3 Research methods

The majority of articles I collected involve some empirical research. Based on the authors' description of research design, I identified 817 articles (61.02%) as empirical, as they present explicit data collection and analysis. The empirical articles in my data include mixed method studies, qualitative studies, and quantitative studies. Regarding specific research designs, these empirical studies involve case studies, interviews, think-aloud methods, comparative experiments, surveys, text analyses, observations, meta-analysis, corpus-based/driven studies, etc.

The other 522 articles (38.98%) are non-empirical, lacking explicit description of data analysis. Some of the non-empirical studies involve examples from the authors' own experiences or observations, but none of them explicitly reports how they collected and analyzed the data to draw the conclusion. Non-empirical studies in my data include a summary of authors' personal experiences, personal thoughts/suggestions, theoretical analysis, conference reports, book reviews, elaboration with examples, introduction to new methods/approaches, etc.

Numerically, empirical and non-empirical studies both increased since 1959. In the early years, most of the articles were non-empirical, and it was not until the mid 2000s that the yearly number of empirical studies surpassed that of non-empirical studies (Figure

3). Since then, the number of empirical studies published per year increased quickly, while the number of non-empirical studies published per year fluctuated and stayed small. During the Prosperous Period, the number of empirical studies has made up 77% of the total number of L2W articles published during that time.

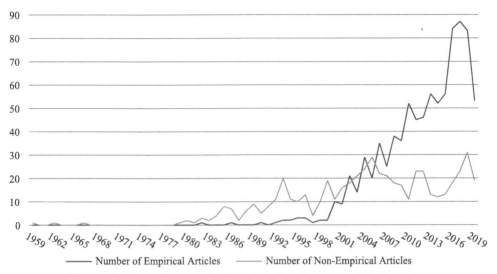

Figure 3. Numerical trend of empirical and non-empirical articles

4.4 Article contexts

A variety of contexts are represented in the articles I surveyed. In the 1,412 articles, 1,125 of them clearly identify one or multiple contexts that the articles address. The majority of the 287 articles with unidentified contexts are non-empirical articles. They are mainly theoretical accounts or personal elaboration with examples.

Among the contexts that are clearly identified in the articles, school context is the most studied. A total of 896 articles looked at contexts related to school settings, ranging from K-12 to college and post-graduate. Compared with K-12 settings, the college context is much more frequently investigated, and the college undergraduate context is the most commonly studied setting with 631 articles. In the articles on college settings, college English majors (both undergraduate and graduate) are the most studied population.

Other contexts that are addressed in the collected articles include academic manuscripts (117 articles), newspapers (31 articles), business discourse (27 articles), technical writing (25 articles), literary works (12 articles), law discourse (11 articles), tourist materials (eight articles), political discourse (eight articles), medical discourse (seven articles), speech scripts (two articles), hiring advertisements (two articles), etc. A total of 21 different contexts are analyzed in the 1,125 articles with clearly identified contexts.

Another feature in terms of article contexts is the number of languages represented in these articles. Although the majority of articles analyze Chinese L1 writers' L2 writing in English, a total of 55 articles investigate other L1s. Among these 55 articles, 38 of them examine international students' writing in Chinese as L2. These international students come from various linguistic backgrounds, including English (e.g., Wu 2017), Thai (e.g., Liu 2018), Korean (e.g., Wu 2019), Japanese (e.g., Ma & Shi 2016), and German (e.g., Chen 2016). There are also articles on Chinese L1 writers writing in non-English languages, such as Russian (e.g., Huang 1989), French (e.g., Zhang 1983), Japanese (e.g., Xiao 2017), and German (e.g., Chen 2017).

5. Conclusion and Future Directions

After analyzing the 1,412 articles on L2W published in 28 major linguistics/foreign language journals between 1949 and 2019 in China, I conclude that (1) L2W in China originated from instructional practice and (2) scholars in China have expanded their knowledge of L2W with an increased number of L2W articles published on various topics, applying different research methods in diverse contexts. I hope the findings of this study will help L2W scholars both in and outside China gain a better understanding of L2W development in China since 1949.

For L2W scholars in China, this study brings a comprehensive review of L2W journal articles in the past 70 years. It shows how various topics expand over time and how different issues are explored. The changes and features identified in my study can serve as a steppingstone for future studies. For L2W scholars outside China, this study provides an insider's perspective on the development of L2W in China. This study provides non-Chinese scholars an access to the research findings that are originally written and published in Chinese and helps scholars from other language backgrounds see what has been going on in L2W studies in China.

By analyzing and synthesizing China's L2W articles in its major linguistics/foreign language journals, I identified features and patterns in the origin and development of L2W in China. By tracing back to the earliest articles and examining the various topics, research methods, and contexts involved in these articles, I suggest that L2W in China is unique in its developmental path and has a promising future.

References

Ai, B. （艾斌）, 2006, "首届中国外语中青年学者科研方法学术研讨会暨科研写作高级研修班" 摭评 [J], 《中国外语》（3）: 78-79。

Bai, L. （白丽茹）, 2012, 大学英语写作中同伴互评反馈模式测量评价表的编制 [J], 《现代外语》35（2）: 184-192。

Bao, G. （鲍贵）, 2010, 英语学习者语言复杂性变化对比研究 [J], 《现代外语》（2）: 166-176。

Cai, J. （蔡金亭）, 2003, 记叙文语篇结构与英语过渡语中一般过去时变异的关系——对语篇假设的检验 [J], 《现代外语》（1）: 59-68。

Cai, L. （蔡兰珍）, 2001, "任务教学法" 在大学英语写作中的应用 [J], 《外语界》（4）: 41-46。

Cai, Y.（蔡永贵）& Yu, X.（余星），2018，基于语料库的《论语》两个英译本的翻译风格研究[J]，《外国语文》（5）：127-136。

Chen, J.（陈建林），2011，基于语料库的引述动词研究及其对英语写作教学的启示[J]，《外语界》（6）：40-48。

Chen, L.（陈立平）& Li, Z.（李志雪），1999，英语写作教学：理论与实践[J]，《解放军外国语学院学报》（1）：66-69。

Chen, Q.（陈琦），2017，汉、德语学术论文注释性言语行为对比研究[J]，《外国语》（6）：40-48。

Chen, Q.（陈倩）、Lin, L.（林伦伦）& Xu, Z.（许竹君），2016，基于广东媒体语料库的中文报刊语码转换语域理论模式分析[J]，《语言科学》（1）：85-95。

Chen, X.（陈潇潇）& Ge, S.（葛诗利），2008，自动作文评分研究综述[J]，《解放军外国语学院学报》（5）：78-83。

Chen, X.（陈晓湘）& Li, H.（李会娜），2009，教师书面修正性反馈对学生英语写作的影响[J]，《外语教学与研究》（5）：351-358。

Chen, Y.（陈钰），2016，留学生论文指导策略的有效性研究[J]，《语言教学与研究》（6）：19-27。

Cheng, S.（程仕娟），2011，国内英语写作研究述评——十年回眸[J]，《黑龙江教育学院学报》（2）：153-155。

Dai, L.（戴镏龄），1962，略谈提高学生外语写作能力问题[J]，《外语教学与研究》（1）：11-12。

Ding, W.（丁往道），1959，略谈笔语和笔语课[J]，《外语教学与研究》（4）：213-214。

Ding, X.（丁雪欢），2006，初中级留学生是非问的分布特征与发展过程[J]，《世界汉语教学》（3）：103-112。

Duan, P.（段平）& Gu, W.（顾维萍），2002，医学论文标题与摘要汉译英常见错误分析[J]，《中国翻译》（4）：47-48。

Duanmu, Y.（端木义万），1986，英语新闻报道中表示"说"的方式和用词[J]，《南外学报》（2）：43-46。

Feng, Y.（冯亚琳），1995，关于德语写作课教学目标等问题的思考[J]，《四川外语学院学报》（1）：86-90。

Gao, J.（高骏骅），1982，他们是怎样批改高年级英文作文的?[J]，《外国语》（5）：63-64。

Gao, L.（高莉）& Li, M.（李敏），2017，英语广告语篇的人称视角表达[J]，《外语教学》38（1）：38-42。

Gao, Y.（高芸），2018，中西医英语科研论文语篇互动性对比研究——基于 SCI 期刊论文的语料库分析[J]，《外语电化教学》（2）：78-83。

Gu, X.（辜向东）& Yang, Z.（杨志强），2009，CET 二十年写作试题分析与研究[J]，《外语与外语教学》（6）：21-26。

Gui, Q.（桂清扬），2005，LSP语料库的设计标准问题——兼谈英语专业高年级专业课学期论文动态语料库设计[J]，《外语电化教学》（5）：29-32。

Guo, C.（郭纯洁）& Liu, F.（刘芳），2005，文化定式对中介语作文的负面影响及其对策研究[J]，

《外语界》（5）：24-28。

Guo, S.（郭姗姗），2009，国内二语写作研究 18 年述评（1991- 2008）[J]，《山东外语教学》（5）：38-41。

Guo, Y.（郭影平），2015，政治文献英译特点探究[J]，《上海翻译》（4）：52-58。

He, W.（何武），2013，中国 EFL 写作研究十年概览（2001-2010）[J]，《英语研究》（1）：66-73。

He, W.（何微微），2018，国内 EFL 写作焦虑研究现状及思考[J]，《湖北第二师范学院学报》（9）：18-21。

Hei, Y.（黑玉琴），2010，应用语言学期刊中书评文章的辩论修辞结构[J]，《外语教学》（2）：23-28。

Hu, J.（胡瑾）& Zeng, L.（曾蕾），2007，国际学术交流英语演讲稿语篇模式分析[J]，《外语教学》（3）：20-24。

Huang, J.（黄静）& He, H.（何华清），2018，人机反馈对学生写作行为的影响研究[J]，《外语电化教学》（1）：19-24。

Huang, J.（黄建滨）& Yu, S.（于书林），2009，国内英语写作研究述评[J]，《中国外语》（4）：60-65。

Huang, S.（黄士增），1989，俄语科技写作教学初探[J]，《解放军外国语学院学报》（3）：69-72。

Hui, L.（惠良虹）、Zhang, Y.（张莹）& Li, X.（李欣欣），2019，移动学习环境下大学生英语学习动机调控实证研究[J]，《外语教学》（1）：59-65。

Li, H.（李航），2017，英语写作自我效能感对非英语专业大学生写作成绩的影响研究[J]，《外语教学理论与实践》（3）：57-63。

Li, K.（李克兴），2000，试析深圳的英语弊病及翻译谬误[J]，《上海翻译》（1）：35-45。

Li, K.（李克兴），2008，法律英语条件句的写作和翻译[J]，《中国翻译》（4）：71-77。

Li, M.（李梦骁）& Liu, Y.（刘永兵），2016，基于语料库的中外学者学术语篇词块使用对比研究[J]，《现代外语》（4）：507-515。

Li, N.（李娜）& Li, Z.（李忠庆），2013，学术文章中的"写作者声音"——基于语料库的跨学科和语言的对比研究[J]，《解放军外国语学院学报》（4）：17-23。

Li, S.（李绍鹏），2015，二语写作发展中的个体差异研究[J]，《语言教学与研究》（6）：27-34。

Li, S.（李双燕）& Cui, Q.（崔启亮），2018，国内技术写作发展现状调查及其对 MTI 教育的启示[J]，《外语学刊》（2）：50-56。

Li, X.（李响），2017，相同体裁语篇的搭配框架研究——以《中国政府工作报告》和《美国国情咨文》为例[J]，《外语电化教学》（1）：70-77。

Li, Z.（李志雪）& Li, S.（李绍山），2003，对国内英语写作研究现状的思考——对八种外语类核心期刊十年（1993-2002）的统计分析[J]，《外语界》（6）：55-60。

Liang, H.（梁汇娟）& Chu, T.（初彤），2013，情绪对二语写作创新影响的调查与实证研究[J]，《中国外语》（2）：61-66。

Lin, C.（林椿）& Xiao, Y.（肖云南），2018，中国大学生英语写作测试中母语与非母语评分员行

为的对比分析 [J]，《中国外语》（5）：72-84。

Lin, W.（林巍），2005，特定的规范化：澳门法律公文翻译探讨 [J]，《中国翻译》（5）：80-85。

Liu, D.（刘丹），2016，基于论辩体裁的英语写作跨文化评价研究 [J]，《外语学刊》（6）：121-124。

Liu, X.（刘旭），2018，泰国大学生汉语名词习得机制探析——以名词句法功能习得为中心 [J]，《语言文字应用》（3）：114-123。

Lu, H.（陆红）& Shi, M.（施鸣鸣），2007，非英语专业硕士生写作元认知水平调查与分析 [J]，《中国外语》（4）：38-41。

Lu, Z.（陆振慧），2002，英汉语篇中指同表达的对比研究 [J]，《外语教学与研究》（5）：24-31。

Luo, J.（罗健），2002，商务英语写作教学探新 [J]，《外语界》（6）：45-48。

Luo, Y.（罗毅）、Cai, H.（蔡慧萍）& Wang, J.（王金），2011，体验式教学理论在英语应用文体写作教学中的应用 [J]，《外语教学理论与实践》（1）：38-42。

Lv, Y.（吕岩），2009，主位推进模式及其在英语写作教学中的应用 [J]，《四川外语学院学报》（2）：60-62。

Ma, G.（马刚）& Lv, X.（吕晓娟），2007，基于中国学习者英语语料库的情态动词研究 [J]，《外语电化教学》（3）：17-21。

Ma, J.（马洁）& Dong, P.（董攀），2018，大数据背景下国内外语写作焦虑研究 [J]，《外语电化教学》（2）：32-37。

Ma, W.（马文津）& Shi, C.（施春宏），2016，基于整句—零句表达系统的汉语中介语篇章现象考察——以日语母语者汉语语篇为例 [J]，《世界汉语教学》（4）：513-530。

Ouyang, H.（欧阳护华）& Tang, S.（唐适宜），2006，中国大学生英语议论文写作中的作者身份 [J]，《解放军外国语学院学报》（2）：49-53。

Qian, S.（钱绍昌），1986，科技英语写作 [J]，《上海翻译》（1）：40-44。

Qin, F.（秦枫），2017，美国写作研究回顾与展望 [J]，《外语电化教学》（2）：40-44。

Qin, X.（秦晓晴）& Bi, J.（毕劲），2012a，二语写作流利性指标的效度——一项基于文本特征的研究 [J]，《外语教学与研究》（6）：899-911。

Qin, X.（秦晓晴）& Bi, J.（毕劲），2012b，大学生英语写作话题知识运用特点研究 [J]，《外语电化教学》（3）：29-35。

Shang, Y.（商艳芝），2013，网络信息技术环境下英语写作创新思维能力的培养——以英语写作精品课的开发应用为例 [J]，《外语电化教学》（5）：52-56。

Si, J.（司建国），2005，提倡"快乐写作"理念，改革高职英语写作教学——体验英语《写作学习语料库》给予我们的启示 [J]，《外语电化教学》（104）：72-74。

Song, R.（宋瑞梅）& Wang, H.（汪火焰），2019，中国博士学位论文摘要句法复杂度研究 [J]，《解放军外国语学院学报》（1）：84-91。

Su, H.（苏航）& Yang, L.（杨磊），2001，结果教学法与过程教学法——谈英语写作教学改革 [J]，《北京第二外国语学院学报》（2）：98-102。

Su, J.（苏建红），2014，Bruton 与 Truscott 二语写作语法纠错之争 [J]，《现代外语》（6）：855-863。

Sun, H.（孙海燕），2017，学习者叙实类外壳名词的搭配构式发展特征 [J]，《外语与外语教学》（2）：81-89。

Sun, L.（孙蓝）& Chen, J.（陈纪梁），2009，研究生英语科技论文写作探究式学习体系的思考与构建 [J]，《中国外语》（4）：66-71。

Tang, H.（汤红娟），2014，基于人称代词动允性变量的儿童英语仿写衔接手段实证研究 [J]，《中国外语》（6）：62-69。

Tian, H.（田海龙），2001，计算机辅助英语写作教学：活动与优势 [J]，《外语电化教学》（80）：11-14。

Wang, C.（王初明），2005，外语写长法 [J]，《中国外语》（1）：45-49。

Wang, J.（王娟），2001，论英汉文体特征的差异 [J]，《解放军外国语学院学报》（3）：27-31。

Wang, J. (2016). An ecology of studies on EFL writing in the Chinese context [A]. In T. Silva, J. Wang, C. Zhang & J. Paiz (eds.). *L2 Writing in the Global Context: Represented, Underrepresented, and Unrepresented Voices* [C]. Beijing: Foreign Language Teaching and Research Press. 48-63.

Wang, L.（王莉），2014，英文学术论文摘要篇章特征的多维研究 [J]，《外语学刊》（3）：111-113。

Wang, L.（王兰忠），2016，基于键盘记录和眼动仪的中文二语写作过程研究 [J]，《外语电化教学》（2）：35-39。

Wang, L.（王立非）& Li, S.（李炤坤），2018，中美商务语篇互文性多维对比研究 [J]，《外语教学理论与实践》（3）：56-62。

Wang, M.（王墨希）& Li, J.（李津），1993，中国学生英语语篇思维模式调查 [J]，《外语教学与研究》（4）：59-64。

Wang, T.（王同顺）、Zhu, X.（朱晓彤）& Xu, Y.（许莹莹），2018，促学性评价对中国大学英语学习者学习动机及写作能力的影响研究 [J]，《外语学刊》（3）：46-53。

Wang, W.（王文宇）& Wang, L.（王立非），2004，二语写作研究：十年回顾与展望 [J]，《外语界》（4）：51-58。

Wang, X.（王学锋），2016，形成性评价对大学生英语写作水平的动态影响研究 [J]，《解放军外国语学院学报》（4）：102-110。

Wang, W.（王文斌）& Zhao, C.（赵朝永），2017，中国学习者产出英语"流水句"现象剖析：英汉时空差异视角 [J]，《外语界》（1）：30-37。

Wang, Z.（王志刚），1986，英语写作理论的新发展 [J]，《外国语》（2）：73-77。

Wang, Z.（王振平），2006，科普著作的文体与翻译 [J]，《上海翻译》（2）：35-38。

Wen, Q.（文秋芳），2009，学习者英语语体特征变化的研究 [J]，《外国语》（4）：2-10。

Wen, Q.（文秋芳）、Ding, Y.（丁言仁）& Wang, W.（王文宇），2003，中国大学生英语书面语中的口语化倾向——高水平英语学习者语料对比分析 [J]，《外语教学与研究》（4）：268-274。

Wen, Q.（文秋芳）& Liu, R.（刘润清），2006，从英语议论文分析大学生抽象思维特点 [J]，《外国语》（2）：49-58。

Wu, J.（吴婧），2003，大学生英语论说文语篇结构特征调查——篇章主题句和段落主题句的使用[J]，《外语教学理论与实践》（2）：35-42。

Wu, J.（吴继峰），2017，英语母语者汉语书面语动态发展个案研究[J]，《现代外语》（2）：254-264。

Wu, J.（吴继峰），2019，韩国学生不同文体写作中的语言特征对比研究[J]，《语言教学与研究》（5）：1-12。

Wu, X.（吴雪峰）、Liu, Y.（柳烨琛）& Yin, Y.（殷缘），2018，英语写作评分标准模型的建构及其效度研究[J]，《外国语文》（5）：137-146。

Xi, C.（滕春红），1993，英语语法与写作——对美国堪萨斯大学中国留学生英文水平的调查[J]，《外语教学与研究》（4）：65-69。

Xiao, J.（萧洁汶），1986，两篇旅游文章的文体比较[J]，《外语教学与研究》（1）：52-54。

Xiao, J.（肖建安）& Wang, Z.（王志军），2001，名物化结构的功能及变体特征[J]，《外语与外语教学》（6）：9-11。

Xiao, K.（肖开益），2017，基于说服心理学的日语自我呈现文的写作方法分析——以写作内容与写作顺序为中心[J]，《解放军外国语学院学报》（3）：95-103。

Xu, F.（徐昉），2011，英语写作教学法的多视角理论回顾与思考[J]，《外语界》（2）：57-64。

Xu, F.（徐昉），2012a，中国学习者英语学术词块的使用及发展特征研究[J]，《中国外语》（4）：51-56。

Xu, F.（徐昉），2012b，实证类英语学术研究话语中的文献引用特征[J]，《外国语》（6）：60-68。

Xu, J.（许家森），1990a，大学英语4/6级考试作文中的连贯性原则[J]，《中国翻译》（4）：48-53。

Xu, J.（许家森），1990b，大学英语四级考试作文中的统一性原则[J]，《中国翻译》（1）：42-44。

Xue, F.（薛凤敏），2013，从写作过程看二语写作测试任务设计的影响因素[J]，《语言教学与研究》（4）：1-7。

Yan, X.（晏晓蓉）& Cui, S.（崔沙沙），2011，国内二语写作研究近况及展望——基于2006—2010年9种外语类核心期刊的统计分析[J]，《北京第二外国语学院学报》（12）：24-30。

Yang, J.（杨建昌），1982，浅谈外国留学生汉语专业的写作课教学[J]，《语言教学与研究》（3）：110-113。

Yang, L.（杨俐），2007，《外国人汉语过程写作》的编写理念[J]，《语言教学与研究》（6）：63-66。

Yang, L.（杨鲁新），2010，高校英语专业教师写作教学信念与教学实践——经验教师个案研究[J]，《外语教学理论与实践》（2）：59-68。

Yang, M.（杨苗），2006，中国英语写作课教师反馈和同侪反馈对比研究[J]，《现代外语》（3）：293-301。

Yang, N.（杨娜）& Ran, Y.（冉永平），2017，新闻评论话语的语用论辩视域分析[J]，《外语学刊》（4）：57-62。

Yang, Y.（杨永林）、Liu, Y.（刘寅齐）& Wang, L.（王丽娟），2009，倾听教学一线的声音，探讨写作难的问题———种"问题化"的研讨视角[J]，《外语电化教学》（128）：3-11。

Yao, L. （姚兰）& Cheng, L. （程骊妮），2005，我国20世纪80年代以来英语写作研究状况之研究 [J]，《外语界》（5）：2-16。

Ye, H. （叶红卫），2016，海外英文汉学论著翻译研究 [J]，《上海翻译》（4）：37-42。

Yi, B. （易保树）& Luo, S. （罗少茜），2012，工作记忆对中国英语学习者书面语产出的流利度、准确度和复杂度的影响 [J]，《解放军外国语学院学报》（5）：43-47。

Yin, L. （尹丽娟），2008，从功能句子观角度谈英语流畅段落的写作技巧 [J]，《中国外语》（1）：60-63。

You, X. (2004). "The choice made from no choice": English writing instruction in a Chinese University [J], *Journal of Second Language Writing* 13(2): 97-110.

You, X. (2010). *Writing in the Devil's Tongue: A History of English Composition in China* [M]. Southern Illinois University Press.

Yu, F. （余富盛），1966，怎样培养学生的写作能力 [J]，《外语教学与研究》（2）：57-58。

Yu, F. （于飞）& Zhang, H. （张慧芬），1996，写作教学中的"成果教学法"、"过程教学法"和"内容教学法"浅析 [J]，《外语界》3（11）：38-40。

Yuan, Y. （袁野），2017，基于构式语法的书面及对话语篇分析框架——以网络语体为例 [J]，《外语学刊》（2）：45-49。

Zeng, L. （曾立），2003，英文电子书信体：文体特征与语境 [J]，《外语电化教学》（2）：21-25。

Zhang, A. （张爱卿），1998，大学英语写作能力滞后探源 [J]，《外语与外语教学》（12）：13-15。

Zhang, D. （张德聪）& Zhao, Y. （赵亦民），1993，从东西方文化差异谈汉英写作的区别 [J]，《外语教学》（4）：67-70。

Zhang, F. （张放），1983，法语教学中的写作课 [J]，《外语教学与研究》（2）：53-57。

Zhang, H. （张红霞）& Wang, T. （王同顺），2004，电子档案袋——外语写作测评的新理念和新方法 [J]，《外语电化教学》（95）：41-44。

Zhang, J. （张坚），2000，过程教学法与英语写作教学 [J]，《北京第二外国语学院学报》（3）：89-95。

Zhang, K. （张凯）& Wang, T. （王同顺），2014，口头反馈对中国学习者英语冠词和介词习得效果研究 [J]，《外语教学理论与实践》（2）：64-70。

Zhang, L. （张乐）& Wei, N. （卫乃兴），2013，学术论文中篇章性句干的型式和功能研究 [J]，《解放军外国语学院学报》（2）：8-15。

Zhang, M. （张美芳），2006，澳门公共牌示语言及其翻译研究 [J]，《上海翻译》（1）：29-34。

Zhang, X. （张锡惠），1992，大学英语写作探讨 [J]，《四川外语学院学报》（2）：108-112。

Zhang, X. （张雪梅），2006，大学英语写作教学现状之调查 [J]，《外语界》（5）：28-32。

Zhang, X. （张新玲）、Zeng, Y. （曾用强）& Zhang, J. （张洁），2010，对大规模读写结合写作任务的效度验证 [J]，《解放军外国语学院学报》（2）：50-54。

Zhang, Z. （张志），1979，介绍一本论英语科技文件写作方法的书 [J]，《外语教学与研究》（2）：75-78。

Zhao, C.（赵朝永）& Wang, W.（王文斌），2017，中国英语学习者语域变异多维分析：英汉时空特质差异视角[J]，《外语电化教学》（4）：71-78。

Zhao, H.（赵奂），2018，译写融合与中国事件的国际话语书写方案——中外主流媒体十九大报道话语书写方式研究[J]，《外国语文》34（5）：16-23。

Zhao, Y.（赵颖），2012，基于学术语篇语料库的过渡标记语语用失误调查[J]，《中国外语》（6）：57-63。

Zhao, Y.（赵永青）& Sun, X.（孙鑫），2009，英语写作过程中注意的分布和意识程度的研究[J]，《外语与外语教学》（1）：32-36。

Zheng, C.（郑超）& Chang, C.（常春娥），2014，是传递意义还是炫耀形式——外语写作过程中的形—意缠结现象[J]，《现代外语》37（4）：513-524。

Zheng, D.（郑丹），2017，基于英汉学术期刊论文语料库的转折关系对比研究[J]，《外语学刊》（2）：55-60。

Zheng, L.（郑丽娜），2014，母语为英语的学习者汉语语序参数重设研究[J]，《语言教学与研究》（6）：11-19。

Zheng, X.（郑新民）& Jing, F.（景飞龙），2017，我国外语类学术期刊实证研究论文首尾呼应效果探析——体裁分析和元话语研究的视角[J]，《外语与外语教学》（4）：42-51。

Zhou, Q.（周奇），1990，谈谈段落主题句的拟写——大学英语写作教学探微[J]，《山东外语教学》（3）：21-23。

Zhou, Y.（周越美）、Sun, X.（孙晓龙）& Zhang, R.（张韧弦），2009，写作课程的无纸化考试研究[J]，《外语界》（3）：59-65。

Zhu, J.（朱菊芬）& Ye, M.（叶敏），1996，融大学英语写作训练于英语精读教学之中[J]，《外语与外语教学》（92）：35-38。

Zhu, Y.（朱岩岩），2011，对我国英语写作研究发展的调查和思考——基于我国外语类核心期刊统计分析（1980-2010）[J]，《外语界》（6）：56-62。

Zou, S.（邹申）& Chen, W.（陈炜），2010，TEM4评分效度与计算机辅助评卷[J]，《外语电化教学》（1）：56-60。

About the Author

Yue CHEN is a PhD candidate in the English Department at Purdue University, USA. Her research interests include second language writing, writing assessment, and pedagogy. Email: chen1398@purdue. edu

国内二语写作研究现状与发展趋势[*]
——基于国家社科和教育部人文社科立项课题的分析

周 杰

山东大学 / 湖南工业大学

提要：本文从立项数年度分布、项目类别、项目负责人职称、承办单位性质及地区分布、项目内容及热点五大方面，对 2006 至 2021 年国家社科基金和教育部人文社科基金二语写作项目立项数据进行历时的比较分析，以探讨国内二语写作研究现状和发展趋势。结果表明，当前研究立项呈整体上升趋势，但存在增长不稳定、项目类别分布不均、地域差距明显、研究内容失衡等问题。研究热点体现在"学术英语""写作能力发展""反馈""语料库""评价""等级量表"等方面。本文尝试对发现的问题给予合理建议，为二语写作研究课题的申报和立项提供指导和建议，以期推动国内二语写作研究的发展。

关键词：国家社科基金；教育部人文社科基金；二语写作；研究现状；发展趋势

1. 引言

国家社会科学基金（以下简称国家社科基金）和教育部人文社会科学基金（以下简称教育部人文社科基金）是国内目前最具有权威性和导向性的社科类基金。能否成功申请两大基金课题立项，在很大程度上反映了各高校、机构乃至地区的科研进展、水平和实力。同时，这些立项的项目具有前瞻性，能体现社会科学和学术主流的发展方向。因此，多角度梳理和分析两大基金的立项趋势，能较好地提高课题申报成功率，引导和指导学科研究的发展。

二语写作是语言学研究的重要领域。国际范围内的二语写作研究历经半个世纪的发展，已逐步发展成为相对独立的学科体系。国内关于二语写作的研究始于 20 世纪 90 年代中期，虽起步较晚，却在短时间内实现了较快发展（王俊菊 2013）。尤其在进入 21 世纪后，越来越多的学者和科研人员开始关注和参与这一领域的研究，使得研究成果在数量和质量上有所提升，研究范畴更为多元，研究内容更为深刻。国内诸多学者开展了基于国家社科基金或教育部人文社科基金立项统计的分析，如对外语研究项目的阐述（贺显斌 2006）；对语言学类立项项目的探讨（苏新春、刘锐 2015；苏红 2018）；对国家社科基金外国语言学研究立项的分析（王立非、江进林 2011；吴进善 2015）；对国家社科基金中国语言学研究立项的统计分析（吴珊

---

[*] 本研究为国家社科基金重点项目"二语写作理论建构与本土化研究"（17AYY022）和湖南省教育科学研究工作者协会"十四五"规划 2021 年度高等教育重点课题"服务'三高四新'战略的湖南高端语言服务人才培养研究"（XJKX21A001）的阶段性成果。

2012）；比较国家社科基金中国、外国语言学及文学项目的立项情况（刘泽权、朱利利2018）；对比国家社科基金、全国教育科学规划项目及教育部人文社科基金中的语言学项目立项现状（康勇、葛明贵2018）等。

　　然而，对语言学学科下的二语写作研究立项情况进行分析的研究尚不多见。因此，本研究基于2006至2021年国家社科基金和教育部人文社科基金立项的统计分析，从历时和共时角度回顾国内二语写作研究的发展状况，分析其研究热点与发展趋势，挖掘存在的问题，给予合理的建议，为今后二语写作研究者的课题立项提供数据支持。

2. 研究设计

2.1 数据来源

　　本研究对2006至2021年国家社科基金和教育部人文社科基金立项名单进行了统计，前者的项目信息来源于全国哲学社会科学工作办公室网站（http://www.npopss-cn.gov.cn），后者来源于教育部社会科学司网站（http://www.moe.gov.cn）。

2.2 数据收集与分析

　　本研究主要关注以英语为第二语言的写作研究项目（其他语种或对外汉语项目，如"基于语料库的留学生中文学位论文语言差异研究"，不包括在内），采取计量语言学中的关键词统计方法。

　　主要步骤如下：首先，在国家社科基金和教育部人文社科基金"语言学"项目历年立项名单中通过"二语""英语""英文""外语""外文""第二语言""作文""论文""书面语""书面表达"等关键词进行检索。检索结果，如2021年国家社科基金立项项目"中国大学生表达性英语写作育人机制研究""'跨文化修辞'视角下的中国研究生英语学术语篇特征历时研究"、2021年教育部人文社科基金"中美硕博学位论文摘要的语类特征对比研究"等，通过筛选，保存为Excel文件。

　　然后，将与二语写作相关的立项课题名称按时间顺序、项目类别（如重点项目、一般项目、青年项目等）、项目负责人职称（正高级、副高级、中级等）、项目承办单位或机构的性质（国家"双一流"大学、985高校、211高校、省属重点高校等）和地区分布（华东、华中、东北、华北、西南、西北、华南地区）、项目内容及热点分别进行统计、归纳和分析。其中，研究热点主要通过统计和对比分析两大项目立项标题中的关键词和高频词的分布情况得出。关键词的提取原则是：去除"研究""实践""调查"等与研究主题无关的词；去除"的""和""或"等虚词；去除具体的人名、地名、民族名等；同一题目中出现多个关键词分别统计；同一题目中同一关键词出现多次，均只记一次；关键词大多以两个字或三个字为主。

3. 二语写作项目立项数据统计与分析

根据以上研究方法进行检索，共获得106条有效项目数据。关于二语写作研究的项目立项分析将从立项数年度分布、项目类别分布、项目负责人职称分布、研究机构性质及地区分布和项目内容分布及热点分析五大方面展开。

3.1 立项数年度分布

本研究将2006至2021年两大国家级项目中有关二语写作立项数按时间顺序分别进行统计，同时合并计算两大基金历年立项数，以探寻整体发展趋势。经统计，国家社科基金和教育部人文社科基金16年间关于二语写作立项数分别为45（占比42.5%）和61（占比57.5%）。如图1所示，从两大基金合计立项数来看，2006至2015年有关二语写作的立项数虽有波动，但整体呈上升趋势，2014至2015年涨幅最大，在2015年达到立项峰值。尽管之后一年数值骤降，但2017至2021年数据回暖，呈平稳上升趋势。通过对比图1两大基金数据线走势发现，国家社科基金在2020年前起伏不定，随后在2021年达到峰值（有8项立项）。而教育部人文社科基金在2011年、2015年和2019年分别达到最高水平，在2012至2013年、2016至2017年间立项数持续走低，在2017年达到历年最低，然后在2019至2020年达到历史最高水平。

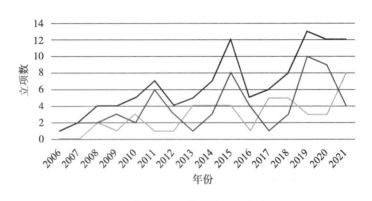

图1 2006至2021年国社科和教育部人文社科项目立项走势图

3.2 项目类别分布

3.2.1 国家社科基金项目类别分布

国家社科基金项目主要分为重大项目、年度项目、西部项目、后期资助项目和特别委托项目（不纳入计算）等类别。其中，重大项目是目前国家社科基金中权威最大、等级最高的项目类别，年度项目分为重点项目、一般项目和青年项目，是国家社科基金的主体。2006至2021年各项目类别累计立项数统计如下：

表1 国家社科基金项目类别占比

项目类别	项目数量	所占比例
重大项目	0	0
重点项目	1	2.2%
一般项目	36	80.0%
青年项目	6	13.3%
西部项目	2	4.4%
后期资助项目	0	0
总计	45	100%

如表1所示，2006至2021年，一般项目的立项数占据绝对优势，为80.0%，大约是其他项目立项总和的四倍；青年项目、西部项目和重点项目较少，均不足10.0%；而国家社科基金自1991年成立以来，还未出现二语写作相关课题的重大项目和后期资助项目立项，这体现出国内二语写作研究领域在承担重大项目研究方面力量不足，亟待加强。在这45个立项中，重点项目虽只有一个，却也不容忽视。山东大学王俊菊教授2017年"二语写作理论体系建构及本土化研究"的立项标志着二语写作研究重点项目从无到有的突破，极大推动了二语写作研究的发展。近年来，国家社科基金中的西部项目立项规模扩大、资助额度增加，但有关二语写作的西部项目仅有2008年立项的两个项目。这意味着自2009年至今，西部地区关于二语写作研究的活跃度不高，这与项目整体发展趋势有所不同。

3.2.2 教育部人文社科基金项目类别分布

教育部人文社科基金分为规划基金项目、青年基金项目、自筹经费项目、西部和边疆地区项目、新疆项目、西藏项目等几大类别。2006至2021年各类别累计立项数统计如下：

表2 教育部人文社科基金项目类别占比

项目类别	项目数量	所占比例
规划基金项目	30	49.2%
青年基金项目	29	47.5%
自筹经费项目	1	1.6%
西部和边疆地区项目	1	1.6%
总计	61	100%

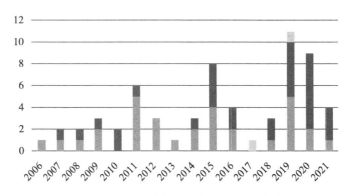

图2　教育部人文社科基金项目类别年度分布

通过表1和表2对比，可以看出国家社科基金和教育部人文社科基金在项目类别、数量和所占比率方面有很大差异。国家社科基金关于二语写作研究的立项中绝大多数为一般项目，青年项目占比较少（13.3%）；教育部人文社科基金立项中规划基金项目占比一半，但青年基金项目占比也相当可观（47.5%），且大体上在每年立项中都占有一定比例（见图2）。由此可见，教育部人文社科基金对青年科研人才的支持力度要大于国家社科基金。青年学者，尤其是刚毕业的博士，经过严格的学术训练，掌握了扎实的学术知识与技能，在申请教育部人文社科基金二语写作相关课题时成功立项比例较大，也反映出国家对新生科研力量培养的重视，但想要成为国家社科基金立项中的主力军还需要不断磨砺。

3.3　项目负责人职称分布

根据国家社科基金年度项目指南要求，申请重点项目和一般项目需要具有副高级以上专业职务；申请青年项目者，若未达到副高级以上标准，可由两名拥有正高级职称的同行专家推荐。

表3　项目负责人职称分布

专业职称	国家社科基金		教育部人文社科基金	
	人数	所占比例	人数	所占比例
正高级	23	54.8%	23	39.0%
副高级	15	35.7%	29	49.1%
中级	4	9.5%	7	11.9%

对45项国家社科基金项目的负责人专业职称进行统计，结果（见表3）发现正高级占比最多，为54.8%；其中王俊菊、王颖和战菊这三位正高级教师在此期间均获得两个国家社科基金项目，因此不重复统计其专业职称；其次是副高级教师，占比35.7%；中级职称教师仅占9.5%。与国家社科基金相比，教育部人文社科基金项

目正高级职称教师人数为23人，占比39.0%，其中何武、卢丹两位教师都获得两次立项，因此不重复统计其职称；副高级职称人数明显高于国家社科基金立项教师人数，达到29人，占比49.1%；中级职称教师人数和所占比例也略高于国家社科基金，达到7人（11.9%）。表3中的中级职称负责人主持的都是青年基金项目。这也从侧面说明，在有关二语写作研究的国家社科基金项目中，仍由学术经验丰富、积淀深厚、颇有建树的学者和专家们主导，青年科研工作者在国家层级的立项项目中取得一席之地绝非易事，需要从基础研究开始，持之以恒。

3.4 承办单位性质及地区分布

3.4.1 承办单位性质分布

所统计的106个项目共涉及68个研究机构，且全为国内大学。按承办单位性质划分，国家"双一流"、985和211工程大学共有21所，国家"双一流"和211工程大学共有16所，仅为国家"双一流"建设高校有四所，省属重点高校有五所。如图3所示，重点高校的二语写作研究立项比例（67.7%）高于普通高校（32.3%），这充分表明重点高校强大的师资力量和齐全的硬件设施能为二语写作研究提供良好的科研环境。

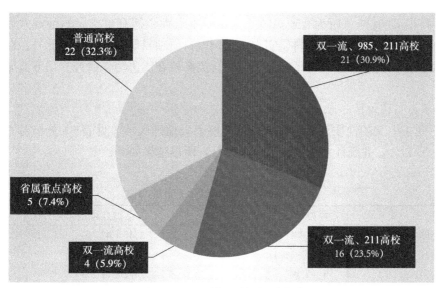

图3 立项研究机构类别分布

立项的普通高校共计22所，在科研立项总数上高于其他类型高校（占比32.3%）（见图3），可见普通高校在国家和教育部社科基金二语写作研究项目中做出了重要贡献，拥有很大的发展空间和潜力。"双一流"、985和211高校与"双一流"、211高校的基金立项占比较为均衡，由此反映出我国关于二语写作研究的立项呈现出高水平大学引领和带动其他大学，各高校科学研究共同进步，课题持续深入探寻、协调发展的局面。

按照研究机构立项数量由高到低排列，前10名统计结果如下：

表4 研究机构立项数排名

序号	研究机构	机构类别	立项数目
1	东北师范大学	"双一流"、211 高校	6
2	山东大学	"双一流"、985 和 211 高校	5
3	华中科技大学	"双一流"、985 和 211 高校	4
4	华中师范大学	"双一流"、211 高校	4
5	南京大学	"双一流"、985 和 211 高校	3
6	浙江大学	"双一流"、985 和 211 高校	3
7	吉林大学	"双一流"、985 和 211 高校	3
8	西安外国语大学	普通高校	3
9	重庆邮电大学	普通高校	3
10	鲁东大学	普通高校	3

如表4所示，2006至2021年间有关二语写作研究立项数目最多的是东北师范大学，六项；其次是山东大学，五项；再次是华中科技大学和华中师范大学，均为四项。在前10名中，有七所大学均是国家"双一流"建设高校（其中五所既是985又是211高校），其他三所为普通高校。这说明重点大学拥有更雄厚的师资力量、更优秀的学术氛围、更强大的科研实力，是国家科研项目研究的主力。此外，在高等院校类属方面，综合性大学、师范类和语言类高校在二语写作研究立项方面显现出优势。

3.4.2 承办单位地区分布

不同于上文的性质划分，作者尝试按照七大地理区域（见表5）分布对立项高校进一步划分，并统计每个区域的立项数目，所得结果如下：

表5 承办单位及区域立项数分布

区域	承办单位数（百分比）	区域立项数（百分比）
华东地区	30（44.1%）	45（42.1%）
华中地区	9（13.2%）	17（15.9%）
东北地区	5（7.4%）	12（11.2%）
华北地区	8（11.8%）	9（8.4%）
西南地区	6（8.8%）	9（8.4%）
西北地区	5（7.4%)	8（7.5%）
华南地区	5（7.4%）	7（6.5%）

如表5所示，不同地区的承担单位数和立项数分布有很大不同。在这七大地理区域中，华东地区作为人口和高等院校密集地，占据地理、经济等优势，无论是涉及的高校和研究机构数还是立项数都远远领先于其他地区，分别占总数的44.1%和42.1%。其中山东省、上海市和江苏省表现突出，立项数分别为13、12、10项。

这三个省市中任一省的立项数都超过了华北地区、西南地区、西北地区和华南地区，足以体现他们强大的科研实力和蓬勃的科研活力。然而，与上海同为高等教育中心的北京，纵有10余所"双一流"、985或211高校，经济发达，但仅有三个立项。华中地区和东北地区的立项形势良好，分别立项17项和12项。而经济和教育一直相对落后的西北地区，立项数却能高于华南地区。这说明，初步了解华东、华中和东北这三个区域的二语写作研究成果，就基本掌握了国内二语写作研究的发展动态。

3.5　项目研究内容分布

3.5.1　二语写作项目的标题分析

本研究借鉴了王文宇和王立非（2004）、刘弘和凌雯怡（2012）对于国内二语写作研究内容的划分，将二语写作立项课题按研究内容分为写作测评、写作教学、写作过程、写作文本、写作影响因素、论文写作、写作思维、写作理论和其他九大类。

表6　项目内容分布

主要类型	子类	项目数	占比
写作测评	写作能力评估；写作中心构建评估；评估模型构建；写作测评方式	24	22.6%
写作教学	教学模式；课堂教学策略；教材；教学活动设计；教师和同伴评改、反馈等	22	20.8%
写作过程	学习者写作策略和技巧；学习者写作能力过程发展；写作动态系统发展及发展模型	16	15.1%
写作文本	错误分析、修辞分析、对比分析等；语篇特点；写作体裁	15	15.0%
写作影响因素	影响学生及写作能力的内外因素	12	14.2%
论文写作	英语论文的写作与发表；论文的写作特征、模式、质量研究等	8	7.5%
写作思维	写作认知和思维研究	5	4.7%
写作理论	基于语言学、心理学等理论基础的写作研究	2	1.9%
其他	与二语写作相关但重点不同的研究	2	1.9%

如表6所示，2006至2021年我国两大基金关于二语写作研究内容主要集中于写作测评和写作教学上，且两者占比总和接近50%；其次是写作过程、写作文本和写作影响因素，所占比例皆在10%以上；有关论文写作、写作思维和写作理论的立项较少。与立项数占比排名后三位相比，前五位研究内容的子类更为多元和细化，每一个子类基本都有相对应的立项课题。由此可见，前五项不仅在立项数目上占有优势，在立项课题涉及点上也比较广泛和全面。

3.5.2 立项热点分析

借助词频软件，本研究对立项标题中关键词的频次进行了统计。由于关键词较多，限于篇幅，本文仅就两类国家级项目中排名各前10位的关键词进行对比分析，结果如表7所示。

表7　二语写作国家社科基金和教育部人文社科项目关键词词频统计结果

国家社科基金			教育部人文社科基金		
排名	关键词	频次	排名	关键词	频次
1	学术英语	9	1	语料库	9
2	写作能力发展	7	2	评价	9
3	反馈	4	3	学术英语	8
4	学术论文写作	3	4	等级量表	6
5	写作教学	3	5	写作过程	4
6	语篇	2	6	写作能力发展	4
7	隐喻	2	7	反馈	3
8	跨文化修辞	2	8	二语产出	3
9	测试效度	2	9	大学英语写作	3
10	本土化	2	10	语篇	3

由表7可知，国家社科基金和教育部人文社科基金项目都关注的热点包括"学术英语""写作能力发展""反馈""语篇"等。其中国家社科基金还聚焦"学术论文写作""写作教学""隐喻""跨文化修辞""测试效度"和"本土化"，教育部人文社科项目更侧重于"评价""等级量表""写作过程""二语产出"和"大学英语写作"等主题。

如表7所示，"学术英语"是一大热点，在两大项目关键词词频统计中均排名前三。十多年来，国家社科基金项目立项涉及学术英语多元互动反馈体系构建与应用、学术英语写作立场建构、学术英语写作合作式教学模式、学术写作中的思辨对比、学术写作能力发展、学术写作教学等方面。教育部人文社科基金项目的立项涉及学术英语写作深度学习环境分析、学术英语写作语料库建设、学术英语写作迁移现象、学术英语写作与批判性思维培养等方面。

"写作能力发展"作为两大项目都关注的热点之一，其研究体现在不同方面。例如，考察不同层级的学习者写作能力发展，如博士生、蒙英双语专业大学生等；分析其影响因素，如基于过程写作的档案袋评估、大学英语课堂协作写作、综合评价模型、系统互评模式、文本声音构建等；采用不同工具，如文本挖掘、历时语料库等；讨论不同体裁的写作能力，如议论文论证能力发展特征；开展写作能力的认知诊断评估等。

"反馈"也是两大基金的立项热点。现有立项中既考察了不同类型的反馈，如多元互动反馈、形成性评价反馈、在线反馈、同伴互评等，也有探析反馈机制、反馈效果与作用、反馈模式等研究。

"语料库"作为重要的研究工具成为一大研究热点，尤其体现在教育部人文社科基金立项中，涉及多个领域，如大学生书面语语言特征变化与应用、藏汉中学生英语书面语对比、英语写作教学体系、英语学习者写作能力发展、英语写作评价语言、抄袭行为和语言错误分析等。而在国家社科基金立项中主要体现于蒙英双语专业大学生英语写作能力发展研究。

"评价""评估"这组词反映了二语写作研究又一大热点。研究内容涵盖写作教学形成性评价反馈模式、英语写作能力的认知诊断评估、写作评价系统研究、自动评估模型构建、在线同伴英文作文评价量表、批判性思维评价效度、写作促学评价机制、高校写作中心构建与评估、语篇连贯性评价及写作评价语言研究等。

"等级量表"一词频繁出现在教育部人文社科基金立项项目中，涉及基于机器学习的写作自动评估模型构建、基于量表的大学英语写作促学评价机制、量表框架下高考英语综合写作效度验证、量表评价体系构建等。

此外，"写作过程""写作教学""语篇""测试效度""二语产出""隐喻"等出现频次较高的关键词都反映了二语写作近年来的热点。值得注意的是，"本土化"一词两次出现在国家社科基金立项名单中，其一是2017年重点项目"二语写作理论体系建构及本土化研究"，其二是2020年一般项目"外语教学中体裁理论的本土化研究"，还有2021年基于王初明教授"续论"立项的"读后续写在我国高考英语中的应用研究"，这些反映了国内学者开始重视国内二语写作研究理论建构及其实际应用。

4. 二语写作研究项目总结和发展趋势

本研究从五大方面统计分析了2006至2021年45项国家社科基金和61项教育部人文社科基金的二语写作研究项目的标题特点，描述和总结了国内二语写作研究的发展现状及未来发展趋势。

4.1 立项数目整体呈上升趋势，但发展不稳定

从立项数来看，合计立项数基本呈稳步上升趋势，但在2012和2016年出现了两次"倒退"现象，后者尤为明显。在经历了多年（除2012年）的稳定增长后，国家社科基金立项数在2021年达到峰值，教育部人文社科基金在2015年达到峰值却在下一年骤降，退回到几年前的发展情况，但之后数据回暖，发展态势良好，在2019年达到历史最高值。该结果表明，随着我国的经济和科技发展水平不断提高，教育水平和科研实力也逐步增强，呈现繁荣发展的景象。两大基金自设立以来，资助力度逐渐加大，规模不断扩大，研究成果数量不断增加，质量也稳步提高。但二语写作研究项目增长幅度并不明显，且波动幅度较大。因此，高校应该不断培养和提升科研人员实力，高校老师应该与时俱进，响应国家战略，把握学科发展动态，了解其发展现状，符合其建设需求，力求实现科研突破。

4.2 立项类别分布不均

从立项类别看，国家社科基金立项数差别悬殊，一般项目占绝对优势，是其他几类立项数总和的四倍；重大项目和后期资助项目自国家社科基金设立以来没有实现破零的进展，发展停滞；西部项目自 2009 年后也再无进展；2017 年重点项目和自筹基金项目实现从无到有的突破。重大项目立项的空缺反映出二语写作研究在重大理论和联系现实问题方面的不足。项目负责人的职称分布情况也展现出青年学者在二语写作研究项目立项中处于弱势。相比之下，教育部基金立项数相对均衡。虽然规划基金项目仍具有明显优势，但青年基金项目发展势头强劲，基本上在每年立项中都占有一定比例，并逐年增加，到 2020 年达到峰值。近年来国家虽在各类项目上加大资助力度，增加立项数量，但从两大基金的整体来看，有关二语写作研究的青年立项仍旧不理想，这无疑给青年教师及博士等科研工作者施加了极大的科研压力。因此，应该合理优化各类立项结构，通过加强年轻人员与权威学者的沟通和交流，提升青年研究者科研实力，为国家注入源源不断的科研活力。

4.3 地域立项差距明显

从地域来看，在有关二语写作研究的立项中，仅华东地区就占比近半，为科研主力。究其原因，该地区内山东省、浙江省等都是教育和人口大省，高校林立、地理位置优越、经济发达，为科研创新和进步提供了良好的发展条件。此外，华中和东北地区立项数也较为可观。然而，首都北京所在的华北地区立项数不高，经济发达的华南地区立项数却不如地理和经济等都不占优势的西南和西北地区。因此，各地区间应加强沟通与合作，及时交流科研成果，把握学科最新发展动向，提升二语写作研究的重视度和普及度。可采用"以强带弱"模式，即具有地理、经济、科技等优势的地区，在保证自身平稳较快发展、不断创造出优秀的科研成果的同时，努力带动西部等较不发达地区进行科研建设和创新，推动二语写作研究的协调和长足发展。

4.4 研究侧重点不同，理论研究偏少

通过对课题研究内容进行分类，我们发现二语写作研究立项课题的研究重点各异，且占比差距较大。写作测评与写作教学是主要立项研究内容，对它们的子类研究也比较广泛和全面，未来研究可以关注二语写作在现实生活中的引领和示范作用，注重解决实际问题。研究热点涉及学术英语、写作能力发展、反馈、语料库方法、写作评价、等级量表等方面，研究者应加大关注力度。研究对象多元化，既包括中学生、大学生、硕士、博士等不同水平的学生，又包括汉族、藏族、蒙古族等不同民族学生，未来研究可以关注低龄儿童、失语症患者等不同群体。研究方法倾向于使用"数据库""资源库"等进行多维动态的历时追踪研究，此外还可以借鉴其他学科的先进研究方法，如眼动跟踪、人种志等方法。尽管现有立项中涉及从不同理论视角来探讨二语写作问题，如跨文化修辞、积极心理学、体裁理论、图尔敏理论、动态系统理论、自我调节理论、社会文化理论、潜伏语义分析理论、向心理论

等，但有关本土化写作理论构建的研究较少。理论构建起一个学科的整体框架，指导整个学科的发展。未来国内二语写作研究者既要大力借鉴国外先进理论，开展跨学科的理论实践，也要将理论应用与国内研究实际问题相结合，从而不断修正或创新理论，还要结合本土二语写作研究积极创建本土化的理论体系。

5. 结语

本文统计了2006至2021年国家社科基金和教育部人文社科基金关于二语写作研究的立项数据，从立项数年度分布、项目类别、项目负责人职务、承办单位性质及地区分布和项目内容及热点分析五大方面深入探究了二语写作研究的发展趋势和研究现状，发现存在项目类别分布不均、地域差距明显、理论研究过少等问题。这说明国内的二语写作研究发展较晚，在研究内容、研究方法和理论体系等方面发展不够成熟。本文针对性地提出了改善建议，以期有助于二语写作研究者进一步提高项目数量和质量，创造出更优秀的研究成果。

参考文献

贺显斌，2006，国家社科基金1993—2004年外语研究立项分析[J]，《现代外语》（2）：193-196。

康勇、葛明贵，2018，从课题立项看我国语言学研究趋势与热点——基于国家社科、全国教育科学规划、教育部人文社科基金（2013—2017年）的历时统计分析[J]，《安徽理工大学学报：社会科学版》（2）：77-82。

刘弘、凌雯怡，2012，国内外二语写作研究现状与特点的比较研究[J]，《云南师范大学学报（对外汉语教学与研究版）》（3）：29-40。

刘泽权、朱利利，2018，国家社科基金2013—2017年语言、文学类项目立项现状与态势[J]，《西安外国语大学学报》（4）：21-26。

苏红，2018，语言学国家社科基金项目（1991—2016）研究动态分析[J]，《外语研究》（1）：33-38。

苏新春、刘锐，2015，国家社科基金语言学立项课题分析[J]，《新疆师范大学学报（哲学社会科学版）》（3）：118-123。

王俊菊，2013，国内二语写作过程研究的现状剖析[J]，《山东外语教学》（5）：7-11。

王文宇、王立非，2004，二语写作研究：十年回顾与展望[J]，《外语界》（3）：51-58。

王立非、江进林，2011，"十一五"期间国家社科基金外国语言学立项热点及分布分析[J]，《外语教学与研究》（5）：772-779。

吴珊，2012，中国语言学研究现状及发展趋势——近十年（2001—2010）国家社科基金资助项目的统计分析[J]，《北京航空航天大学学报》（1）：93-97。

吴进善，2015，国家社科基金外国语言学课题立项情况历时统计分析[J]，《哈尔滨学院学报》（2）：102-106。

作者简介：

周杰，湖南工业大学外国语学院，讲师，山东大学外国语学院博士生。主要研究领域：语言习得、二语写作。电子邮箱：zjliz2001@163.com

注释文献

二语写作书目（2021）

1. **曹春玲，2021，《全人教育日语写作技巧与实践》[M]。武汉：华中科技大学出版社。**

本书编写的宗旨是提高学生及读者的日语写作技巧和实践能力。本书主要以国内日语专业四级考试为基础设定，包括日语原稿用纸的横向和纵向的使用方法与实践、日语写作的六大顺序、日语的礼貌文体和文章文体的理论与实践、日语原文范文分析与欣赏等。教学方法是先读解范文文本，再进行写作。本书文本内容表达自然流畅，充分体现了用日语写作身边事的真实感。

2. **邓鹏鸣、肖亮，2021，《体裁与二语写作研究》[M]。北京：外语教学与研究出版社。**

本书共分五个章节。第一章主要描述了三十年来国内外体裁与二语写作研究概貌。第二章对国内外体裁与二语写作研究的理论进行了回顾与评析，系统介绍了体裁理论的主要学术流派，并对体裁知识、体裁意识、体裁能力及二语体裁写作教学法相关理论予以阐述。第三章对国内外体裁与二语写作实证研究进行了回顾与评析。第四章描述了体裁与二语写作研究中常用的研究方法，如个案研究法、访谈法、观察法、问卷调查法、测试法、语料库研究方法等。第五章归纳整合了体裁与二语写作研究的焦点，指出了该研究领域的发展趋势，并针对体裁与二语写作研究发展趋势提供了选题建议，以期对该领域的未来研究带来启发。

3. **郭书彩，2021，《基于语料库的中国大学生英语议论文中动名词搭配研究》[M]。北京：外语教学与研究出版社。**

本书着重研究学习者对限制性搭配（restricted collocations）的使用。限制性搭配是 Howarth（1996）提出的搭配连续体的四个类别之一，其他三个类别分别是自由组合、比喻性习语和纯习语。该书有两个主要研究目的：一是尽可能完整、准确地呈现学习者在英语书面语中动名词搭配的使用情况；二是探究学习者动名词搭配的使用是否以及在何种程度上与四个语言因素相关。这四个语言因素分别为搭配的限制程度、搭配在学习者母语（即汉语）与英语中的一致性、搭配中虚化动词的使用以及搭配在英语本族语者语言中的出现频率。

4. **刘东虹，2021，《中英议论文体的语篇修辞性研究》[M]。北京：光明日报出版社。**

本书的首要特点是将写作修辞学理论与实证研究相结合。每章介绍不同的写作修辞学理论，并呈现以该理论为框架的实证研究。其次，本书对写作修辞学理论进行了系统、详细的介绍和探究，对于被误读的理论进行了理性分析和澄清。此外，本书中的实证研究视角新颖，不再局限于英语写作教学法和作文反馈方式的研究，而是聚焦语篇本体，从写作修辞学的各种角度进行调查分析。

5. 刘秋成，2021，《高校英语写作中的声音构建研究》[M]。长春：吉林大学出版社。

探讨英语学习者的声音构建及其如何实现自我构建，能够揭示学习者在学习写作过程中的发展变化，促使其成为有自我的学习者和写作者，从而构建一个清晰有力的个人声音去感染读者和听众，最终赢得同行的认同和支持，达到自我宣传和推销的效果。本书综合对话理论、语言学、文学批评和外语教学理论，通过考察声音构建的特点和语言因素，结合中国大学生英语写作中声音缺失的原因，从语用策略、文化传统和学科规范等方面提出了声音构建的策略。

6. 任凤雷，2021，《学习者因素和外语写作过程研究》[M]。芜湖：安徽师范大学出版社。

本书重点研究外语写作的构成及学习者写作动机和写作策略在外语写作过程中的影响。本书分为两大部分：写作动机研究和写作策略研究，探讨这两个因素对于外语写作过程的影响，以及对于外语写作教学的意义。作者认为，外语写作动机从写作努力程度、写作态度和投入程度方面影响写作者的行为；而写作策略可以协调各种影响写作过程的因素，比如写作动机、写作环境、任务难度、情感因素和外语写作水平等，提高外语写作效率和写作效果。

7. 孙莉，2021，《学术写作中的身份元话语研究》[M]。南京：南京大学出版社。

学术英语写作中的作者身份成为近年来学界研究的热点话题之一。本书通过与国际期刊作者的论文进行对比，在语用身份理论视角下考察中国硕、博士研究生在学术英语写作中身份元话语的使用及其身份建构特征，旨在揭示中国英语学习者的学术语用能力状况。本书的研究背景涉及三个方面：学术英语写作中作者身份研究的必要性，学术英语写作中元话语与身份建构的相关性以及二语写作中元话语使用及其身份建构与学术语用能力的关系。

8. 张允，2021，《英语教师写作书面反馈能力测评研究》[M]。天津：南开大学出版社。

本书以职前高中英语教师为测试开发对象，探讨如何有效测量其英语写作书面反馈能力，设计并完善相关测试任务及评分方案。本书主要内容包括：我国基础阶段英语教师队伍的现状、中小学教师资格定期注册制度、教师书面反馈在二语写作教学中的作用、基于问题的职业资格测试开发模型、二语教师提供写作书面反馈时应完成的关键任务、测试任务设计方案及相关要求、评分方案的设计与完善等。

9. 周开林、王曦、郑燕飞，2021，《医学英语论文摘要写作》[M]。北京：对外经贸大学出版社。

　　本书针对中国学生医学英文摘要撰写过程中存在的问题予以指导，提高其英文摘要的质量，进而提高文章被检索和录用的概率。本书先从摘要的定义和作用方面进行了概述，举例介绍了医学论文英文摘要主要分类和写作的雷区，提炼了高质量摘要的特征；然后结合众多实例介绍了医学论文英文摘要正文的写作要求，重点介绍了结构式摘要每部分包含的要素，同时比较了中外医学英语摘要的特点，阐述了中外医学英语摘要在用词和句式表达方面的异同。

二语写作期刊文章（2021）

1. **李晓红，2021，学术英语写作中短语框架的功能特征——基于中英博士论文引言语料库的对比研究[J]，《外语电化教学》（1）：98-104+16。**

　　本文基于中英博士论文引言语料库，从功能层面探讨中国英语语言学专业博士论文引言中短语框架的使用特征。研究发现，语篇功能短语框架的大量使用受制于高度规约化的引言结构；指示功能短语框架中，评述文献类框架常用于评价以往研究一致趋同的局限性并引出作者的单声评价；立场功能短语框架缺乏表达不同命题态度的多样化型式。笔者认为，在高水平学习者的英语学术写作教学中，应注重如何运用丰富的短语框架有效地发表学术声音和准确地传递认知立场。

2. **陈丹丹，2021，动态评价视角下网络同伴互评对英语写作质量的影响[J]，《外语电化教学》（1）：17-23+3。**

　　该研究基于动态评价理论开展为期12周的教学实验，开发写作学生评价表并借助线上平台开展写作同伴互评活动，重点探讨同伴互评在大学英语写作动态评价中对写作质量的影响。衡量本研究写作质量的维度为教师基于文本按照评分要求的主观评判——写作成绩，以及借助文本分析工具Coh-Metrix 3.0展开对文本本身的探究。在学生写作成绩上，该研究通过前测和后测比较实验班和对照班组间和组内的成绩差异，发现对照班和实验班写作后测成绩有显著差异，实验班成绩得到更为显著的提升；运用Coh-Metrix文本分析工具量化文本质量，重点探究影响议论文写作质量的四个文本特征：易读性、词频、连贯性和句长，结果发现同伴互评可显著影响文本的词频和句长维度。

3. **关成勇、郭万群，2021，混合式教学环境下基于POA的英语应用文写作多元评价辩证研究[J]，《外语电化教学》（2）：30-36+5。**

　　该研究采用辩证研究范式，以问卷调查、文本分析、课堂观察、在线测试等为研究工具和方法，以产出导向法为教学理念，以线上线下混合式教学为环境，旨在构建、实践并完善英语应用文写作多元评价理论框架。研究发现：（1）多元化的主体应以师生主体为主、机器主体为辅；（2）多数评价方式应遵循"逐级提示"策略，包括师生合作评价、在线测试、驱动问答点评、促成问答点评、教师随机指导、教师集中讲评等；（3）不同的评价方式实现不同的评价目的，包括"以评促学""以评为学"和"以评促教"；（4）多元评价能有效提升学生的参与度与获得感，促进"以评促学""以评为学"和"评学融合"；同时，多元评价也促使教师反思改进，促进"以评促教"和"评教融合"。

4. 屈琼、刘媛媛、兰宁艺，2021，国内二语写作反馈研究现状与趋势的可视化分析[J]，《外语电化教学》(3)：37-43+6。

　　本文以国内1992—2020年间中国知网数据库中有关二语写作反馈研究的中文期刊文献为数据来源，利用文献计量分析法梳理国内二语写作反馈研究的基本情况，并运用CiteSpace信息可视化技术绘制二语写作反馈研究的相关科学知识图谱。研究结果表明，近年来国内二语写作反馈研究呈波动上升态势，仍有较大发展空间；研究的核心领域主要包括同伴反馈、写作过程、写作能力、教师反馈以及任务难度等；新兴研究热点主要集中在基于网络平台的二语写作反馈与多元反馈研究上。

5. 肖平飞、刘欣婷，2021，直接聚焦与直接非聚焦书面纠正性反馈对英语写作介词习得的影响研究[J]，《外语电化教学》(3)：44-49+7。

　　本文主要探讨直接聚焦和直接非聚焦书面纠正性反馈以及元语言解释能否提高学生英语写作中介词运用的准确性。实验结果表明，直接聚焦与直接非聚焦书面纠正性反馈都有助于学生在英语写作中有效地习得英语介词。在即时后测中，直接聚焦反馈效果优于直接非聚焦反馈；在延时后测中，直接非聚焦反馈效果优于直接聚焦反馈；元语言解释对学习者英语介词的习得也具有一定的积极影响。此外，英语学习者语言水平的差异对目标结构效果也具有一定的影响。

6. 许宏、付钰，2021，写作模糊综合评价研究——以全国高校俄语专业八级水平测试为例[J]，《外语电化教学》(3)：70-75+11。

　　写作评价具有较强的主观性和模糊性，如何保证评分结果一致且可靠始终是高风险语言测试亟须解决的难题。本文基于对现行写作评分方法的分析，主张运用模糊综合评价法对写作评分标准进行量化处理，并以全国高校俄语专业八级水平考试为例构建写作质量评估的模糊数学模型，分析该模型的优缺点，以期提供一套更加科学、客观、准确、全面的评分方法。

7. 徐翠芹，2021，写作停顿视角下的中国英语学习者记叙文和议论文写作认知加工过程研究[J]，《外语教学》(1)：35-40。

　　写作停顿是观察二语写作认知活动动态交替的窗口。本研究采用Inputlog7.0记录南京大学60名本科二年级学生的英语记叙文和议论文写作过程，并将写作过程划分为10个相等时段，通过各时段停顿频次和停顿时长的变化来考察体裁因素对二语写作认知加工过程的影响。研究发现，学习者在记叙文和议论文写作初始阶段均表现出频次低、时间长的构思停顿，说明初始阶段是学生进行内容检索规划的认知加工过程；但记叙文初始阶段冗长，表明学习者在记叙文写作初期的构思障碍。随着写作进一步展开，记叙文写作集中出现频次高、时间短的撰写停顿，体现为语言匹配内容的语言加工过程；而议论文写作中的停顿频次和停顿时长则显著变化，体现出撰写停顿和规划停顿的交叉，表明议论文产出过程中内容检索规划和语言匹配内容的双重加工过程。结合访谈数据，本文进一步考察了写作停顿凸显的二语写作问题和二语写作过程管理，以期反馈二语写作教学。

8. 朱慧敏、杨连瑞、刘艳梅，2021，二语写作句法动态发展变异特征研究[J]，《外语教学》（1）：41-46+65。

本文基于动态系统理论及可视化数据分析技术，追踪研究了两位初始水平相当的非英语专业大学生在两个学年内产出的议论文，考察个体内不同句法指标动态发展变异特征和个体间的差异性。研究结果显示：两位学习者基于 T 单位的句法指标——平均长度、从属子句数量、复杂名词性短语数量整体呈上升趋势，具有非线性及变异性发展特征；学习者个体内三个句法指标变异度和变化点存在非同步性，个体间句法指标的发展模式及变异特征同中有异；呈显著性变异和分段显著发展的句法指标均有质的提高。研究结果验证了变异性能够有效促进二语写作发展。

9. 李梦骁、韩忠军，2021，中外学者期刊论文评价性词汇使用的对比研究[J]，《外语教学》（2）：29-34。

基于 Martin 和 White 的评价理论，本研究对比了中外学者在期刊论文讨论部分使用态度评价、介入评价、级差评价的异同。研究发现：与本族语学者相比，在使用数量上，中国学者过低使用态度评价、接纳评价和级差评价；在使用规律上，中国学者使用三类评价性词汇的形式变化都明显少于本族语学者。上述情况可能会在一定程度上影响传情达意的充分性，阻碍学术语篇之间互动性，损害修饰命题的适切性。

10. 初萌、王丽萍、吴红云，2021，硕士研究生学术英语写作文献知识的实证研究[J]，《外语教学》（2）：60-63。

本研究基于问卷调查，分析了 309 名英语专业和非英语专业研究生基于文献阅读的英语学术论文写作方面的知识。研究发现：（1）两类学习者对文献选取、阅读与引用知识的掌握情况均有较高的自我评价；（2）英语专业研究生对文献引用知识的了解情况更好，而非英语专业研究生对文献阅读知识的了解情况更好，且他们的文献选取知识显著强于英语专业研究生；（3）高年级研究生的文献阅读和引用知识显著强于低年级研究生；（4）两类学习者均缺乏文献引用策略知识，且均需加强文献引用过程中的读者意识。

11. 赵小东、邓耀臣，2021，中国英语学习者写作中联加状语使用型式研究[J]，《外语教学》（2）：64-69。

本研究采用语料库方法，以系统功能语法为理论框架，从主、述位结构视角分析中国英语学习者写作中联加状语（linking adverbial，LA）使用型式。结果发现，中国英语学习者主位结构中使用的LA显著多于英语本族语者，但在主语后、动词之间、动词与其他成分之间等述位结构中却明显少于后者。此外，中国英语学习者使用的LA呈现位置"偏好"特征，倾向于在多重主位结构中较多使用转折类、因/果类LA与连词、评述状语及联加状语连用情形；除添加类外，中国英语学习者使用的其他三大类LA频率从主位到述位基本呈L形曲线分布，述位位置变化小，多样性低。中国英语学习者写作中高频LA（除also和then外）也呈类似L型线分布趋势。

12. **何莲珍、阮吉飞、闵尚超，2021，基于文本特征的校本写作考试与《中国英语能力等级量表》对接效度研究[J]，《外语教学》（3）：52-57。**

本研究以某高校校本英语考试为研究对象，采用分析性判断法作为标准设定方法，建立校本考试与《中国英语能力等级量表》之间的对接关系。结果表明，该校的英语水平考试写作卷及格线对应量表5级，符合考试定位。外部效度验证结果表明：总体而言，对应的量表级别越高，文章长度越长，词汇更加丰富多样，句法更加复杂，但与语篇连贯性无直接关系。本研究是校本考试对接量表的一次有益探索，为对标研究提供方法参考，对于量表的修订完善具有一定的借鉴意义。

13. **陈静、陈吉颖、郭凯，2021，混合式学术英语写作课堂中的学习投入研究[J]，《外语界》（2）：28-36。**

混合式学习是线下学习与线上学习相结合的新型学习模式。本研究采用个案研究方法，通过课堂观察、文本分析及半结构化访谈探究了7名中国大学生在混合式学术英语写作课堂中的行为、认知、情感投入的特点与影响因素，发现学生在混合式学习过程中展现出多样的行为投入、深入的认知投入和客观的情感投入，学习投入受到个体因素和环境因素的共同影响。研究为混合式外语学习的教学设计与课堂实施提供了可行性建议，以期促进混合式学习在我国外语教学情境中的有效应用。

14. **高霞，2021，不同水平学习者英语作文句法复杂度研究[J]，《外语教学与研究》（2）：224-237+319**

本研究采用TAASSC工具自动标注并提取不同水平学习者英语作文的三类句法复杂度参数，对比和分析宏观句法层面、微观从句和短语层面复杂度参数与作文等级的关系。研究发现，三类参数是同一语言维度的不同侧面，含三类指标的回归方程的作文等级解释力最强。从句和短语复杂度参数加强了宏观句法复杂度指标的预测力，为不同等级作文的区别性句法特征描述提供了有效补充。传统的从句复杂度指标并非作文质量的有效预测指标。这些发现为EFL学习者语言复杂度评价和发展描述提供了重要参照，对二语习得理论、外语教学和测试有一定启示。

15. **高霞，2021，中国学者英文学术论文中的非正式语体特征研究[J]，《外语与外语教学》（2）：92-102+150。**

　　基于中西学者学术论文可比语料库和中国学者学术论文历时语料库，本研究对比分析了中西学者间和中国学者不同历史时期论文中非正式语体特征使用的异同。研究结果显示，中西学者论文中高频使用的非正式语体特征相似，均为第一人称代词、指示代词和句首连词/连接副词。中国人文社科学者论文中非正式语体特征使用频数显著低于西方学者，中西方理工科学者非正式语体特征使用无显著差异。同时，近20年间中国学者论文中非正式语体特征使用频数显著增加，尤其是理工科学者。这或许表明中国学者对非正式语体特征的使用态度日趋宽容，但与西方学者相比，仍趋于谨慎。

16. **朱慧敏，2021，二语书面语句法发展及其动态增长模型建构研究[J]，《外语与外语教学》（2）：103-114+150。**

　　句法是二语书面语研究的重要维度。目前，对其内部指标动态发展进行历时个案研究并尝试动态建模的还很欠缺。本文以动态系统理论为框架，借助L2SCA和CPA，采用移动极值图、移动相关系数图、动态建模等可视化数据分析手段，辅以回溯访谈，追踪2名英语专业学生4个学期的议论文，考察二语书面语句法子系统内平均T单位长度、从句与T单位比、复杂名词性短语与T单位比个指标的发展轨迹并拟合动态增长模型。研究发现：这三个指标均具变异性、交互性、非线性和不可预测性发展特征，表现为支持、竞争、波动和高度协同，且存在个体差异；变点分析显示，不同学习者的不同指标分阶段显著发展；动态增长模型进一步检验了观测值发展趋势，求解了时间序列指标的增长率，科学预测了学习者在理想条件下最大发展潜力。

17. **韩晔、杨鲁新，2021，硕士生对多稿多轮同伴反馈认知投入的个案研究[J]，《外语与外语教学》（3）：92-101+150。**

　　国内同伴反馈实证研究主要检验同伴反馈的效果，但学生作为接收者对同伴反馈的投入情况仍不清楚。本研究采用个案研究法，追踪了一组（三名）非英语专业硕士生在同一写作任务的三轮同伴反馈中的认知投入。研究发现，学生对同伴反馈的理解程度有所加深但仍然不足。学生对元认知策略与认知策略的使用情况在共时、历时维度上都呈现出鲜明个体差异。本研究发现可为推进同伴反馈作用机制研究提供参考。

18. **靳红玉、王同顺，2021，任务复杂度、工作记忆容量与二语写作表现——学习者能动性的作用[J]，《外语与外语教学》（3）：102-113+150。**

　　任务复杂度是贯彻任务型教学"聚焦于形"原则的重要考量因素。本研究采用阐释性顺序设计方案，探究了任务复杂度、工作记忆容量对二语写作表现的影响，以及学习者能动性的作用。量化考察结果显示，任务复杂度和工作记忆容量对被试语言表现的复杂度和准确度均有显著主效应，但不存在显著交互效应。质化研究发现，受外在动机驱使，低工作记忆容量被试采取多种策略对复杂任务进行了改编，导致任务复杂度两个水平在工作记忆容量两个水平上的语言表现差异不显著。因此，任务设计须兼顾认知和社会因素，以实现"聚焦于形"的最大化。

English Abstracts

Icy LEE The Chinese University of Hong Kong, China

Abstract: Recent years have witnessed the emergence of blogs as a tool for promoting second language (L2) teachers' development. However, the majority of studies have addressed the pre-service rather than in-service context. The study reported in this paper aims to examine the use of blogging in an in-service teacher education programme in Hong Kong, China. Drawing upon data gathered from blog entries and comments as well as written self-reflections by 20 novice EFL teachers, this study investigates the extent of the teachers' participation in the class blog, the focuses of their blog entries and comments, as well as their perspectives on the benefits and problems of blogging. The paper concludes that blogging can enhance collaborative learning, promote professional exchange and serve as a multi-purpose tool that facilitates novice EFL teachers' professional development.

Keywords: blogging; in-service teacher; teacher education

Neomy STORCH University of Melbourne, Australia

Abstract: In this paper, I focus on learner agency in two activities associated with feedback on L2 writing: learners' engagement with and response to teacher feedback and learners' stances as givers or receivers of feedback in peer response activities. This paper begins by discussing what agency means and its key attributes. Adopting an activity theory perspective, I show how these attributes can be mapped onto a model of activity. Then, drawing on a number of studies that I and my colleagues have conducted with English language learners, I interpret the salient learner behavior observed in these studies using the construct of learner agency. Using activity theory I highlight the individual and contextual factors that could explain these observed behaviors. I conclude by suggesting some strategies that could encourage learners to take a more active role in feedback activities and call on teachers to reflect on their practices in order to promote learner agency in L2 feedback activities.

Keywords: feedback; learner agency; L2 writing; enactment

Hani ALBELIHI Qassim University, Saudi Arabia
Ge LAN City University of Hong Kong, China

Abstract: This corpus-based study sought to investigate the association between noun phrase complexity and language background in the introductory sections of English dissertations written by L1 English and L1 Arabic doctoral students. A corpus was built based on 100 dissertations, including 50 dissertations for each group. Based on the index of writing complexity features in Biber et al. (2011), 11 noun modifiers were extracted to represent noun phrase complexity in the writings of the two groups. A Chi-square test and residual analysis were then applied to explore how language background influenced the 11 noun modifiers. The results show that language background largely influences four specific noun modifiers: premodifying nouns, PPs (other), prepositions followed by -ing clauses, and infinitive clauses. More specifically, the L1 students used premodifying nouns more frequently to construct compressed noun phrases in their dissertations, whereas the L2 students produced more diverse patterns of noun phrases based on prepositional phrases (other), prepositions followed by -ing clauses, and infinitive clauses. Finally, pedagogical implications are provided, such as the suggestion that online corpora be used to teach noun phrases in graduate writing classrooms.

Keywords: corpus analysis; academic writing; grammatical complexity; noun phrases; second language writing

Ye LIU Qilu Normal University
Jihua DONG Shandong University

Abstract: Based on the self-built corpora consisting of research articles in linguistics and engineering, this paper examines the disciplinary differences in stance markers from the following three aspects, namely epistemic stance, attitudinal stance and authorial presence. It is found that writers of both engineering and linguistics have the tendency to establish an authoritative identity, but there are significant differences in the specific stance expressions used. This study is conducive to an in-depth understanding of the characteristics and conventions on how interdisciplinary authors construct academic discourse and convey knowledge. This study can help researchers master the disciplinary conventions in constructing academic stance and establish rapport with the expected readers. It can also provide empirical reference for the content design, curriculum organization and classroom activities related to academic English writing and other courses.

Keywords: academic discourse; stance construction; disciplinary variation

Yingliang LIU Wuhan University of Technology
Yi WEI Xiantao Middle School of Hubei Province

Abstract: As a common way of citing sources, reporting verbs are used to report others' opinions and express authors' attitudes and stance in academic writing. The paper examines the use of reporting verbs in Chinese students' MA theses by comparing with published journal articles. It was found that compared to journal article authors, Chinese students used a limited number of reporting verbs, overused Think verbs, and misused some negative verbs (e.g., claim, believe). The study reveals the features of reporting verbs used by L2 learners and pedagogical implications are provided.

Keywords: academic writing; reporting verbs; corpus; stance

Wansuo YU Taiyuan University of Technology
Yuan HAO Taiyuan University of Technology

Abstract: Reporting character speeches is one of the important devices employed in the characterization of the character narrative discourse. However, few studies have been undertaken on the use of speech-reporting chunks which are utilized to introduce what characters say. The present study explored the differences in the complexities of speech-reporting chunks occurring in the character narrative discourses produced by in-school senior English majors by means of contrasting speech-reporting chunks retrieved from the self-constructed corpus of SEM (senior English majors) character narratives with those from the ACS (American college students) equivalents. The present study also conducted interviews with student writers to find out the underlying reasons for the differences. The results indicate: (1) Chinese senior English majors are apt to use high-frequency head words in their speech-reporting chunks. Their total number of speech-reporting chunks is substantially smaller than that of American college students although they have developed an awareness of using various categories of speech-reporting chunks. In addition, the most difficult words in their speech-reporting chunks are mostly high-frequency ones. (2) Senior English majors tend to use a great number of shorter-length speech-reporting chunks, comparatively invariant in structure and variety, and also lacking in chunk diversity and complexity, than their American counterparts. These findings have some implications for the teaching of the use of speech-reporting chunks in the character narrative writing.

Keywords: senior English majors; character narrative discourse; speech-reporting chunks; chunk complexity

Ruiying NIU Guangdong University of Foreign Studies

Abstract: Writing English argumentative essays is a basic skill that English learners must master. This skill is mainly trained through instruction. The core of teaching argumentative writing is cultivating students' argumentation competence. Yet, both English native and English second language writers face the problem of argumentation inadequacy. This paper aims to find the solution to the problem from current research studies in the literature. For this purpose, this paper first defined argumentation and argumentation development, followed by introducing the theoretical perspectives on argumentation development research in writing. Then the current empirical studies on written argumentation development were reviewed. The review revealed that current studies had mainly taken the psycho-cognitive perspective, and examined the influence of teaching methods and writing strategy training, writing criteria, and student-dominant activities on students' written argumentation development, with positive results being obtained; only a limited number of studies took the sociocultural perspective and investigated the learning process; more studies had been conducted with English native learners than those with English as a second/foreign language learners; and classroom-based studies were particularly lacking. Facing this status quo, this paper points out the directions for future research on written argumentation development.

Keywords: English argumentative writing; argumentation; theoretical perspectives; research focuses; research directions

Yue CHEN Purdue University, USA

Abstract: After decades of development, L2W has become a thriving field of study in China, with many scholars publishing a good number of journal articles on this topic each year. By reviewing China's L2W articles published in major linguistics/foreign language journals between 1949 and 2019, this article identifies L2W's four developmental periods during these 70 years and nine major topics discussed in the literature. A total of 1,412 articles were reviewed and analyzed. These articles also demonstrated an increasing favor of empirical research over non-empirical research in recent years and a strong preference of undergraduate students as their discussion context.

Keywords: second language writing; numerical trend; major topics; research methods; contexts

Jie ZHOU Shandong University / Hunan University of Technology

Abstract: Aiming to understand the current situation of L2 writing research in China and to find the development trend of it, this paper conducts a statistical analysis of L2 writing research grants from 2006 to 2021 provided by National Social Science Fund and the Humanities and Social Sciences Fund of the Ministry of Education. The analysis was conducted from five aspects: annual number of projects, project categories, titles of project principal investigators (PI), regional distribution and project content. The results show that the research projects reviewed in this study have some problems, such as unstable increase in project numbers, uneven distribution of project categories, obvious regional disparity and unbalanced research content. The heated issues include academic English, writing ability development, feedback, corpus, evaluation, rating scale and so on. This paper offers suggestions on various problems and provides specific data support for future researchers, in order to promote the development of L2 writing research in China.

Keywords: National Social Science Fund; Humanities and Social Sciences Fund of the Ministry of Education; L2 writing research

征稿启事

　　《二语写作》是国内第一本关于二语写作教学与研究的学术集刊。由中国英汉语比较研究会写作教学与研究专业委员会主办，山东大学二语写作教学与研究中心承办，外语教学与研究出版社出版，编辑部设在山东大学外国语学院。本刊已被中国知网（CNKI）数据库收录。

一、办刊宗旨

　　《二语写作》重点探讨二语写作理论、写作修辞、写作教学、写作教师教育、写作测试、ESP/EAP 写作、机辅写作、技术与写作等相关领域的研究问题。本刊接受中、英文稿件，欢迎不同语境下的研究成果，除英语外，亦刊登非英语和对外汉语等领域的二语写作研究成果。本刊倡导理论创新，关注研究方法，强调学术的高度、深度和厚度，尤其注重跨学科视角下的研究与探讨，旨在为我国二语写作研究学者、教师和研究生提供学术交流的平台，推动我国二语写作教学与研究的发展。

二、重点栏目

　　本刊设有"理论视角""写作研究""写作教学""写作测评""跨学科研究""研究述评""新秀论坛""学术动态""新作评介"等重点栏目，真诚欢迎国内外专家、学者和广大外语教师及研究者赐稿，稿件语言中英文均可。

三、稿件要求与投稿说明

　　1. 来稿应具有科学性、原创性，论点鲜明、论据充分、数据准确、逻辑严谨、文字通顺、图表规范。每篇论文以 8000 字左右为宜，最多不超过 1 万字，中英文均可。

　　2. 来稿请详细注明作者简介、作者单位、地址、邮编、联系电话及电子邮箱。稿件不涉及保密问题，署名无争议，稿件一律文责自负，本刊有权对来稿做文字修改。

　　3. 本刊恕不退稿，请作者自留底稿，切勿一稿多投。

　　4. 请不要把稿件邮寄给个人，以免影响审稿和发表。

　　5.《二语写作》实行同行专家匿名审稿制度。审稿周期为三个月。三个月后，若没有收到编辑部反馈，作者可自行处理。

　　6.《二语写作》不收版面费。稿件发表后，赠送作者当期样刊两本。

四、投稿方式

　　投稿网址：https://eyxz.cbpt.cnki.net

五、联系方式

　　地址：山东省济南市洪家楼 5 号山东大学外国语学院《二语写作》编辑部
　　邮编：250100
　　电话：0531-88375183
　　QQ 群：232248241、976907510、222462129

Chinese Journal of Second Language Writing
Guide for Authors

The *Chinese Journal of Second Language Writing* is devoted to publishing reports of research and discussions that contribute to understanding of issues in second and foreign language writing and writing instruction. Areas of interest include L2 writing instruction, L2 writer development, features of L2 written texts, L2 writing processes, L2 writing teacher education and professional development, feedback and assessment, ESP/EAP writing, technology and writing, and any other topics closely relevant to L2 writing instruction and research. Review articles are considered for publication if they deal with critical issues in second and foreign language writing. Manuscripts should take care to emphasize the pedagogical implications of the work.

Before submitting your manuscript, make sure that your submission adheres to the author guidelines and follows the formatting instruction. Please pay particular attention to the reference section, the formatting of headings, tables, figures, and author's biography.

Formatting and references

1. Length

Manuscripts should be 8,000 to 10,000 words in English or Chinese, including references, tables, figures, notes, and appendices.

2. Headings

- *CJSLW* uses only three header levels. Format them as follows:

1. First Level Heading (Size 12, Boldface, First Letter Caps)
1.1 Second level heading (Size 10, Boldface)
1.1.1 Third level heading (Size 10, Italics)

3. Tables

- Please submit tables as editable text and not as images.
- Tables should be numbered consecutively with single numbers, e.g. Table 1, Table 2, Table 3 ...

4. Figures

- Figures should be numbered consecutively with single numbers, e.g. Figure 1, Figure 2, Figure 3 ...
- Both tables and figures should be referenced in text and be placed next to the relevant text.

5. Keywords

Up to 5 key words are required upon submission. Only abbreviations firmly established in the field should be included.

6. Acknowledgements

Please submit the acknowledgements after your paper is accepted.

7. Funding sources

Authors are required to identify who provided financial support for the conduct of the research and/or preparation of the article. List funding sources in the following way:

Funding: This work was supported by Grant Name [grant number].

8. Author biography

This part includes author's full name, title, affiliation, research interest(s) and email address. Please clearly indicate who is the corresponding author if there are more than one author.

9. References

List your references by following the format shown in the examples.

Examples:

Atkinson, D. 2002. Toward a sociocognitive approach to second language acquisition [J]. *The Modern Language Journal* 86(4): 525-545.

Creswell, J. W. 2013. *Qualitative Inquiry and Research Design: Choosing Among Five Approaches* [M]. Thousand Oaks, CA: SAGE.

Friedlander, A. 1990. Composing in English: Effects of a first language on writing in English as a second language [A]. In B. Kroll (ed.). *Second Language Writing: Research Insights for the Classroom* [C]. Cambridge: Cambridge University Press. 109-125.

Jiang, Yan. 2000. The Tao of verbal communication: An Elementary textbook on pragmatics and discourse analysis [OL]. http://www.polyu.edu.hk/~cbs/jy/teach.htm (accessed 30/04/2006).

Whalen, K. & N. Ménard. 1995. L1 and L2 writers' strategic and linguistic knowledge: A model of multiple-level discourse processing [J]. *Language Learning* 45(3): 381-418.

Robertson, M., M. Line, S. Jones & S. Thomas. 2000. International students, learning environments and perceptions: A case study using the Delphi technique [J]. *Higher Education Research & Development* 19(1): 89-102.

Authors are requested to submit their papers electronically by using the *Chinese Journal of Second Language Writing* online submission web site (https://eyxz.cbpt.cnki.net).

If you have further questions, please contact: writing-journal@sdu.edu.cn.